UNIVERSITY COLLEGE

Brescia

BERYL IVEY LIBRARY

Law and Society
Recent Scholarship

Edited by Melvin I. Urofsky

A Series from LFB Scholarly

Judicial Power in a Federal System
Canada, United States and Germany

Cristina M. Ruggiero

LFB Scholarly Publishing LLC
El Paso 2012

Library of Congress Cataloging-in-Publication Data

Ruggiero, Cristina M., 1972-
  Judicial power in a federal system : Canada, United States and
Germany / Cristina M. Ruggiero.
     p. cm. -- (Law & society)
  Includes bibliographical references and index.
  ISBN 978-1-59332-443-8 (hardcover : alk. paper)
  1. Political questions and judicial power--Germany. 2. Political
questions and judicial power--Canada. 3. Political questions and
judicial power--United States. 4. Judge-made law. 5. Judicial review.
6. Federal government--Germany. 7. Federal government--Canada. 8.
Federal government--United States. I. Title.
  K3175.R85 2012
  347'.012--dc23
                                    2012020789

ISBN 978-1-59332-443-8

Printed on acid-free 250-year-life paper.

Manufactured in the United States of America.

Table of Contents

List of Tables and Figure

Acknowledgements

I have received immense support and assistance in the writing of this book. Bert Kritzer was patient and encouraging. Donald Downs, Kathryn Hendley, Charles Franklin and Alexandra Huneeus were also supportive and provided feedback. K.T. Albiston, Mark Pollack and Corrie Potter provided valuable comments on early drafts of the work. Anya Seitz and Ingrid Hufgard provided research and translation assistance. I would like to also acknowledge the research and intellectual support I had as graduate fellow at the Institute of Legal Studies at the University of Wisconsin Law School and as a visiting researcher at the Max Plank Institute for Comparative Public Law and International Law. I would also like to thank former president of the German Constitutional Court Jutta Limbach and former German Constitutional Court Justice Renate Jaeger for their communications and allowing me to access to the German Constitutional Court Library and its press archives, as well as Volker Roth-Plettenberg, the director of the library for his assistance. In Canada, I would also like to thank Celine Champagne, chief of library services at the Status of Women Canada, Andree Cote, Director of Legislation and Law Reform at the National Association of Women and the Law, and Carissma Mathen, former Director of Litigation Women's Legal Education and Action Fund as well as staff from Birthright by Choice and CARAL who provided me with materials, reports and articles. There are too many people to mention by name, but the helpful and kind staff at numerous libraries, institutes and organizations, that helped me spend hours upon hours in their archives and stacks while I wore out their photocopy and microfiche machines: the University of Heidelberg, the National Library of Canada, the University of Toronto, the Oregon State

Historical Library, Oregon State University, Lewis and Clark College, and the Utah State Archives, and the Oregon and Utah chapters of NARAL. Lastly, I thank my parents, my daughter Olivia and particularly my husband Jon, for his consistent support and encouragement.

CHAPTER 1
Introduction

PREFACE

In January 1991, the Utah Legislature, emboldened by the United States Supreme Court's *Webster* decision permitting state restrictions on abortion, passed the most restrictive criminal regulations on abortion within the United States. As Governor Bangerter said, prior to signing the legislation, "With the present makeup of the US Supreme Court, and the obvious change in the court's attitude toward abortion, the time is now ripe for states to again take steps to protect our unborn" (Salt Lake Tribune 1991: B1). The law prohibited virtually all abortions prior to 20 weeks of pregnancy and required extensive consent provisions and a 24 hour waiting period. Knowing that the law tested constitutional limits on abortion set out by the US Supreme Court, the state government established a litigation fund in order to defend the law. After exhausting all legal remedies, including an appeal to the US Supreme Court, Utah spent more than a million dollars in its failed attempt to defend the law.

In 1998, six years after the German Constitutional Court overturned a federal law liberalizing abortion procedures, and only two years after the federal law was revised according to the Court's directives, the Constitutional Court found that Bavaria's implementation regulations of the new federal criminal law on abortion violated the Basic Law's Article 12 guarantee of citizens' freedom of occupation. In its decision, the Court ruled that the Bavarian government had violated the rights of doctors by legislating that no more than a quarter of a doctor's yearly earnings could come from performing abortions. In addition the Court ruled that the Länder are preempted from legislating in areas in which the federal parliament has explicitly chosen *not to* legislate (Knapp 1998).

After the Canadian Supreme Court struck down the federal criminal law on abortion because it violated individual rights protected in the Charter of Rights and Freedoms, the federal government twice failed to pass new abortion regulations, effectively deferring the responsibility to regulate abortion to the provinces. In 1993, the Nova Scotia government passed the Medical Services Act, which prohibited the establishment of out-patient abortion clinics within the province. Dr. Henry Morgentaler, who had publically announced he would be establishing an abortion clinic in Halifax, was charged and convicted with violating the Act.   Upon appeal, the Canadian Supreme Court found that the intent and purpose of the law was to criminally regulate abortion. Given that criminal law is the domain of the national, not provincial governments, the Court concluded that Nova Scotia had violated the principles of federalism. Two years after the decision, the Nova Scotia government began paying $50,000 a year in federal penalties for failing to pay for abortions performed in free standing abortion clinics (Canadian Medical Journal 2001: 847).

The role of high courts in the policy process

The examples above address attempts by sub-national governments to regulate abortion policy while highlighting the role high courts play within the policy process. In addition, these examples also reveal how the variations in federal systems condition how sub-national governments seek to respond to these decisions. The increasing influence of high courts in countries such as, Hungary, Italy, Israel, Portugal, Spain, South Africa, and of supra-national institutions like the European Court of Justice, has placed high courts in the position of directing and influencing policy outcomes, often within federalist or multi-layered political systems. While American scholars have differed over the nature and extent of the United States Supreme Court's influence over social policy in the US, given the rising influence of other high courts around the world and the scholarly debate over the nature of the 'judicialization of politics' in recent decades, this book contributes to the judicial research agenda by providing a systematic evaluation of the 'interdependent nature' of judicial power within three federal systems (Canada, United States and Germany) that have, arguably, three of the most 'powerful' high courts in the world.[1]

The 'interdependent' nature of judicial power

By tracing and comparing the role of high courts in policy-making and legislative responses (particularly sub-national legislatures) in three cases, this project is both testing and refining existing concepts of court influence as 'interdependent' (see Ginsburg 2003, Baum 2003, Frymer 2003). This study asserts that the influence of high courts and their decisions are shaped both by 'intrinsic' institutional features, as well as the 'extrinsic' environment (political and federalist) in which these court institutions operate.

Assuming that that court exercise 'interdependent' law making power, significant concerns for those interested in political institutions and in judicial politics are: Why are some high courts more powerful than other courts? Stated another way, why do some high courts seem more or less successful at exercising their 'interdependent' power than others? Are there particular institutional features that enable some courts to act more 'powerfully' than others? What accounts for the variation across and within cases, regarding court decisions and subsequent compliance with said decisions by sub-national legislative actors? By employing a comparative, historical analysis of the three most 'powerful' courts in the world, this project attempts to answer these questions. This study confirms and refines current theories of court power as well as develops an argument about what conditions are necessary to being a 'powerful' court.

In addition to contributing to the comparative judicialization of politics literature, this book contributes to the burgeoning literature, largely within the American context, conceptualizing the 'interdependent' power of courts and examining under what conditions courts may exert influence within the larger political context. This research integrates the assumptions 'strategists' have about courts and

---

[1] This is not an exhaustive list, but to merely note some scholars who have focused recently on these issues within in a comparative context in recent decades: Hirschl (2004), Ginsburg (2003), Stone-Sweet (2000), Epp (1998), Tate and Vallinder (1995), Holland (1991), Capelletti (1989).

court interactions with other political actors and reaches beyond the partisan debate in judicial politics about whether policy preferences or law matters more (attitudinalists/behavioralists vs. legalists), By examining such interactions within and across cases and over time, this book address the interests of those not just interested in American judicial politics but those interested in the interaction of political institutions and comparative politics more generally.

Much of the research focusing on the nature and extent of court influence implicitly discusses the nature of court power as universal, but these conclusions often have been generated from one case, the US Supreme Court. This book takes these theoretical developments beyond a single case to a systematic comparative context allowing us to generalize more confidently which institutional features and conditions facilitate court power. Therefore this project's findings contribute as a 'check' on the assumptions that what is understood about the power of the US Supreme Court is consistent with other high courts.

Lastly, while a number of scholars have suggested that federalism plays a significant role in determining or enabling court power (see Holland 1991, Whittington 2005, Stone-Sweet 2000, Shapiro and Stone 1994) there have not been systematic evaluations of the relationship between federalism and court influence. This study directly examines and compares the influence of this condition across cases. Overall, this book contributes to a larger research agenda on court influence and further refines these concepts in order to more accurately determine whether they hold in other cases.

Project overview and structure of the book

Unlike single country studies, which often assume the structural conditions, this book shows that one must consider the variations in the *multi-dimensional* structuring of institutional relationships in order to understand high court power. The account provided is not merely one of court decisions proposing the direction of policy, but situates court policymaking and influence both within a complex interplay across national governmental institutions, and between national and sub-national institutions, highlighting how variations in institutional features and federal structures can shape the nature of court decisions and condition how actors may choose to respond (or not) to each other's actions. Specifically, I examine and compare the contested issue of court-led abortion policy-making within and across the United States, Germany and Canada.

Using a structured comparative historical method, I assess court power in the policy process through an empirical examination of both the 'intrinsic' institutional features and court rules that shape the influence of high courts, and the 'extrinsic' features of the political and institutional environment, emphasizing the federal arrangements that provide incentives and disincentives for sub-national government response. Thus, I develop my understanding of court influence in regards two dependent, yet interconnected variables: first, the court policy 'output', the nature and extent of major court decisions regarding abortion and second, the legislative responses to those decisions at the national and sub-national level.[2]

This book asserts the following hypothesis: the presence or absence of those (intrinsic) institutional features supporting court power and the significance of those features are often revealed in the nature of the decision a court makes. Stated another way, the greater number of institutional and uncontested supports the Court has at its disposal, the more likely it will seek to make a decision that is comprehensive, detailed and prescriptive, thereby indicating its willingness to promote its policy objectives and impose those policy directives on other political actors. Conversely, if such institutional features are absent, or weak (i.e., vague or subject to constraint from outside the court), a court is more likely to refrain from making comprehensive and detailed policy pronouncements. Comparing the existence and strength of these institutional features across high courts helps us to determine which features may be significant in providing power to a high court.

However, these 'intrinsic' features alone are not sufficient to explain court influence in policymaking. Acknowledging that these decisions were not made in a vacuum, but within a particular political and federal context, this research situates these court actions within this broader 'extrinsic' context and traces the compliance with, and legislative responses to, these court policies by other political actors,

---

[2] While arguably the availability of abortions and performance of the abortion procedure at the individual level would be the ultimate 'outcome', this study focuses on explicating the factors conditioning 'interdependent' court influence in the policy process.

particularly national and sub-national legislatures. Given that all three courts operate within a federal system, the role of federalism is examined to determine how this feature conditions the response to court policy by sub-national actors. Therefore, this project also asserts that particular features of the political and institutional environment also condition the influence or power of high courts by shaping how other actors may choose to respond and the likelihood for court oversight.

Chapter two examines the theoretical debates and empirical research on judicial power and as well as discusses the theoretical and methodological approaches of the project. Chapter three outlines the first step of this project by comparing various institutional features 'intrinsic' of the courts in question in order to suggest that the presence and nature of particular features may increase or decrease the likelihood of a high court to create comprehensive and detailed policy decisions. The greater number of clear, uncontested institutional supports a court has, such as a extensively detailed guarantee of rights (both positive and negative) or the presence of unqualified judicial review, the more likely a court will provide policy directives (through its decisions) that are comprehensive, detailed and prescriptive. Conversely, if those features are absent or weak, a court is more likely to refrain from making comprehensive, detailed and prescriptive decisions. This study also finds that the courts with limited institutional supports are more likely to depend on court/legal 'rules' such as standing or mootness to justify their interventions or non-interventions in the policy process, and more likely to 'defer' authority to legislative institutions.

In addition to influence of these 'intrinsic' features shaping the nature and exercise of court influence, there are 'extrinsic' features of the political and federal environment that facilitate or limit compliance of legislative actors with court directives, which thereby conditions the influence of the courts themselves. The second step in this project, found in chapter four, examines and compares these 'extrinsic' features to determine which and to what degree these features may shape legislative responses and compliance with court decisions. Therefore the third step of this project places these court decisions within the larger political and federal context and traces the response and compliance with these court policies by other political actors, particularly national and sub-national legislatures. Through a detailed historical analysis, chapters five, six and seven present the data for step three. The distribution of both policy and legislative competencies between federal and sub-national governments significantly shape whether and how governments will respond and seek to advance their interests regarding abortion policy. Most notably, the determination of whether abortion is a primarily a health policy or a criminal policy is a necessary but not sufficient condition in determining which level of government is responsible and how said government will legislate abortion. In addition, whether or not sub-national governments are largely responsible for only implementing federal policies or able to institute their own policies also shaped the nature of sub-national government responses to high court decisions.

Sub-national governments who successfully avoided court challenges to their policies were those that strategically sought to enact their preferences working within the policy and institutional competencies available to them, however, when sub-national actors exceeded either their policy or legislative (or both) competencies they were prone to face judicial review. Regardless of ideological or party affiliation, sub-national governments who avoided judicial oversight employed particular competencies, such as utilizing their fiscal authority or promoted their actions as falling clearly under sub-national policy authorities (such as health policy) thereby insulating their actions from legal challenge. Therefore, the *presence* and *nature* of a federal system provides particular avenues in which legislative actors may act and also shapes the conditions that facilitate or inhibit court oversight of such actions. In addition, this study illustrates how and under what conditions judicial and political actors (at both federal and sub-national levels) may, by design or default, defer responsibility for abortion policy to other actors in the political system. The means by which they do so is structured by particular institutional features and competencies available to such actors.

Lastly, chapter eight provides an overall comparison of the cases noting some of significant findings of the previous chapters and areas for future research, and concludes with the proposition that court 'power' is shaped and conditioned by a number of institutional and political features, both intrinsic and extrinsic to high courts. Drawing upon the empirical data presented in the project, I posit three conditions under which such courts are likely to be powerful political actors (1) A high degree of court policy comprehensiveness and specificity, (2) a high likelihood of court oversight/intervention in the policy process, and (3) a limited diffusion or overlap of legislative competencies between federal and sub-national governments. I find that particular institutional features, including the comprehensiveness and nature of constitutional rights guarantees, the structure of judicial review and the constitutional division of powers between the federal and sub-national governments enable these conditions. In conclusion, I suggest how these concepts may apply to a more general approach to understanding institutional power.

CHAPTER 2

The Interdependent Nature of Judicial Power'?

INTRODUCTION

This chapter elucidates the theoretical foundations and assumptions that animate this project as well as notes the assumptions and limitations of the project. This chapter asserts that court power is not unidirectional and instead is 'complex' and interdependent. It also articulates a broader proposition that political actors tend to have similar interests and the particular constellation of institutional conditions, in which these actors operate, provide opportunities or limitations for these actors to act upon their interests. This view is consistent with Paul Frymer's conclusion, drawn from his study of the integration of labor unions in the United States, that "No political branch, then, is either "hollow" or perfect, as each provides activists different opportunities and constraints that vary with historical and political context" (2003: 495). I suggest that under particular conditions, the political supports for judicial power *are not sufficient* for explaining the exercise of judicial review in a pluralist democracy.

POWER, PLURALISM AND THE NEW INSTITUTIONALISM RESPONSE

"The notion of power is often said to be central to the analysis of politics" (Riker 1964: 341). If Riker was correct, then why did explicit 'power' analysis seem to disappear from the research agenda of political scientists in recent decades? While pluralists addressed the issue of power directly, I believe such studies have not disappeared entirely but rather have been re-named or subsumed under the theoretical approach of new institutionalism.[3]

In response to the formalist approaches favored by earlier political scientists, 'modern' theories of power developed primarily out of the 1950's and 1960's research on groups and interests (Baumgartner and Leech 1998: 48). The pluralist approach assumed that "the best political outcomes would arise out of group conflict"(Ibid)[4]. However, by neglecting the institutional context and attempting to pinpoint episodes of decisive outcomes revealing a clear 'winner' the pluralists developed incomplete understandings of power.

More recently, new institutionalist approaches have attempted to remedy the limits of pluralist approaches by refocusing the attention on states and their respective institutions. 'New' institutionalism differs from the 'old' or formalistic institutionalism in that it can be defined to include norms, rules and structures, *influence* or shape the behavior of political actors.[5] In addition, new institutionalism examines how these various features play a role in the policy process and are amenable to cross-national comparisons: "Whereas the earlier institutionalism militated against cross-national comparisons, this approach often

---

[3] There is also a significant literature focusing on individual or 'personal' power as Richard Neustadt has aptly described it. I have chosen not to address this approach since this research project is focused on a macro rather than micro level explanation of the power of political actors. This research does rest on basic micro-level assumptions that political actors have interests and seek to act upon those interests. Yet, given the scope of this project and that the unit of comparison for this work is of high courts as whole, I collapse the interests of the individual judges into the interests of the court. This will be addressed in a later section.

[4] This approach was found in both American and comparative politics research, see Lijpart (1968), Almond (1958), Almond and Verba (1963), Dahl (1961) and Truman (1951).

[5] See Peter Hall (1986), Shepsle_(1986), March and Olsen (1989), North (1990), Dimaggio and Powell (1991), Thelen et al eds. (1992), Orren and Skowronek (1994), Hall and Taylor (1996).

utilizes such comparisons in order to identify the most salient institutional determinants of policy" (Hall 1986: 20)[6]. Even though new institutionalists have not always stated that they are studying power, by examining the nature and extent of institutional influence, their works can be understood as investigations into the nature of power. Therefore, this approach is the ideal theoretical framework for this project, as my assessment of court power compares and examines how institutional features facilitate or constrain high court interventions in the policy process.

New institutionalism comes in multiple variants: sociological, historical, and rational (Hall and Taylor 1996). Much of the political science research to date utilizes either the historical or rational approach. The primary difference between the latter two is that the rational approach assumes actors' preferences are 'fixed' prior to engagement in the institutional context, whereas the historical approach relaxes this assumption and allows for the contention that institutions themselves may shape the interests of political actors. It is fruitful to see these two variants on a continuum. One can begin with a strongly rational perspective where preference construction is completely exogenous to the institutional setting. From this perspective, institutions merely serve to alleviate the transaction costs of actors. We can then move to an extreme historical approach in which actors are at the mercy of conditions in which they operate and have little autonomy. To the chagrin of most political scientists, the real world of politics falls somewhere in the middle.

By comparing across high courts and political environments, and using a small number of cases, this book is not establishing a universal theory of court behavior but a 'middle' level approach by refining the concepts that help us distinguish between the institutional and structural conditions that are likely to support a powerful court. A subset of recent American judicial politics research, 'separation of powers games' has focused on strategic interactions between courts and other political

---

[6] A number of significant comparative works have utilized the 'new' institutional approach; Pierson (1994), Collier and Collier (1991), Immergut, (1992), Tarrow (1994), Mattli and Slaughter (1997).

institutions.[7] Much of the work in this area uses 'game theory' to model the interactions between institutions. However, while accepting some of the premises of strategic judicial behavior, this project does not attempt to provide a purely abstract 'one size fits all model' of judicial power.

Therefore, I offer a more realistic middle ground by simply assuming all political actors, including high court justices, have interests and seek to act upon those interests. They are, after all, political appointees at the highest level of government. High court judicial nominees are often at the center of battles between political parties and among institutions. For example, in the United States, national politics often plays out strategically between the executive and the legislative branch regarding judicial appointments, creating a highly contentious and politicized Supreme Court appointment process (see Watson and Stookey 1995 and Epstein and Segal 2005). Therefore, simply from experiencing such an appointment process, it is reasonable to assume that these judicial appointees are well aware of the significance of their position and the interests that they might serve. Paraphrasing what one judge on the German Constitutional Court remarked to me, "[T]he amount of influence you have increases as you reach the top of the political system, and as a judge, the most influence you can have is on the Constitutional Court" (Jaeger 2000).

The incentive or ability to act upon said interests may be constrained or facilitated by the institutional setting and by the actions of other political actors. This project focuses on the interests of each court, rather than on the interests of individual judges. While there is likely to be variation among the preferences of these judges (e.g., the nature, order or intensity of these preferences), given the project's focus on understanding court power vis-a-vis other institutions, this project

---

[7] Early examples of this research agenda can be found in Schubert (1958), Pritchett (1961) and Murphy (1964). More recent examples can be found in works from Songer, Segal and Cameron (1994), Maltzman and Wahlbeck (1996), Epstein and Knight (1998), Wahlbeck, Spriggs and Maltzman (1998), Maltzman, Spriggs and Wahlbeck (2000), Epstein et al (2004). In addition, a number of law and business scholars have contributed to the field, see Gely and Spiller (1990), Eskridge (1991), Eskridge and Frickey (1994) Farber and Frickey (1991), (1992), Spiller and Gely (1992) and Cross and Tiller (1998).

assumes that the intent to "alter the behavior of others" and preserving one's own institutional relevance or legitimacy as the major interests animating *collective* court behavior (Krasner 1991: 364).[8] While acknowledging the importance of these interests, court behavior may be significantly enabled or constrained by context.

While legal scholars and normative judicial theorists have long argued that judges are supposed to be neutral and not motivated by such interests, research on US Supreme Court behavior has indicated that policy preferences are good predictors of court decision outcomes (Rohde and Spaeth 1976, Segal and Spaeth 1993). By failing to address the institutional conditions and often focusing on single-country studies, it has been somewhat difficult to understand the extent to which acting on policy preferences is shaped by context.[9] Recently, a number of American judicial scholars have produced works examining how the behavior and preferences of courts are shaped by institutional, historical and political contexts.[10]

---

[8] I accept the general proposition that individual behavior by judges is motivated and shaped in part by their political preferences (See Segal and Spaeth generally). In addition, justices may also be motivated by preferences which stem from their judicial philosophy, values or self-perception of their judicial role. Given the scope and comparative nature of this project, to attempt to disaggregate (and discern the impact) of these individual assumptions from a 'collective' political preference over the time period examined would have shifted the focus of this project since it is not a micro-level examination of behavior, but a macro approach examining the institutional factors shaping behavior and outcomes.

[9] As Paul Brace and Melinda Gann Hall pointed out in their examination of the institutional conditions structuring the behavior of US state supreme court judges, "At this stage of scientific inquiry we simply do not understand the role of institutions and context in the process of judicial decision making very well, leaving our theories of judicial choice incomplete. And we have hardly even begun the task of unraveling complex interactions between institutional arrangements and other forces affecting judicial choice" (1997: 1210).

[10] Clayton (1992), Gilman (1993), Clayton and Gillman eds. (1999), Gillman and Clayton, eds. (1999), Lovell (2003), McMahon (2004), Keck (2004), Graber (1993), Whittington (2005), Frymer (2003). Some of these works will be addressed in greater detail in a succeeding section.

ASSESSING JUDICIAL INFLUENCE WITHIN THE AMERICAN CONTEXT-JUDICIAL "IMPACT"

Much of the research examining the 'impact' of the US Supreme Court was initially motivated by understanding the influence of the Warren Court on American public policy, particularly in protecting individual and minority rights (Baum 2003). Many these works focused on understanding the independent 'policy impact' or 'effect' of Supreme Court decisions on implementing institutions; or why court policy (as emanating from court decisions) was or was not implemented by other policy makers. [11] These scholars posited a number of factors to explain the influence and impact of court decisions. Similar to the early pluralist scholars, in attempting to find exact causal relationships, and in studying outcomes for absolute rather than relative gains, these studies provided a variety of explanations of judicial impact.

In addition, a number of these studies focused on the inability of the US Supreme Court to have its decisions effectively implemented. Yet, as Laurence Baum points out, they did not address whether such implementation failures were due to the particular constraints faced by courts or to the fact that such 'failures' could reasonably be expected in any imperfect policy-making environment (Baum 2003: 172-3).

In his book *The Hollow Hope* (1991), Gerald Rosenberg attempted to determine definitively whether or not United States Supreme Court decisions have had a significant independent impact on social policy. His analysis of macro-level data showed that Court decisions themselves have had little direct impact in either raising public consciousness or in implementing policy change. Rosenberg claimed that since the Court was not sufficiently independent from other political actors and lacked formal enforcement powers, it was a 'constrained' rather 'dynamic' institution.

Generating substantial discussion and debate within the field of judicial politics, Rosenberg's work has been criticized for obscuring effects of particular variables, and having a rigid view of causality and court impact (McCann 1996). Schultz and Gottlieb noted that by setting up the 'dynamic' vs. 'constrained' dichotomy, Rosenberg

---

[11] See Wasby (1970), Rogers and Bullock (1976), Johnson and Canon (1984), Canon (1991), Rosenberg (1991), Spriggs (1996), (1997).

created unrealistic expectations about influence and policymaking that no political institution could reasonably achieve: "Rosenberg seems to ignore that Congress, too, is hampered by implementation difficulties that include lower state and federal officials opposing policy changes...Rosenberg's omission masks power" (184-5).

These critiques of Rosenberg echo those made of earlier pluralist scholars, who, by relying on a 'coercive' definition of power, sought to explain the power of actors by observing in isolation the effect of that individual behavior on outcomes. Rosenberg's assumption of the court as a one-stop policy-maker and enforcer obscures any attempt to understand court influence as mediated by the political and institutional context in which policy makers operate and simplifies to an unrealistic degree the complexity of the policy-making process. This book argues *it is more realistic to assume that all government institutions have particular strengths and weaknesses when operating in particular institutional and political environments.* In addition, these institutions do not operate completely independently from one another; therefore interactions among them are likely to shape the impact or influence of said institutions on the policy process.

THE CONCEPT OF 'DEFERENCE' AND UNDERSTANDING JUDICIAL INFLUENCE AS 'INTERDEPENDENT'

Moving beyond top-down and bottom-up approaches to understanding judicial influence, a burgeoning strand of 'interbranch' research has examined, particularly within the American context, a court's power within the political system. This research focuses broadly on the question, "How can scholars meaningfully study the inherently complex (and variable) role of law and courts in American politics and policy-making?" (Barnes 2007: 28). As Jeb Barnes point out, these works start from the presumption that "American politics and policymaking emanate from interaction among overlapping and diversely representative forms" where 'separate institutions share power' (Barnes 2007: 25

Adapting terms that Karen Orren and Steven Skrowonkek used to conceptualize American political development literature, interbranch analysis often combines both cross-sectional and longitudinal inquiry. Such analysis can "locate courts and decision-making within particular institutional contexts", while "analyzing how these institutional arrangements unfold and engender specific outcomes" (Ibid 28). In addition to examining courts both cross-sectionally and longitudinally, this project draws from the three variants of interbranch analysis: micro institutional analysis, strategic-separation of powers studies/games, and regime politics studies.[12]

As noted earlier, 'separation of power' researchers examine the strategic interaction among political actors through a series of discrete iterations or 'games'. These researchers usually assume that individual justices and courts as a whole seek to impose their policy preferences, like any other political institution. However, since they assume that policy formation arises from the interaction between institutions, "it follows that [in order for] any set of actors to make authoritative policy—be they justices, legislators, or executives—must take account of this institutional constraint by formulating expectations about the preferences of relevant actors and what they want them to do when making their decisions" (Epstein, Knight and Martin 2004: 174). These expectations limit what a court may decide or rule based upon the configurations of the interests of other actors involved and the likelihood that such actors may respond negatively to the court's decision. As Barnes points out, much of this work hypothesizes that the "[United States] Supreme Court will be most strategically constrained when the other branches are ideologically cohesive and will enjoy greater policy-making discretion as ideological divisions among the elected branches widen" (Barnes 2007: 31).

Whereas 'separation of powers' research focuses on discrete iterative points in time, 'regime politics' studies examine the interaction between courts and other political actors over a longer and more fluid time period. In addition, while separation of power game researchers often assume institutional actors are relatively independent and are competing with each other to impose their preferences on the policy process, 'regime politics' focuses how political actors 'use' the Court in order to achieve their policy preferences (Ibid 32). Much of this research builds upon Dahl's seminal work asserting that US

---

[12] This project is aligned with within the 'micro institutional analysis' framework because it "rel[ies] on detailed case studies that trace the policy-making process in [a] specific area" (Ibid 34). The following sections review the separation of powers and regime approaches in more detail.

Supreme Court decision-making is largely consistent with the 'dominant law-making majority' and Mark Graber's more recent 1993 article explaining why political elites would support US Supreme Court policy-making through a theory of 'deference'. [13]

Graber asserts that political elites may often explicitly or tacitly "support judicial policymaking both as a means to avoid political responsibility for making tough decisions and as a means of pursuing controversial policy goals that they cannot publically advance through open legislative and electoral politics" (Graber 1993: 37). He notes that such 'deference' to the Supreme Court can be traced to the two party structure of the American political system where "mainstream politicians may advance their interests by diverting difficult, crosscutting issues to such 'peripheral mechanisms' as the national judiciary"(Ibid). While Graber theory reflects Rosenberg's view that Supreme Court influence is dependent on other political actors, I would argue that the institutional structure and lack of entrenchment of the judiciary in the American political process also contributes to the 'peripheral' nature of the (US) national judiciary. As this project demonstrates, 'deference' occurs in other democratic, federalist systems, but the nature of deference and the degree of court influence differs due to the structural conditions and institutional features present.

The majority of the research that has come after Graber has supported the proposition that fragmentation and diffusion of a political system enables court influence. However, this project finds that the presence of parliamentary system as compared to a more 'diffuse' presidential system is not sufficient in constraining court influence. For example, even with a parliamentary system, the absence of institutional rules supporting court interventions and exercises of judicial review limits the influence of the Canadian Supreme Court relative to the German Constitutional Court, which also operates within a parliamentary system (one that some may argue is more fragmented than Canada's because it employs a proportional rather than a 'first past the post' electoral system).

Graber, as well as number of other scholars, note this 'deference' may be revealed when political actors "wavi[e] the flag of federalism"

---

[13] "The Non-Majoritarian Difficulty: Legislative Deference to the Judiciary" *Studies in American Political Development*, 7: 33-73.

by asserting sub-national governments are responsible for resolving such controversial issues, since such officials may not be divided politically on the issue (Graber 1993: 41).[14] [15] While I would agree that federalism provides this opportunity, the way this actually plays out differs depending on the structural features of the federal system itself.

In addition, Graber proposes that "justices are more willing to declare laws unconstitutional after receiving explicit or implicit permission from elected officials" (41). I argue that they are also more willing to do so when there are institutional supports enabling such action, not only when there is 'permission'. Permission may be necessary in the American case, because particular *institutional supports are absent*. In addition, the Canadian case shows that when deference is institutionalized through the reference procedure[16] and has been is *underutilized* by political actors, this condition may actually inhibit a court from declaring laws unconstitutional. In summary, Graber's assertions may not hold for other high courts within different political and institutional contexts. I believe that while political supports for judicial review may be significant they *may not be sufficient* in explaining the influence of high courts in federalist systems.

---

[14] A number of judicial scholars have speculated on the role federalism has in shaping the influence of high courts; however, they have not systematically examined the role federalism plays in shaping court influence. See Stone Sweet 2000, Shapiro 2002, Guarneri and Pederzoli 2002, Whittington 2003, 2005. This project, in part, attempts to systematically determine the nature of this influence.

[15] Graber also proposes other conditions when judicial review may be beneficial to political elites: when a majority coalition is not possible, or when legislative rules make it difficult to choose among competing proposals, or when party moderates seek to take 'safer' positions on controversial policies or justify implementation of said policies because they can point "to their obligation to obey the law, while insisting that they disagree with the Court's holding" (Graber 1993:43).

[16] As will be discussed in greater detail in the next chapter, the reference procedure allows the federal government to appeal directly (and provincial governments' indirectly) to the Canadian Supreme Court to determine the constitutionality of government act or proposed law prior to its enactment.

By testing Graber's propositions, a number of recent projects have supported the view that judicial review and court intervention is both a means for elected elites to avoid responsibility (a 'non-decision' or 'deferral') and for such elites to advance policy when they *want* to but are blocked from doing so for various reasons. For example, George Lovell, in his book *Legislative Deferrals*, revealed how Congress empowered the US Supreme Court by crafting ambiguous legislation enabling the Court to limit the rule that strikes were not allowed, even though such legislation was seemingly intended to protect workers, thereby deferring the resolution of a controversial issue to the Court (Lovell 2003). Moreover, Kevin McMahon's study showed how President Roosevelt utilized his appointment power in order to appoint liberals justices to the federal judiciary in the south and then promoted litigation in order to strike down Jim Crow Laws that would be reviewed by these justices (McMahon 2003).

Echoing Graber's assertions, Keith Whittington detailed a number of historical cases in order to examine US Supreme Court interventions in the policy process (Whittington 2005). Through his analysis, he suggests three conditions, federalism, entrenched interests (within majority coalitions) and fragmented political coalitions, under which judicial review 'friendly' to governing elites is likely to emerge (Ibid).

Collectively, such research reveals how legislative and/or the executive actors, motivated by their political preferences, defer to courts or enable court policy interventions and influence through the various *institutional capacities* these actors have at their disposal.[17] While these actors are motivated by their policy preferences, they are both enabled and constrained by the institutional (and political) conditions in which they operate. Such actors will seek to use whatever resources available in order to achieve their interests. As earlier 'judicial impact' works examined how individuals or interest groups used the courts to achieve certain policy objectives, these more recent works examine ways in which government actors have sought to use the courts to achieve their interests.

Some of these propositions regarding the political supports of judicial power have begun to be explored comparatively, with particular focus on the political conditions that have animated and

---

[17] See Powe 2000, Gilman 2002, Frymer 2003, as other recent examples.

expanded 'new constitutional' regimes. Ran Hirschl asserts that hegemonic political elites have supported the expansion of judicial review in Israel, Canada, New Zealand and South Africa in order to advance their neoliberal policy goals to the detriment of collective rights and values, and that high courts in these countries have reinforced these policy goals through their decisions (Hirschl 2003).[18] Similarly, Tom Ginsburg finds, in what he refers to as 'new' Asian democracies, that the existence of party diffusion or competition at the time of the constitutional founding lead elites to 'insure' their interests by creating a high court with the power of judicial review (Ginsburg 2003). However, if one party is dominant at the time of the founding, it will not find it necessary to imbue a high court with strong powers of judicial review, thereby such a court will be less likely to assert (or develop) its authority and will likely support the dominant majority or authoritarian regime (Ibid).

Consistent with the view that political elites seek to 'use' the Supreme Court to achieve their policy objectives, Carlo Guarneri and Patrizia Pederzoli find that political elites in Europe also seek to use courts to achieve ends they could not obtain through the electoral process (Guarneri and Pederzoli 2002). In particular, they "identify a tendency of political parties or factions to turn to prosecution in court as a way of eliminating political opponents by showing them to be guilty of corrupt practices" (Goldstein 2004: 614). Guarneri and Pederzoli conclude their work by suggesting that judicial activism is less likely in majoritarian regimes where executive power is centralized, and is more likely in non-majoritarian regimes, where "power is shared, dispersed and limited" due to partisan representation in the legislature, separation of powers among institutions and/or federalism (Guarneri and Pederzoli 2002: 161). Lastly, Alec Stone, in his comparative study of European courts, posits that the judicialization

---

[18] Hirschl has been criticized for failing to examine the particular institutional conditions that may have shaped the outcomes he describes, such as the differences in constitutional texts that these Courts interpret. In addition, he attempts to make a causation by 'correlation' argument by indicating that economic inequality had declined concurrently with the entrenchment of a bill of rights and judicial review (see Goldstein 2004: 626).

of politics is likely to occur when legislative processes are more fragmented, creating conditions in which 'abstract review' is likely to be engaged and constitutional courts may be able to act as 'third legislative chambers' (Stone 2000).[19]

While this fragmentation of the governing process may be a necessary condition in some contexts, it may not be a sufficient to explain the influence of high courts in federal systems. As this project shows, the national legislative process in the United States is heavily veto laden, particularly since it is a presidential rather than parliamentary system. However, when comparing the US Supreme Court and the German Constitutional Court, the German Court produces decisions that are more comprehensive, proscriptive and detailed and the Court itself is more integrated into the policy process than the US Supreme Court, even though the German Court operates within a parliamentary and not a presidential system.

Essentially, these works, both within the US and comparative contexts, focus on elucidating the political conditions supporting judicial review and suggest the significance of party or 'structural' diffusion in the political system which, by extension, shape court intervention and influence in the policy process. Mark Graber summaries these points emphatically,

> Judicial review is established and maintained by elected officials. Adjudication is one of many means politicians and political movements employ when seeking to make their constitutional visions the law of the land. Elected officials provide vital political foundations for judicial power by creating constitutional courts, vesting those courts with jurisdiction over constitutional questions, staffing those courts with judges prone to exercising judicial power, assisting or

---

[19] As Leslie Goldstein points out, Stone-Sweet's account suffers from excessive jargon and abstractness that make it difficult to evaluate his claims (Goldstein 2004: 618). More significantly, while Stone-Sweet provides various anecdotal accounts which illustrate his arguments, it difficult to evaluate his conclusions because he does not systematically examine one policy, set of policies or even time periods across all the courts in his study.

initiating litigation aimed at having those courts declare laws unconstitutional, and passing legislation that encourages justices to make public policy in the guise of statutory or constitutional interpretation. Judicial review does not serve to thwart or legitimate popular majorities; rather that practice alters the balance of power between numerous political movements that struggle for power in a pluralist democracy. (emphasis added) (Graber 2005: 427-8).

This book both accepts and challenges this understanding of judicial review by comparing the presence and nature of the institutional and federal features that arose from political bargains and how such features have shaped both court intervention in the policy process as well as the response of legislative actors to those interventions. By employing a systematic historical comparative method of analysis, this project provides a modest 'test' of Graber's conclusion that "judicial review does not serve to thwart or legitimate popular majorities…". In some cases judicial review may serve this purpose (whether it *should* is a different question and one that this project can only speculate on). Depending upon the constitutional order that has been created and the institutional capacities granted to high courts, this may very well be the case. For example, in Germany there are rights guarantees in the Basic Law that are incontrovertible and cannot be amended. The presence of these rights guarantees, and the institutional rules establishing judicial review in conjunction with other institutional features of the German high court, result in a situation where the Court twice struck down the policy that was supported by a majority of the national legislature (and the public as well). In addition, given the institutional structure legitimating this exercise of court influence, other political actors largely complied with the Court's directives.

Graber concludes his review by issuing a call to the judicial scholars of this new paradigm who "recognize that judicial power rests on political foundations" (Ibid). "Rather than worry about whether courts are behaving in a counter-majoritarian fashion, scholars should explore the ways in which judicial review promotes and weakens the political accountability of elected officials" (Graber 2005: 428). This project's comparative examination of judicial interventions in the policy process highlights how judicial review, as it operates within a particular political system, may interact with the political accountability of elected officials. As the following chapters demonstrate, in both the United States and Canada, elected officials implicitly (United States) or explicitly (Canada) attempted to defer policy-making to Courts.

In neither case was judicial review established concurrently with the constitutional establishment of the Court itself. However, in Germany this process of 'deferral' is part of the constitutional design. Elected officials may and do employ deferrals to judicial authority through the feature of abstract (judicial) review, which allow the Court to thwart or legitimate the claim of those officials. Yet, if this judicial authority was constitutionally provided for, then are such acts of judicial review truly 'weakening political accountability'? Perhaps they do not. A likely explanation as to why Graber states such acts of judicial review may 'weaken or limit accountability' may be the fact that he is speaking from the American context, where judicial review itself was not explicitly provided for in the constitution. Judicial review was developed de facto in the US as opposed to de jure in the German case. As Graber and others have pointed out, elected majorities themselves have established constitutional courts and their corresponding powers in order to serve their interests. Since the United States Supreme Court itself 'established' judicial review and its exercise was subsequently affirmed by political elites, the lack of constitutional foundation for judicial review in the American case has spawned much of the controversy and research to prove why it *should* (normative arguments) and *does* exist (the current research elucidating the political supports for judicial review). By determining there are 'political' supports for judicial review this research implicitly supports normative arguments that judicial review is part of a political, i.e., 'democratic process' and therefore legitimates its existence.

The German case adds a helpful dimension to addressing these assumptions about the purposes and consequences of judicial review. In Germany, judicial review was constitutionally enshrined, in part, *to limit* the democratic majority and uphold the values and rights inherent in the constitution (the historical conditions of Nazism as a clear antecedent). In addition, the nature of such review in Germany explicitly allows political elites to engage in judicial review through the abstract review procedure. The exercise of judicial review neither runs counter to the system itself, nor does it have to be justified as supporting the acts, interests or values of the democratic majority. This purpose or understanding of judicial review is often what the Constitutional Court relies on in order to justify its assertive, proscriptive decisions on abortion. However, the presence of constitutional guarantees in conjunction with the fact that Court decisions are recorded as 'law' and other political actors are bound to follow these decisions are also significant for ensuring compliance by other political actors. Each time the Constitutional Court issued a major ruling on abortion, the federal legislature largely 'complies' with the courts directives by enshrining said directives in revised legislation in a relatively timely fashion.

As noted above, Germany judicial review by 'deferral' is de jure; whereas US it is 'de facto'. Canada operates within a middle ground where political elites can make a 'reference' to the Court, which is also 'de jure'—thereby deferring controversial issues to the Court for constitutional review. However, the Canadian Supreme Court's decision is only advisory and is not legally binding as it is in the German case. During the debate over abortion in Canada, the governing coalition could have utilized the reference procedure, but did not. Instead it attempted to 'defer' to the court through other, less transparent or 'accountable' means. The Court recognized it was put in a situation where other political elites were not formally asking the Court to provide a constitutional evaluation, thereby potentially threatening the Court's legitimacy. In addition, the Court itself had few institutional supports for the independent exercise of judicial review that would support an 'activist' decision. Here the institutional mechanism enabling direct intervention into the policy process was not employed and the existing institutional features intrinsic to the court itself were weak, creating the conditions which made it unlikely that the Court would make a ruling that provided substantive, 'activist' directives on what abortion policy should look like.

To return to the previous discussion regarding the conclusions about judicial influence drawn largely from the American experience in which political actors seek to 'use' courts to advance their interests, it must be understood that if we accept the proposition that high courts are political actors then we should also assume that Courts will act in ways analogous to how other political actors treat courts. Stated another way, we should also recognize the ways in which Courts 'use' or 'defer to' other actors or when it serves *the Court's interests*. This supports the animating proposition of this book that court power is not *unidirectional* and instead is 'complex' and interdependent. It also suggests that if these institutional actors have similar interests, then examining the constellation of institutional and structural conditions will provide particular opportunities or constraints in which these actors may act upon said interests. As stated in the introduction to this chapter, this view is consistent with Paul Frymer's conclusions from his study of the integration of labor unions in the United States; "No political branch, then, is either "hollow" or perfect, as each provides activists different opportunities and constraints that vary with historical and political context" (2003: 495).

Therefore, I return to my earlier point that *it is more realistic to assume that all government institutions have particular strengths and weaknesses when operating in particular institutional and political environments.* Even though courts operate within particular limits (they cannot initiate policy, for example) by systematically comparing across high courts operating in democratic, federal systems we can draw conclusions about how these institutional features shape the role courts and judicial review plays in the policy process, and by extension, the 'interdependent' nature of judicial power. By comparing the nature of policy interventions of federal high courts with judicial review, we can more confidently conclude what institutional and political configurations contribute to the influence of high courts in federal systems.

CHAPTER 3

Comparing 'Intrinsic' Court Features

INTRODUCTION

In recent years, a number of researchers have identified factors they believe have contributed to the rise in 'judicialization' of politics or the influence of courts within the political process. [1] These have included variables such as the appointment process, tenure or court size, as well as the legal education and recruitment of judges (see Guarnieri 2002, Stone Sweet 2000, Ginsburg 2003, Hilbink 2007). Since this project focuses on the role of high courts in the policy process, particularly focusing on the relationship between high courts and sub-national legislatures, these variables were not found to be particularly significant. Compared to most of the courts examined in these recent works, the United States, Canadian and German high courts are relatively 'mature' constitutional/high courts in stable, constitutional, democratic systems. Given that recent works focus on relatively 'newer' courts or courts in transitional democracies, it may be likely that such conditions produce a different constellation of variables which indicate court influence. I suggest that particular features/variables are more 'significant' under certain conditions. Therefore, it reasonable to hypothesize that the confluence of variables shaping court influence changes over time and in different contexts.

I evaluate the significance of these intrinsic features in light of their *entrenchment and specificity*. Entrenchment is defined as permanence; court features/functions that are relatively secure from

27

alteration or removal by other political actors. These institutional features may be externally defined, i.e.; emanating from constitutional or legislative acts, or internally imposed norms or rules that a court established itself. The greater the entrenchment and specificity of such features/functions the greater the likelihood that a court reasonably can expect that other actors will accept the exercise of these functions as legitimate. Therefore a court is more likely to exercise such authority without restraint. For example, if a constitution clearly specifies the nature and extent of a particular court function, such as having final review of administrative acts, the entrenchment and specificity of this function increases the likelihood that the court will fully exercise this authority and diminishes the likelihood that another actor would challenge the court's exercise of such authority (even if the result is inconsistent with the policy preferences of the said political actor).

Conversely, if there is an absence of entrenched features/functions or if they are vaguely defined in the constitution, this condition puts a court in a relatively 'weaker' position as compared to other high courts with clearly defined and constitutionally based functions. With such functions absent or vague, a court will have to establish its own justifications or rules for exercising its authority. Self-made 'rules' may open a court to critique or challenges by other actors, depending on the context. If a court must create or rely on such 'rules', then it may be less willing (as compared to other high courts) to intervene in the policy process. If it does intervene, a court operating within this context would be more likely to render circumscribed and/or vague decisions in order to preserve its authority. Such a court may also be 'deferential' to other branches and less willing to make proscriptive statements.

It is also important to consider the nature and availability of entry points into the policy process in order to understand and compare the relative influence of high courts. If a court has fewer 'on-ramps into the policy process, this limits the opportunities a court has to exercise its influence. With more opportunities available, a court may be more likely to intervene and shape the direction of policy. In addition, the timing of the court's entry into the process is relevant. If a court can intervene earlier in the process before legislation is finalized or implemented, then other actors may have to accept and incorporate the court's ruling into the final legislation. If a court can only enter the policy process after legislation has been implemented, this increases the likelihood that other actors will respond slowly (or not at all) to the court's decision, particularly due to high level of coordination needed to pass legislation in the first instance.

The following sections briefly outline the features found to have a significant impact in the cases examined: the structure of judicial system, jurisdiction, justicability, judicial review and individual rights guarantees.

FEATURES SHAPING THE NATURE OF AND ACCESS TO JUDICIAL REVIEW

The Structure of the Judicial System

The structure of the judicial system is an important institutional feature facilitating the consolidation of court power. Two general models can be used to highlight this concern. Under 'all courts' review all courts in a political system may address constitutional questions (Tate 1992: 7). In the constitutional or unitary court model, a single court adjudicates constitutional questions. Unitary court review increases the range of potential constitutional issues presented to that particular court, but reduces the overall number of constitutional cases and issues that may be addressed (Ibid.). Therefore, since a greater numbers of policy issues may be addressed in the all courts model, judicial scholar C. Neal Tate asserts, "[T]he policy influence of the judiciary must surely be maximized when a nation employs the all courts model" (Ibid.).

While Tate may have a point, he does not consider that as the number of courts with judicial review increases, particularly within federal systems, this is likely to lead to wider variance in policy positions across courts. Increased variance may likely lead to inconsistent policies, thereby enabling sub-national institutions to avoid compliance with high court policy. In addition, this variation also increases the likelihood that the position of the national court could be supplanted or altered by lower/sub-national court decisions. The 'all courts model' may actually decrease the likelihood of sub-national compliance with high court policy, subsequently decreasing the influence of the high court. In contrast, the unitary scenario requires lower courts to forward constitutional issues to the high court, thereby allowing only one court to impact the policy process limiting the ability of lower courts to deviate from such policies. Therefore, this system encourages policy uniformity since a high court does not have to contend with lower courts providing competing constitutional interpretations and rulings.

Jurisdiction

A significant feature of the nature and exercise of judicial review is a court's jurisdiction; it is the "authority of a court to hear and decide cases" (Pacelle 169). Jurisdictional rules generally outline what kinds of *substantive* issues, legislation or disputes the court may potentially address. The extent of this jurisdiction is a function of the external or internal rules governing it, and the ability of outside actors to limit said jurisdiction. The wider the scope of a court's jurisdiction, the more opportunities it has to be involved in the policy process.

A relatively narrow jurisdiction provides fewer opportunities for a court to exercise its authority. In addition, if other political actors may limit a court's jurisdiction, then the court is constrained even further. The court will likely have to justify its case selection process, putting the court in a relatively weaker position than a court with clear and uncontested control over its jurisdiction.

Justicability

Questions of justicability focus on the *procedural* nature of the disputes a court may adjudicate within its jurisdiction. Justicability rules address issues such as; the types of 'questions' a court may hear (case or controversy), the eligibility of petitioners to bring a case to court (standing), and whether there is a 'live' issue at stake (mootness). Issues of justicability often, but not always, manifest as court created (and enforced) rules or norms. A court uses these rules to determine whether to hear a particular case. While employment of these rules may initially serve an administrative function by limiting the flow cases (i.e. work) the court has to adjudicate, their exercise may also shape court influence. As US Supreme Court Justice Powell noted in *US v Richardson* (1974), "[r]elaxation of standing requirements is directly related to the expansion of judicial power" (418 US 166, 188).

Courts may establish and define these rules both to extend and circumscribe their presence in the political process. As Paul Frymer found, court interpretation of legal rules, such as those regarding class action lawsuits, enabled civil rights groups to bring cases against labor unions to force integration, when such groups were unable to do so before (Frymer 2003: 490). Similarly, the presence and nature of justicability rules may determine the extent to which particular petitioners can access the court, which again can shape the number of opportunities a court has to enter and alter the policy process.   In addition, a court with clear, entrenched authorities may find it less necessary to delineate its own authority. Whereas a court faced with a vague definition of its own powers, like the United States Supreme Court, may create rules to shore up its own independent authority and to insulate itself from potential constraints imposed upon it by other actors. As an early scholar of the United States Supreme Court, Robert K. Carr noted, "[N]early all the specific limitations which are said to govern the exercise of judicial review have been announced by the Supreme Court itself."(Carr 185).

This project accepts the assumption that courts, as strategic actors, want to maintain and exercise their institutional authority. The presence of these justiciablity rules may signal a court's interest in insulating and protecting its influence by anticipating negative responses or rebukes from other political actors. Tom Ginsburg names this behavior as a strategy of a court to limit its power in order to consolidate it (Ginsburg 2003). The fewer entrenched capacities a court has in order protect itself from such attacks, the more likely a court is going to establish its own protections through the creation of such rules.

Granted, it may not be possible to ascertain a court's intent in exercising such a rule in a particular case, for as stated previously, one could make the observation that the court applies such standards in order to address administrative concerns rather than to insulate it from outside challenges to its authority. Regardless of intent, collectively, employing such rules of standing, mootness and ripeness, 'case and controversy' and 'political question' *may effectively limit* the court's jurisdiction and reduce the opportunities for court interventions in the policy-making process. In addition, the existence of these rules also provides justifications for other political actors to support and demand particular behavior of the court (when it suits their interests). These rules provide a double edged sword; for example, employing a particular rule may enable a court to deny hearing a case on its merits, but it will also be seen as inconsistent if it does not choose to do for a similar case. Therefore, overall these rules may effectively be more 'constraining' then liberating on the court.

To summarize, the development and application of these internal norms may indicate the willingness a court has in broadening or limiting its jurisdiction, thereby a possible indicator of its desire to exercise authority within the policy process. Therefore, since courts seek to maintain their legitimacy and authorities, courts that employ these rules are likely to be more 'restrained' in their decision-making than courts that do not have such rules.

Nature of the Judicial Review Process

Judicial review is the most significant function (and in the case of the German court, the only function) that these three courts perform. Simply, judicial or constitutional review enables courts to determine authoritatively whether governmental acts or legislation are compatible with constitutional principles. In order to evaluate how judicial review shapes a court's scope of authoritative action, it is also important to consider *when* judicial review occurs in the policy process. While most judicial politics scholars often discuss review as a discrete function of either *a priori* or *a posteriori* review, it is useful to consider judicial review on a continuum aligned with the policy process.[20] Along a continuum, judicial review may occur prior, during or after the promulgation of legislation or exercise of constitutional authority by a government actor (see Figure 1). If a court may intervene earlier in the process, such court action may require or influence other actors to change the direction of policy. Courts, which can intervene only after legislation has been created, enter a policy arena where the political and/or policy 'lines have already been drawn' on a particular issue. Therefore there may be more resistance to the court's decision and less willingness to accept the court's position. Thinking about judicial review in this fashion better facilitates an examination of the opportunities the court has to enter and alter policy process, and

---

[20] A priori review enables court review of legislation or governmental acts before the creation of the law, implementation of it. A posteriori is after promulgation or implementation.

provides insight into why a court may or may not be successful in shaping the direction of policy.

Figure 1: Judicial Review as aligned with the policy-making process

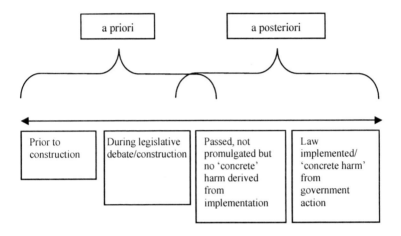

| Prior to construction | During legislative debate/construction | Passed, not promulgated but no 'concrete' harm derived from implementation | Law implemented/ 'concrete harm' from government action |

Scope and Nature of Individual Rights Guarantees

The opportunity a constitutional court has to exercise its authority (and subsequently shape policy) depends in part on range of rights guarantees provided by the constitution. An essential function, for the courts in this book, is the adjudication of rights. The greater the comprehensiveness and detail of the rights listed in the constitution, as well as the number of constitutional rights listed overall, the greater number of potential opportunities (and justifications for) for Court policymaking. If there are fewer rights, which are also vaguely defined, then this also presents challenges for the court in either accepting cases and/or ruling in a definitive manner.

In addition to the quantity and specificity of rights present, the nature or quality of these rights guarantees is also significant for understanding court influence. Rights may also be described as 'negative' or 'positive' guarantees. 'Negative rights' are guarantees *from* government intervention or encroachment. The majority of all the individual rights guaranteed in the US Constitution are negative rights;

for example, the fourth amendment is a right to be free from 'unreasonable searches and seizures". Positive rights are rights which exist only with the intervention of government action. The protections of said rights are often understood as an 'obligation' or 'duty' of the government. For example, Article 1, Sect. 1 of the German Basic Law, obliges the state to 'respect and protect' the dignity of man.

One could argue that these distinctions are merely semantics; in order for any rights to truly exist there needs to be some level of government oversight or intervention. However, these distinctions are important for understanding court interpretation of said rights and how a court's decisions may influence the policy process. If constitutional rights guarantees are largely construed in a negative fashion, this will constrain a court's ability to make proactive decisions. Such a court will only make 'negative' decisions, determining what governments *cannot* do under constitutional constraints, not directing what government actors *must or can* do. The court can only 'veto' a potential policy or government action. Whereas, if 'positive' guarantees are present, when interpreting these guarantees a court may be able to state in its decisions what government actors *must* do in order to meet the requirements of a constitutional guarantee. Therefore, positive rights guarantees provide more opportunities for courts to make more proactive decisions that may be potentially more binding or constricting on government actors.

CANADA

Establishment of the Court

A legislative act initially established the Supreme Court of Canada, whereas both the German Constitutional Court and the American Supreme Court were created via a constitutional document. Given Canada's colonial history, the broad outlines of judicial power were not initially granted to the Supreme Court but to England's Judicial Committee of the Privy Council.[21] Section 101 of the British North

---

[21] The Privy Council is the highest court of appeals in the UK for commonwealth countries. Canadian appeals to the Privy Council were abolished in 1933 and 1949 (for criminal and civil cases respectively).

American Act[22] states that the Canadian Supreme Court should be established, but it does not detail the court's features, functions or its independence from other government institutions (Russell 1987: 68).

Initially, the Supreme Court functioned only as an intermediate court of appeal, whose decisions could be appealed to the Privy Council, or could be bypassed entirely with a direct appeal to the Privy Council (Russell 87: 336). As Peter Russell has noted, "During this long period of subordination, the Supreme Court was a thoroughly second-rate institution and was treated as such by the federal government.... Far from viewing the Supreme Court as the head of a separate branch of government, politicians and officials were more inclined to see the Court and its justices as instruments of the federal government."(Russell 87: 337). The Supreme Court of Canada was not the country's court of last resort until Judicial Committee of the Privy Council jurisdiction over Canada was fully abolished in 1949, (Manfredi 12).

Although the Canadian Supreme Court's political stature improved after the removal of the Privy Council's jurisdiction, and began operating relatively independently from other government actors, the Supreme Court's function as the highest court of appeal in Canada has never been established constitutionally. None of Canada's constitutional acts, including the 1982 Constitution Act, which established the Canadian Charter of Rights and Freedoms, document this function. Only the Supreme Court Act, a legislative act subject to Parliamentary revision, provides details about the Court's composition. It outlines appointment procedures, judicial qualifications and tenure requirements, in addition to the Court's jurisdiction (Russell 67).

The lack of an external constitutional basis regarding the Court's existence and its functions provides a weak foundation for the Court's role in the Canadian political system and for its interventions in the

---

[22] The BNA Act was 'constitutionalized' in 1982, becoming part of the 'Constitution Acts' of Canada. Prior to 1982, the BNA Act was a governing document that only the British Parliament could amend or remove. I will refer to the Constitution Act(s) and the BNA act interchangeably.

policy process. Some court observers believe the absence of constitutional entrenchment of the Supreme Court and its functions has hindered its development as an institution on par with Parliament and the 'Executive' (Russell 1987 generally). Others have argued that the subsequent creation of additional Canadian legislative and constitutional acts, particularly the Charter of Rights and Freedoms, has provided sufficient support for the Supreme Court of Canada to function as Canada's high court of last resort (Manfredi 2001).

Section 52 (1) of the Constitutional Act of 1982 (Charter Act) declared the supremacy of Supreme Court interpretations of the Charter of Rights and Freedoms, and section 24(1) of the Charter explicitly provides for judicial enforcement of Charter rights and freedoms. However, these are relatively recent developments. The Canadian Supreme Court, having been a second rate institution for most of its existence, with minimal constitutional basis establishing its existence and its functions, is a relatively weaker institution on this measure as compared to the other two courts in this study.

Judicial Structure

Canadian judicial scholar Peter Russell summarizes it well, "Comparatively speaking, the Canadian judicial system ranks as one of the most integrated, or least federalized. The judicial provisions of the Canadian Constitution lean strongly in the direction of the judicial system of a unitary state" (Russell 1987: 49). Therefore, although the Canadian system has a federal design in other respects, its judicial system operates more like a unitary system.

Section 92.14 of the BNA Act provides that provinces shall administer and organize the provincial civil and criminal courts. Each province has a two-tier court system, which includes lower provincial courts (such as traffic, family, etc.), and superior courts, which are trial courts and appeals courts respectively (Malcolmson 160). In contrast to the US 'dual court' model with two largely separate judicial systems (state courts vs federal courts); appeals based solely on provincial, federal, or constitutional law may be brought before the Canadian Supreme Court. This comprehensive jurisdiction of the Court effectively combines ten provincial systems into one national system (Hogg 177).

In addition, another 'unifying' feature of the Canadian system is the fact that the federal government has the authority to appoint provincial 'superior' courts judges, while the provinces have the power to establish and administer the lower provincial courts. None of the Canadian constitutional documents detail why the federal government has the power to make these appointments. Peter Hogg believes that since such courts adjudicate questions of constitutional, federal, private and provincial laws, the federal government's role is appropriate (Hogg 179). Additionally, other Canadian constitutional scholars note that since the Canadian framers decided the federal government would have jurisdiction over criminal law, it needed to have the power to appoint superior court judges in order to consistently enforce a national criminal law.

In addition to provincial inferior and superior courts, the BNA Act also established solely federal courts. Parliament has the right to establish courts for the 'better administration' of Canada and to establish a 'General Court of Appeal for Canada'-the Canadian Supreme Court. Under Section 101, Parliament has also established the Federal Court of Canada which has specific jurisdiction over areas such as maritime law and copyright law and hears appeals from federal regulatory agencies and administrative courts (Malcolmson 160).

In summary, Canada has a fairly unified court system. Lower courts are the responsibility of the provinces, but superior courts, which are more likely to address issues of national policy importance, tilt more towards the federal government than towards part of the provincial authorities. As we will see in chapter five, these 'superior' courts tended to support Supreme Court precedent and make decisions based on constitutional and federal principles rather than provincial laws.

Jurisdiction

Among the three high courts in this study, the Supreme Court of Canada enjoys the broadest grant of jurisdiction. As noted above, the Canadian Supreme Court is a general court of appeal for Canada's entire judicial system (Russell 1987: 50). From its founding, the Supreme Court of Canada's jurisdiction has included appeals on the legality of local, provincial, criminal and federal law, in addition to review of constitutional questions (Russell 1987: 64).

The Court is constitutionally required to hear provincial and federal references and take criminal cases in which there was dissent in the lower court decision; otherwise the Court can choose what cases to hear under 'leaves to appeal' (similar to writs of certiorari in the American case). This broad jurisdiction provides the Court a variety of opportunities to engage in the policy process.

Justiciability

As compared to the United States Constitution, none of the Canadian constitutional documents limit the judicial power to the settlement of 'cases and controversies' or to certain 'matters' (Russell 1987: 91). In addition, the Canadian Supreme Court rejected the establishment of a 'political question doctrine', although it has created standing and mootness 'rules'. In *Operation Dismantle v the Queen (1985)*, Chief Justice Dickson stated that "...disputes of a political or foreign policy nature may be properly cognizable by the courts" (1 SCR 441). The Canadian Supreme Court has since refused to put questions of foreign or defense policy outside the court's jurisdiction simply because such questions may be inherently political or coincide with legislative or executive powers (Manfredi 78).

Until 1974, the Supreme Court of Canada's approach to standing was similar to that of the US Supreme Court. Prior to that time, the Court's standing doctrine originated from *Smith v AG Ontario* (1924), where the Court stated that "an individual has no status in action...unless he is specifically affected or exceptionally prejudiced by it" (1 SCR 331). The Court began to expand its definition of in *Thorson v the Queen* (1974). Thorson, a retired judge, challenged Parliament's authority to pass the 1969 Official Languages Act, which established Canada as officially as a bilingual state and required federal institutions to provide services in both French and English (Morton 98). Accepting Thorson's appeal, the Supreme Court justified its grant of standing by asserting that Official Languages Act was "declaratory and directory" in nature; it "created no offences and imposed no penalties: --there were no persons under the traditional rules [of standing]" (1 SCR 138). Although the Court did not overturn *Smith*, it asserted that "courts retain discretion to hear constitutional challenges to federal legislation in special circumstances.... and that there is a right of the citizenry to constitutional behavior by the Parliament" (1 SCR 138, 162-3).

The Court further broadened its standing doctrine in the case of *Nova Scotia Board of Censors v McNeil* (1976) by expanding the class of persons considered to be 'directly affected' by government action. An editor of a provincial weekly paper, McNeil protested Nova Scotia's denial of permits to theater owners who wanted to show the movie "Last Tango in Paris". He challenged the validity of the permit denial based on his taxpayer status (Morton 99). The Supreme Court acknowledged although the government action directly impacted theater owners, it accepted McNeil's petition due to the fact that "members of the Nova Scotia public are directly affected in what they may view in Nova Scotia" (2 SCR 271). The Court further elaborated by stating, "...that there appears no other way, practically speaking, to subject the challenged Act to judicial review" (Ibid). Since one could easily argue that a class of persons directly injured by the law already existed- theater owners, it is clear that this case further expanded the rule of standing.

The Court further extended citizen access to the court by allowing an individual who was neither directly nor indirectly harmed to bring a case to court in its *Borowksi* decision of 1981. Joe Borowski sought to challenge the federal criminal code regulating abortion on behalf of the 'unborn'. The Court justified granting standing to Borowski by asserting that the 'unborn', who were to face the greatest harm resulting from application of the law, obviously could not be parties to proceedings (Morton 102). After reaffirming its position on standing as outlined in *McNeil decision*, Justice Martland's majority opinion concluded with the Court's broadest definition of standing yet, "I interpret these cases as deciding that to establish status as a plaintiff in a suit seeking a declaration that legislation is invalid, a person need only show that he is affected by it directly or that he has a genuine interest as a citizen in the validity of the legislation and that there is no other reasonable and effective manner in which the issue may be brought before the court" (Morton 102, citing the case).

Ironically enough, although the Court granted Borowksi standing to challenge the federal law on behalf of the unborn, it is Borowksi again, seven years later with the Court now addressing the case on its merits, who led the Court to set its justiciability standards regarding mootness. In 1988, the Court stated it could not reach the substantive question presented by Borowski's case, which was to determine whether a 'person' under section 7 of the Charter of Rights and

Freedoms included the unborn thereby rendering the Criminal Code (sect. 251) unconstitutional. The Court stated that since its 1988 *Morgentaler II* decision had rendered the federal criminal law on abortion unconstitutional, Borowkski's claims were moot (Morton 271). The Court justified its determination of mootness by stating that had it rendered a decision on case, it would have looked like a 'private reference'. This means that the Court would have appeared as if it were trying to "preempt a possible decision of Parliament by dictating the form of legislation it should enact" had the court entertained Borowski's claim (1 SCR 342). Given the court's limited entrenched institutional authority, it would have been "a marked departure from the traditional role of the Court" had the court issued such a ruling (Morton 271). Employing the mootness standard here was consistent with the Court operating with self-restraint.

Yet while the Court employed the mootness doctrine in order to refrain from appearing to dictate policy to Parliament, the Canadian Supreme Court, has at times, one could argue, inconsistently applied this doctrine. As will be discussed in greater detail, in *Tremblay v Daigle* (1989), the Court overturned an injunction granted to Tremblay by the Quebec Supreme Court under the Quebec Charter of Human Rights and Freedoms and the Quebec Civil Code, to prevent his girlfriend, Daigle, from obtaining an abortion. After the Supreme Court had accepted the case, but before it had ruled, Charlene Daigle obtained an abortion in the US, thereby technically making the case moot (Jackman 1 and Morton 282). Yet, the Court issued a unanimous ruling overturning the now moot injunction, asserting that a Court decision was necessary in order to provide a consistent legal rule regarding the general legality of such injunctions under other provincial jurisdictions.

What explains the difference between these two cases in application of the mootness doctrine? The difference can plausibly be explained by the fact that in the *Borowski* case the Court was confronted with limiting the authority of Parliament, a political actor with the power to limit the court's authority, whereas, in *Daigle*, the Court was overruling the actions of an inferior provincial court, over which the Supreme Court has clear legal authority (jurisdiction over provincial law and courts). This is consistent with the view of this project; that if a court has clear, entrenched authority and/or is less likely to face sanction from another actor, the court is more likely to exercise its influence, as opposed to when such authorities are absent or subject to external limitation.

Nature and Timing of Judicial Review

<u>A Priori Review- Reference procedure</u>

The Supreme Court of Canada may intervene in the policy process through both 'a priori' and 'a posteriori' judicial review functions. While this has given the Court greater opportunities to intervene and thereby exercise its influence in the policy process, the Court's a priori review function- the 'reference procedure' is neither as broad nor as final as the German Constitutional Court and is conferred upon the Court by parliamentary statute and not a constitutional act. The 1875 Supreme Court Act empowered the federal government to refer questions to the Supreme Court of Canada 'on any matter whatsoever'. The Supreme Court Act allows the Governor in Council (Prime minister) to refer to the Court questions of:

> (1) interpretation of the Constitution Acts, (2) the constitutionality or interpretation of any federal or provincial legislation; (3) appellate jurisdiction respecting educational matters; and (4) ...important questions of law or fact concerning any matter, whether or not in the opinion of the Court *ejusdem generis* [similar or consistent with] with the enumerations contained in subsection (1), with reference to which the Governor in Council sees fit to submit any such question" *(Supreme Court Act, R.S. 1985, c. S-26, 53 (1, 2))*.

Canada's reference procedure provides the opportunity for direct interaction between the executive and the judiciary. The executive may exercise a reference to the court _prior to_ the exercise of power by Parliament or provincial legislature or _in absence of_ specific legislation being promulgated.[23] When the constitutional validity of

---

[23] Provincial governments cannot directly make a reference to the Supreme Court. All of the provinces, however, have laws enabling provincial governments to make references to provincial courts of appeal. Once a

legislation passed either by Parliament or by a provincial legislature is in question, the Supreme Court "may also give notice to any persons or class of persons who may have a special interest in the question and invite them to submit appeals for intervenor status" [24] (*Supreme Court Act R.S. 1985, c. S-26, 53 (5, 6))*.

The Supreme Court Act also states that advisory opinions are to "have no more effect than the opinions of the law officers" (Ibid). Effectively, this is not always the political reality, as both courts and governments have granted equal importance to judicial decisions stemming from both reference and concrete cases (Russell 1987: 91). The reference procedure has played a significant role Canadian politics enabling the Canadian Supreme Court to address highly significant and controversial policies that otherwise might not have reached the Court.[25] The Court can decline to answer vague reference questions, which grants the Court some justification in avoiding questions that may be too political (Russell 1987: 92). However, the Court has rarely done so and although the reference procedure has not been employed as frequently today as it has in the past, both provincial and federal governments still make use of the procedure.

One could argue that allowing references to the Supreme Court violates the Constitution Act's (BNA Act) determination that the

---

provincial court has issued an opinion (not a 'decision') that court may 'appeal' to the Supreme Court. The Supreme Court Act, determines that such cases must be heard by the Supreme Court (right to appeal 'without leave') (*Supreme Court Act*, S-36).   Therefore, provincial governments (executive) may 'indirectly' seek references from the Supreme Court of Canada, through this mechanism. (Hogg 2002: 237).

[24] Intervenor status is akin to amicus curare 'friend of the court' in the United States context.

[25] Since 1892 there have been 76 federal references. Among the most recent and controversial references have been: the *Anti-Inflation Act Reference* (1976), the *Manitoba Language Rights Reference* (1985), the *Ng Extradition Reference* (1991), the *Quebec Sales Tax Reference* (1994) and *Secession of Quebec Reference* (1998). In addition, the Court has also heard significant references from provincial governments as made through their provincial courts, such as the *Constitutional Patriation Reference* (1981), the *Quebec Veto Reference* (1982), and the *Provincial Court Judges Reference* (1997) (Canada, 2003).

Canadian Supreme Court is a "general court of appeal" and in fact this point was appealed to Privy Council in the *A-G Ontario v A.G Canada* (*Reference Appeal case*) (1912). However, the Privy Council ruled that the reference was not a 'judicial' function, since such decisions were "only advisory and will have no more effect than the opinions of the law officers", therefore the Court may produce such opinions without violating the Constitution Act. The Supreme Court recently reaffirmed this interpretation of the Constitution Act in the *Secession of Quebec Reference (1998)*. Peter Hogg asserts that both the Privy Council's ruling and the Supreme Court's decision support the "proposition that no separation of powers doctrine is to be read into the Constitution of Canada", reinforcing the notion of parliamentary supremacy in Canada (Hogg 238).

The reference procedure has enabled the Canadian executive to 'defer' controversial policies to the court, often as a means to advance policy interests that they are unable or unwilling to pursue in other arenas. While the Court may be used as an instrument to serve the interests of other political elites, the exercise of the 'reference' procedure can also facilitate the Court's influence in the policy process and impose constraints on those actors seeking a reference. In 1984, Pierre Trudeau's Liberal government referred a question regarding Manitoba's failure to protect language rights, compelling the Supreme Court to address this controversial issue (Russell 92). By using the reference procedure, the Trudeau government successfully used the reference procedure and the Court's subsequent ruling supporting the government's position as a means to pressure Manitoba into following the federal law on language rights. In addition, Trudeau's decision to seek a referral put pressure on future Liberal PM John Turner to take a stand on the issue, who had been unwilling to do so prior to the reference (Ibid., citing *Toronto Globe and Mail* March 23 1984).

This example illustrates how the reference procedure allows political actors to shift politically controversial policy-making issues to the Court in order to advance their interests. However, the reference procedure also enables the Supreme Court of Canada to intervene and address issues that may otherwise not reach the Court, thereby exemplifying the complex 'interdependent' nature of Court influence. In addition, in allows the Court an earlier entry point into that process, prior to enactment of a law, when there is likely to be more 'flexibility' or 'flux' in the policy process, as opposed to interventions resulting from concrete cases. Yet, as the Court's decisions in reference cases are not formally binding, the procedure conceivably still leaves room for other actors to deviate from the Court's determinations, which diminishes the Court's authority. However, there are costs to seeking references that can enhance the Court's influence. By seeking a reference, the executive will still be bound to 'respond' to the Court's ruling as these decisions become part of the public debate over said policy. If the executive does not agree with the decision or chooses not to follow it, it is likely that opposition leaders would press the issue, and the government would to be forced to justify their position in the court of public opinion. Therefore the Court's decision, while not formally binding, is likely to have some influence in shaping the direction of the (future) policy issue at hand.

The Court is aware of the impact the reference procedure may have on the policy process, whether it is utilized or not. During the oral arguments of the *Borowski* case, the Supreme Court chastised the federal government for *not* seeking a reference regarding the federal government's proposals to reform the recently declared unconstitutional federal criminal abortion law. The Mulroney government didn't want to ask the Court for a reference because it knew that if it did, it would impact the debate over its proposals for reforming the law. As Justice Lamer asked during oral arguments, "There is no law prohibiting abortions and there is none prohibiting pregnancy... What are we going to latch on to...a proper judicial function as distinct from a policy pronouncement?...I can only express an opinion as to what maybe the law should say" (SCC, Transcript of Appeal Proceedings 10/3/1988 pg. 17).

The Court recognized that if the government refused to ask for a reference granting legitimate authority to the Court to issue a clear policy recommendation, then the Court was unwilling to do so implicitly through its *Borowski* decision. Some scholars have asserted that the reference procedure is comparable to 'a priori' review procedures of other high courts and may enable the Canadian Supreme Court to act as a 'third legislative chamber' (Stone-Sweet 1999). However, it seems in practice, at least in the instance of abortion, that the existence of 'reference procedure' in the Canadian political system also provides justification for the Court *to refrain from* decision-making thereby allowing the Court to serve its own interests in preserving its authority and preventing other actors from deferring controversial issues to the court it does not want to address.

In addition, since the reference procedure can only be engaged by the executive, perhaps this contributes to the Court's unwillingness to make prescriptive decisions as compared to the courts in this study. This is because at worst the Court can be seen as a puppet of the executive (reinforcing parliamentary supremacy) and must depend on other actors to hold the executive 'accountable' for adhering to its decision. In contrast, in Germany the 'a priori' abstract review procedure can be employed by a number of political actors (including opposition party members) who have competing interests, and Court decisions are legally binding on all actors. Therefore the abstract review procedure reinforces the Constitutional Court's independence and influence in the political process, since it cannot easily be seen as beholden to particular elites.

To summarize, while the reference procedure can be an opportunity for the Court to enter the political process because it can only be engaged directly by the federal executive or 'indirectly' by provincial governments, and it only allows the court to provide 'advisory' rulings, these features may limit the influence of the Canadian Supreme Court in the policy process as compared to the German Constitutional Court.

A posteriori or 'concrete' review

In contrast to the Basic Law's grant of judicial review to the German Constitutional Court, the mechanism of concrete judicial review does not derive specifically from a constitutional source in Canada.[26] The

---

[26] To briefly summarize for those unfamiliar with the Canadian case, parties seeking to appeal a case to the Supreme Court must submit a written 'leave to appeal' (similar to a writ of certiorari) to the Court. Each year, the Court considers 550-650 applications for 'leave to appeal'. The Court grants leave to about half of those cases each year. Leaves to appeal are similar to the United State Supreme Court's grant of certiorari and are required for all cases except for criminal cases and provincial references. As stated by the *Supreme Court Act*, the Court grants leaves to appeal when a case raises issues "of its public importance or the importance of any issue of law or any issue of mixed law and

basis for judicial review in Canada has been derived historically from British common law and tradition, and the Court has exercised the power of judicial review since its founding (Ward 256, Russell 93). British common law is also the historical antecedent to the United States Supreme Court, which claimed judicial review in *Marbury v Madison.* Yet in neither the Canadian nor the American case has the power of judicial review constitutionally entrenched, placing these courts in a relatively weaker position relative to the German Constitutional Court.

As stated above, Canada's ratification of the 1982 Constitution Act included the Charter of Rights and Freedoms which includes a supremacy clause similar to that of the United States Constitution. The introduction of the Charter into Canadian politics strengthened justifications for the Court's involvement in constitutional questions and the application of judicial review. If an individual's right has been violated, article 24 (1) of the Charter explicitly allows for specific judicial enforcement and remedy: "Anyone whose rights or freedoms, as guaranteed by this Charter have been infringed or denied may apply to a court of competent jurisdiction to obtain such remedy as the court considers appropriate and just in the circumstances." However, even with the 'supremacy' of the Charter and the express guarantee for individuals to appeal rights claims, the lack of constitutional basis for judicial review still means that the Court must often justify its exercise of this authority in its decisions. Necessitating this step constrains the Court from making proscriptive policy pronouncements and makes it a weaker court relative to the German Constitutional Court, whose power of judicial review is constitutionally established and uncontested.

---

fact involved in that question, one that ought to be decided by the Supreme Court or is, for any other reason, of such a nature or significance as to warrant decision by it, and leave to appeal from that judgment is accordingly granted by the Supreme Court" (1985, c. S-26, s. 40). A three judge panel of the Canadian Supreme Court determines whether a case involves a question of public importance or raises an important issue of law necessitating Court consideration.

Individual rights guarantees

Compared to either Germany or the United States, 'rights politics' has generally played a smaller role in Canada, since the constitutional Charter of Rights and Freedoms was only introduced in 1982. Even with the existence of Canadian Bill of Rights prior to the Charter's enactment, it was only a legislative document under which the Supreme Court was unwilling to exercise judicial review. The 34 articles in the Charter are clustered into eleven sections including fundamental freedoms, democratic rights, mobility rights, legal rights equality rights, language rights, minority rights, education rights in addition to issues of enforcement, and application of said rights (see Table 4 at end of this chapter for a more detailed list). The introduction of the Charter has provided for "a systematic review of public policies from a 'rights' perspective. It provides another set of points of access to the decision making system, and it means that the agenda of law reform can be influenced through judicial as well as executive and legislative channels "(Tuohy 41). Most observers of the Court and Canadian politics generally agree that the introduction of the Charter into Canadian politics has been significant and has enlarged the role of the Supreme Court and the judiciary as a whole.

While the Charter provides a greater number of rights than the American Bill of Rights, they are similar in that the rights listed are largely 'negative' rights. Unlike the Basic Law in Germany, there are no explicit guarantees of 'positive' rights. However, the Charter does provide two conditions on the protection and balancing of these rights; first, is Section 1 of the Charter, which sets out a clear statement that these rights may be 'reasonably limited'; second, is Section 33, the 'notwithstanding clause' which allows the federal and provincial governments to shield laws from challenges or judicial rulings stemming from Charter claims about expression, legal and equality rights. However, this 'override' does not extend to democratic, mobility, language or sexual equality rights. Therefore, in addition to allowing governments to trump individual rights under certain conditions, Section 33 has privileged some rights over others by "distinguishing between rights that may be overridden and those that may not" (Tuohy 41).

Section 1 of the Charter effectively forces the Supreme Court into a two-step process of judicial review when reviewing Charter claims.

Section 1 states, "The Canadian Charter of Rights and Freedoms guarantees the rights and freedoms set out in it subject only to such reasonable limits prescribed by laws as can be demonstrably justified in a free and democratic society." The first stage of Charter review requires the Court to determine whether the law or act violates a Charter right. If it does, then the review must consider whether the law or act is justified in a 'free and democratic society'. In order to apply the Section 1 requirements, in *R. v Oakes (1986)* the Court developed a test for determining the reasonableness of a Charter limitation. When the Court first introduced the test, it stated that the test should be stringently applied, with clear proof supporting every stage of analysis. Over time, the court has relaxed the standard, stating that the test is merely a guideline or framework rather than one with stringent requirements (Funston and Meehan 161). The test can be summarized as follows:

> Does the impugned state action have an objective of pressing and substantial concern? If so, is this objective proportional to the impugned measure?
>
> a) Is it rationally connected to the objective?
> b) Does it impair the right or freedom as little as possible?
> c) Is there proportionality between the objective and the effects of the measure which limits the rights or freedom? (Ibid.).

The Court, when using the *Oakes* test, may strike down a law in whole or in part. Therefore, when performing the act of judicial review under Section 1 the Supreme Court of Canada must explicitly acknowledge this tension between minority rights and majority rule. In addition, since such governmental limits need only to be 'reasonable', this tampers down the absolutist nature of rights adjudication in Canada. To be fair, the US Supreme Court often performs the same task of balancing individual rights and community interests without external instruction. One may also argue that limitations imposed by the condition of a 'free and democratic society' as laid out in Sect.1 are sufficiently vague that this is not a particularly burdensome constraint. Yet, the statement does provide some guidance as it refers to democratic principles, giving the Court external justification for a cautious examination of the policy considerations of elected branches.

Section 33 more explicitly makes the case for allowing 'majority' interests to 'override' particular individual guarantees. As noted above, Section 33 can only be applied to laws which would impact particular rights. To engage a Section 33 override, the federal or a provincial government must simply enact a regular law expressly declaring that for five years, the law is to operate 'notwithstanding' the relevant Charter provision. In regards to the relevant Charter provision, the relevant legislature may renew its 'suspension' of the Court's decision by passing another declaration. Historically, the ratification of the Charter was predicated in part on the inclusion of the notwithstanding clause. In addition, the debates over the ratification of the Charter made it clear that the clause was to be a check on the Court's power providing another indication of the court's weak political position relative to other political institutions.

Peter Hogg summarizes the effect of Section 33 on exercise of judicial review: "The fact that the elected legislative bodies have been left with the last word answers a good deal of the concern about the legitimacy of judicial review by unelected judges" (Hogg 701). One may argue, however, that for Section 33 to have such an effect, it must be utilized often enough to be an effective reminder of the Court's limited power. To support this claim, the notwithstanding clause has been only employed by one government. During the early years after the passage of the Charter, the Parti Quebecois government in Quebec systematically used the override to cover all possible provincial legislation in response to the ratification of the Charter. Quebec had been vigorously opposed to the Charter. However, when the Liberals gained control a few years later, Quebec ended this practice (Hiebert 1996: 139).

With Section 33 rarely employed, some Canadian court scholars such as Christopher Manfredi, believe the notwithstanding clause is an ineffectual check on the SCC's power (Manfredi 188). While I would agree with Manfredi that the exercise of Section 33 is highly unlikely and poses a minimal threat to the Court's influence, nonetheless, I would argue that when making comparisons to other constitutions and rights guarantees, excluding the amendment process, neither the US Constitution nor the Basic Law explicitly provide a means for the legislature to 'suspend' or override court decisions. Therefore, at the very least, the presence of Section 1 and Section 33 effectively reinforce the notions of both parliamentary supremacy and the 'provisional' nature of rights in Canada. In addition, since Charter rights are subject to limitations from the outset, combined with the fact that such rights are largely negative rights, all these factors contribute to the conditions under which the Canadian Supreme Court would exercise Charter review in a more limited and circumscribed manner than the other two courts in this study.

UNITED STATES

Establishment of Court

Article III of the American Constitution outlines the major authorities of the US Supreme Court. It states that "...The judicial power of the US shall be invested in one Supreme Court...". The article does not define 'judicial power' beyond the fact that is covers all cases and controversies "arising under this Constitution, the Laws of the United States, and Treaties made, or which shall be made, under their Authority..." (Article III). The court's jurisdiction under this grant of authority is largely appellate, and subject to limitations by Congress and Supreme Court discretion. The Constitution also states that "The Judges, both of the supreme and inferior Courts, shall hold their Offices during good Behavior". While not an explicit declaration of judicial independence, it does provide an entrenched guarantee of their position, with a limited exception.

Beyond these statements, the Constitution does not further outline the exercise of the court's functions. Article III is relatively brief compared to the specific authorities of Congress listed in Article I and the Executive's powers in Article II. Over time the Court has created its own rules and justifications to augment its powers outlined in the Constitution, most notably, the power of judicial review. However, the exercise of these court created authorities has not always been accepted by other political branches, and at times has created intense controversy over the Court's exercise of its powers. The US Constitution does not provide a clear basis upon which the US Supreme Court can justify its exercise of judicial review. Over time, the Court has had to find ways to justify or shore up its institutional capacities, which places the court in a relatively weak position as compared to the German Constitutional

Court and somewhat stronger position than the Canadian Supreme Court.

Judicial Structure

The United States judicial system embodies the principle of dual federalism. There are two distinct judicial hierarchies: a federal court system of original courts and courts of appeal, and a state system for state law and appellate courts. The federal government organizes and administers federal courts, while states systems may differ in their organization or administration, in addition to the variations in the state laws themselves.

The US Constitution and federal statues outline the basic divisions between the jurisdictions of the two systems. Most cases heard in federal courts include those based on the US Constitution, treaties and other federal laws (Baum 1998: 23). In addition, federal jurisdiction also covers any case in which the federal government is a party, or cases in which the parties are from different states and when the suit is $75,000 or more (diversity jurisdiction) (Ibid.). This federal jurisdiction is neither exhaustive nor exclusive. For example, litigants in a diversity jurisdiction case may choose to bring a case either a federal or a state court. In addition, most cases filed in the United States do not fall under federal jurisdiction and are tried in state courts (Ibid.). As compared to Canada and Germany, substantive criminal law is primarily a state matter in the US (though there is an ever increasing body of federal criminal law) and such cases are largely adjudicated in state courts.

Court organization in the federal system begins with district courts. They are arranged to cover the entire US. Other courts at this level include courts of specific jurisdiction, such as the Court of International trade, Tax Court and the Court of Veterans Appeals (Baum 1998: 28). Next are the district Courts of Appeals, the Court of Appeals for the Federal Circuit covering some of the lower specialized courts, and the Courts of Appeal for the Armed Forces and the Intelligence Surveillance Court of Review. Above all these federal courts sit the US Supreme Court.

There is a fair amount of organizational variation among the state court systems, but there are some general patterns. Most states have major and minor trial courts, and intermediate and supreme appellate courts. They also have a final court of appeals, usually named a supreme court, most of which have discretionary jurisdiction. Some of these courts have mandatory jurisdictions, and a few have *only* mandatory jurisdictions. A few states have separate final court of appeals for criminal and civil cases.

Lastly, virtually all state and federal courts have the ability to exercise judicial review and render interpretations of the US Constitution, should constitutional claims be raised in a particular case. Such decisions may be appealed through either the state or federal court system ending with possible review by the Supreme Court. However, should cases within the state court system address issues only regarding the interpretation of state law or state constitutions, such cases are not appealable to the US Supreme Court and the highest state court has final jurisdiction over such cases.

Given the diversity of the court system, combined with the fact that lower courts may adjudicate constitutional questions, there are many more potential opportunities for policy issues to eventually appear at the Supreme Court. Since control over this system is 'diffuse', with fifty separate state systems with their respective high courts, this also means that some policy issues may never reach the Supreme Court, particularly if such issues are resolved solely on the basis of interpretations of state constitutions and laws by lower state courts. As will be discussed in greater detail, litigation regarding state abortion policy arose in both Utah and Oregon. The cases that arose in Utah were challenges to state laws based on the US Constitution and pursued in federal courts, up to and including the US Supreme Court. In Oregon, while the petitioner made claims that state administrative actions violated the US Constitution guarantees (as well as state law and the state constitution), the Oregon Supreme Court resolved the case definitively on the basis of state constitutional law, therefore shielding the case from being appealed to the US Supreme Court.

Jurisdiction

The United States Supreme Court has limited original jurisdiction and relatively broad appellate jurisdiction, subject to Congressional limitations as outlined in Article III of the Constitution. The Court's original jurisdiction is limited to cases involving ministers, consuls and ambassadors to the US, and controversies between states. Otherwise the Supreme Court may hear:

> all Cases, in Law and Equity, arising under this Constitution, the Laws of the United States, and Treaties made, or which shall be made, under their Authority; to all Cases affecting Ambassadors, other public Ministers and Consuls; to all Cases of admiralty and maritime Jurisdiction; to Controversies to which the United States shall be a Party; to Controversies between two or more States; between a State and Citizens of another State; between Citizens of different States; between Citizens of the same State claiming Lands under Grants of different States....

The appellate function accounts for almost all the cases on court's docket.

Although Article III of the Constitution indicates that cases in which 'a state shall be a party' are part of the Court's original jurisdiction, in *Cohens v Virginia* the Court itself limited the scope of its original jurisdiction. In the case, the Court ruled that lower courts could first hear most cases involving a state, and that the original jurisdiction requirements applied only to controversies among two or more states. Congress subsequently created legislation codifying this limitation (Perry 25). Therefore, *Cohen* and the ensuing congressional legislation excluded a large class of cases that otherwise would have been a required part of the court's docket. In addition, Congress further empowered the Court's discretion over its docket by removing most automatic appeals categories in 1988 (Ibid). For most of the Court's history appeals cases had comprised almost 25 percent of the cases heard by the Court (Ibid.). Given these changes, today the overwhelming majority of cases arrive at the Court through writs of certiorari.

Prior to 2006, Congress has not exercised its right to unilaterally limit the Court's jurisdiction; however, it has done so in the past, most notably in *Ex Parte McCardle* (1869), in which the Court accepted Congress' removal of part of its appellate function. In this case, the Court rejected a challenge to congressional legislation removing the Court's ability to hear appeals arising under the 1867 Habeas Corpus Act. Within the last fifty years, members of Congress have introduced dozens of legislative proposals attempting to limit the USSC's jurisdiction in some manner (Pacelle 82). Members of Congress have often proposed such legislation as a threat or response to court decisions that they disagreed with (Pacelle 85). Two of the most significant attempts that ultimately failed occurred in 1957 and 1958 after the Warren Court had struck down desegregation in public schools and upheld a number of other individual rights against government encroachment (Biskupic & Witt 340). More recently, through the Detainee Treatment Act of 2005, and the Military Commissions Act of 2006, Congress attempted to remove the Supreme Court's jurisdiction to review habeas corpus petitions filed by Guantanamo detainees. The Supreme Court declared in both *Hamdan v Rumsfeld (*2006) and *Boumediene v Bush* (2008), that Congress did not have the authority to strip the Court of its jurisdiction.

The constitution only provides for 'exceptions', but it does not, however, specify as to the nature and the extent to which Congress may carve out exceptions to the Court's jurisdiction. It is unclear the extent to which Congress can remove parts of the Court's jurisdiction over constitutional rights. Nonetheless, this power of Congress provides a constitutionally justifiable opportunity to limit the Court's scope by removing the Court's appellate review of certain policy issues. The constitutional authority of Congress to make exceptions to the Court's jurisdiction merely highlights how the ability of the Court to intervene in the policy process can depend upon Congress' powers. During the time period covered in this study, there was no serious threat posed by Congress to circumscribe the Court's jurisdiction. While it seems unlikely that there would be conditions under which Congress could reasonably remove a significant portion of the Court jurisdiction, recent controversies over 'enemy combatants', 'writs of habeas corpus' and access to federal courts may remind us (and the Court) that there may be such conditions where Congress would choose to take such action.

Justiciablity

Article III of the Constitution allows the Supreme Court to address issues that are an actual 'case' or 'controversy', although it provides no further clarification as to what constitutes a case or controversy. The Court, through its own rulings, has largely chosen to interpret this statement in a limited fashion. The Court has rejected the view that the 'case or controversy' requirement expressly includes the authority to provide advisory opinions to other branches of government. During the first years of the United States existence, Chief Justice John Jay denied President Washington's request, via Secretary of State Thomas Jefferson, for the Court to determine whether the Franco-American treaty conflicted with the Proclamation of Neutrality (1788) (Pacelle 88). In 1911, the Court denied review of *Muskrat v US*, because the case presented no adverse controversy between the two parties to the case. Congress had expressly authorized certain Native Americans to sue the US, in a direct attempt to force the Court to determine the constitutionality of legislation regarding Native American land ownership. The Court determined it could not provide a ruling in this case because it would be "no more than an expression of opinion upon the validity of the acts in question" (*Muskrat v United States (1911), 219 US 346 at 342).*

It is plausible to assume that the Court, especially in its early history, sought to consolidate its authority and independence by rejecting these cases in order to insure that the Court did not appear beholden to or serving the interests of a particular branch of government. Perhaps, if the constitution had provided more clarity, the Court would not have found it necessary to limit itself in this fashion. The Court closed off a more direct avenue of court intervention in the policy process by refusing to develop an interpretation of the 'case and controversy' requirement that would have enabled it to issue advisory opinions on behalf of either the President or Congress. In subsequent decades, both the President and Congress sought to force court intervention in the policy process in order to achieve their policy objectives (see Whittington, Lovell, and McMahon generally). While in these instances the Court may have been willing or sympathetic to these interests, it seems that such interventions came at the expense of the court's independence and influence. Therefore, the Court has often ended up do the bidding of other branches by other means, even though it initially had attempted to avoid such situations.

In addition to asserting the Court's authority of judicial review Chief Justice Marshall declared in *Marbury v Madison,* "Questions in their nature political are not for us to decide". This phrase established the court's 'political question' doctrine and another self-imposed qualification on the Court's judicial power. While is it is not clear precisely what the doctrine does or does not cover, the Court has applied the 'political question' to refrain from such cases that involve questions of foreign policy, raise questions of legislative process or procedure, or attempt to use the 'guarantee of a republican form of government' as a claim against state actions (Biskupic & Witt 41). Yet there are some notable examples where the Court has ignored its own doctrine and has issued rulings in politically controversial cases; such as the apportionment of legislative districts (*Baker v Carr 1962*) and more recently in the case of *Bush v Gore (2000)*. While these exceptions are few, by failing to consistently apply the political question doctrine, the Court has opened itself up to critiques and challenges regarding whether its exercise of judicial review is legitimate.

The Supreme Court also has established rules of standing, mootness and ripeness, in addition to the political question and 'case or controversy' rules. Summarizing the rulings from a number of decisions, the Court has developed the following rules of standing: 1. a person party to the case must have suffered an actual, or imminent, not potential harm, 2. the challenged government action or law must have directly caused the harm, 3. the judiciary must be able to provide redress, 4. Congress may specifically confer standing to an individual or class of persons, by statute, but this designation is still subject to points 1-3.[27] Over time the Court has expanded, contracted and provided various exceptions to these principles.[28]

The Court has also established rules of mootness and ripeness, which focus on the nature of the dispute rather than the nature of the

---

[27] See *Flast v Cohen (1968), Sierra Club v Morton (1972), US v SCRAP (1973), Allen v Wright (1984) Lujan v Defenders of Wildlife (1992)* as examples.

[28] See most recently, *Massachusetts v Environmental Protection Agency (2007)* and *Hein v Freedom from Religion Foundation (2007)*. In the first case, the Court allowed a state to challenge the EPA's inaction in regulating greenhouse gases and essentially asserted that states should get special consideration in regards to standing and that the rising sea levels due to climate change were a sufficiently imminent or actual harm. However, in the latter case, the Court ruled that an interest group could not have standing to challenge an executive branch program, and that taxpayer standing only extended to congressionally funded programs.

litigant. A case is moot if it has lost its adversarial nature, or the question has been resolved before its presentation to the court. Echoing its earlier position on 'advisory opinions', the Court has stated that its role is to "decide actual controversies by a judgment which can be carried into effect, and not to give opinions upon moot questions or abstract propositions, or to declare principles or rules of law which cannot effect the matter in issue in the case before it" (*Mills v Green, 159 US 651 at 653 (1895)*). There have been a few exceptions to the mootness standard, particularly in criminal cases where a defendant may still face adverse consequences due to a conviction even if he has served his sentence, and in situations of a short duration, which are "capable of repetition, yet evading review" (*Roe v Wade, Doe v Bolton, 410 US 113, 179 (1973)*).

Finally, ripeness requires that question(s)/claims presented in a case are significantly concrete and the issues and all questions of fact are clear; "a claim is not ripe for adjudication if it rests upon contingent future events that may not occur as anticipated, or indeed may not occur at all" (Wright, Miller, et al 112). Constitutional claims against a potentially harmful law which has been enacted but never applied or enforced, would likely be found not yet ripe for review. However, the Court has at times addressed the merits of 'declaratory judgments' regarding the constitutionality of state laws (see *Epperson v Arkansas 1968*).

To summarize, these rules have generally signified the Court's unwillingness to provide decisions that appear to be advisory or abstract. These largely self-imposed rules, while serving the Court's interests of maintaining its independence and insulating itself from challenges to its legitimacy have also encumbered the Court's ability to intervene in the policy process, both by limiting the types of cases it can address and setting up a high standard for the Court to adhere to. Essentially, if we assume that constitutional interpretation and adjudication inevitably force the Court to address the 'authoritative allocation of values and interests' (public policy) in some way, these rules have become unreasonable standards that the Court cannot sustain. If a jurisprudence of advisory opinions had been developed over time rather than a set of inconsistently applied self-imposed rules (or if the constitution had provided clarity on this point in the first place), perhaps US Supreme Court influence on American politics would look very different today.

Nature and Timing of Judicial Review

Since the initial passage of the Judiciary Act in 1925, the US Supreme Court's docket has been largely appellate, discretionary and consisting of writs of certiorari. There are five ways that cases may come before the Supreme Court; (1) original jurisdiction, (2) certification, (3) extraordinary writ, (4) writ of appeal[29], and (5) writ of certiorari. Today the numbers of cases arising from original jurisdiction, certification and extraordinary writ are few. Certification is a virtually obsolete procedure in which lower courts request the Supreme Court provide binding instructions on a question of law. The lower courts initiate this procedure themselves (Perry 27). As discussed in the previous section, the US Supreme Court does not hear 'abstract' questions or issue advisory opinions. Therefore, the Court has only an 'a posteriori' review function.

Formally, petitions for writs of certiorari are appeals to review the judgment of a lower court. Grants of certiorari are purely at the discretion of the Court. Historically, on average, the Court has accepted 100 of 7,000 certiorari petitions per year.[30] The court has specific rules for the certiorari process outlining how the petition is to be formatted, what it is to include, how the fees are to be paid. The majority of the petitions *accepted* by the Court are formally filed and paid cases, although the Court also allows writs filed *in forma pauperis* which come from litigants who are unable to pay the application fees. Most of these cases are filed by prisoners and the Court rarely grants a hearing to these cases, though a few significant Court decisions have originated from *in forma pauperis* filing, most notably, *Gideon v Wainright* (1963).

The small odds of the Court choosing to hear the case, the filing requirements and the resources necessary to pursue a case through the entire justice system restricts the range of issues the Court could potentially address.[31] Since the Court's original jurisdiction is narrow

---

[29] The Judiciary Act was amended in 1988, virtually removing this practice.

[30] In the last few years, this number of cases granted certiorari has decreased even further, to about 90-80 cases per term.

[31] Pursuing a case through the court system up to the Supreme Court can place substantial monetary costs upon potential plaintiffs, since litigants must pursue their case through a number of lower courts, trial, appellate, etc., before having

and there are no other direct avenues to Court review, the Court is largely dependent upon litigants who can overcome these burdens in order to supply them with cases to review. Therefore the time consuming and costly process of litigating a case up to the Supreme Court limits the opportunities for the Court to intervene in the policy process.

In addition to these administrative rules, the most important substantive guideline to the Court's grants of certiorari is Rule 10. Since grants of certiorari are at the discretion of the Court, these guidelines are "neither controlling nor fully measuring the Court's discretion", but merely "indicate the character of reasons that will be considered by the Court" (Stern and Gressman, et al. 222, citing Supreme Court Rules). Last updated in 1995, the current certiorari rules state that the Court considers: (1) whether there is conflict between Federal Court of Appeals, or a conflict between a Court of Appeals and a state court of last resort, or a Court of Appeal has greatly departed from the 'accepted and usual course of judicial proceedings' or sanctioned such a departure by a lower court; (2) a state court of last resort had decided an important federal question of law which conflicts with a Federal Court of Appeals or another state court of last resort; (3) a Court of Appeals or state court of last resort has decided an "important question of federal law that has not been, but should be, settled by this Court or has decided an important federal question in a way that conflicts with the relevant decisions of this Court "(Ibid.).

Although these rules are broad, one could argue that they provide the Court with clear and documented justification for its decision to accept or reject hearing a case. Consistent with the Court's justicability rules, Rule 10 can be understood as a means to insulate the court from

---

the opportunity for Supreme Court review. Attorney and other legal fees, in addition to other support resources can prohibit many litigants from attempting to take their case to the next level (see Epp 1998 generally). The resources in which plaintiffs utilize in order to overcome these institutionalized barriers to Supreme Court litigation has been characterized by Charles Epp as the 'support structure for legal mobilization' (Epp 1998). While this support structure is an important precondition in considering how issues may arrive at the Court's doorstep, given that this book focuses on the Court centered institutional features which structure Court influence in policymaking, it is beyond the scope of this project to detail the development of this support structure.

external criticism if one assumes that the Court is motivated more by ideological policy considerations as opposed to addressing important discrepancies in the law during the certiorari

process. Yet, since these rules are 'self-imposed' and as Stern, et al note, "It is the discretionary element of the Court's certiorari practice and the Court's apparent disregard of its own standards on some occasions that have caused much of the internal and external criticism of the Court's exercise of its certiorari jurisdiction."(224).

As noted above, the Supreme Court only has the power of *a posetori* concrete judicial review. The US Supreme Court assumed judicial review in its (arguably) most famous decision, *Marbury v Madison* (1803). In a crafty decision, the Court asserted that since (1) it was the Court's role to interpret the law generally and resolve disputes over conflicting laws (judicial power in Article III) and (2) since the Constitution was the 'supreme law of the land' (Article IV), the Court had the authority to interpret the Constitution and determine whether acts of other government actors are consistent with it.

The controversy over judicial review (and the court's interpretation of it) lies in whether the court's constitutional interpretation is *supreme and definitive*. Is the Constitution what the Court 'says it is' and is that decision final and binding on other constitutional actors? Should the Court have such authority when its members are not 'elected' and may issue decisions that are 'counter-majoritarian'? The constitution itself did not make this clear and has contributed to the debate over the legitimate exercise of judicial review. As noted previously, the lack of a solid constitutional ground for the exercise of judicial review has led scholars and justices themselves to articulate external justifications of judicial review and its application in order to justify the Court's exercise of review and to shield the Court from criticism, particularly in regards to the charge of judicial policy-making, which is often assumed to be an inappropriate function for the court.[32]

---

[32] John Ely, Richard Posner, and others have argued for various theories of constitutional interpretation in order to provide a coherent justification for the application of judicial review. To discuss the content and the merits of these theories is beyond the scope of this project, though one may clearly argue that the Court itself engages in this activity (framer's intent, non-interpretivism, etc). While many individual judges have applied these approaches, none have been

In addition, others scholars have asserted that instead of trying to justify the 'means', one could argue that the ends or outcomes of judicial review are sufficiently democratic, reinforce majority views and/or are beneficial to society, therefore the exercise of judicial review is not controversial (see Peretti 1999 as one example). One could also argue that judicial review has gained sufficient political and public support over time that it has become a relatively uncontested authority of the Supreme Court. While I would agree that the Supreme Court is unlikely to deviate so widely from majority values/interests as to create a seismic rift between it and other branches due to the political supports enabling judicial review, when examined in a comparative context to other high courts it is the lack of external, uncontested constitutional supports which undermine the Supreme Court's influence in the policy process as compared to other high courts. Having created untenable inconsistently applied self-imposed standards, rules and justifications in which to legitimize the exercise of judicial review places the US Supreme Court in a position of relative weakness as compared to high courts with more externally entrenched and explicitly defined authorities. As the subsequent sections will detail, the German Constitutional Court has explicit powers of judicial review, a number of institutionalized means in which it can intervene (exercise review) in the policy process and the ability to render decisions that are binding on other actors.

Individual Rights Guarantees

The United States Bill of Rights formally includes the first 10 Amendments to the Constitution, yet there have been subsequent amendments, most notably the 14th amendment, which also comprise the guarantees of individual rights in the US. As compared to the Canadian Charter or the German Basic law, the US Constitution does not provide any overall statements or values limiting the extent of the rights guaranteed in the document. Relatively speaking, the US Constitution provides fewer rights overall, and one could argue that many of the rights are more open-ended, and less specific, than similar

---

consistently employed by the entire court in order to qualify as a substantial internal norm.

rights protected in these comparable constitutional documents, particularly as compared to the Basic Law. Therefore, the extent and full nature of those rights has been largely determined by the Supreme Court through its decisions. For example, the US Constitution prohibits infringements upon individual's 'freedom of speech', whereas the Basic Law guarantees, "Every person shall have the right to freely express and disseminate their opinions in speech, writing and pictures and to inform himself without hindrance from generally acceptable sources" (Basic Law, Article 5, section 1). With fewer and more open-ended rights, this has meant that in order for the Supreme Court to justifiably review the constitutionality of government acts, it has, at times, applied interpretations of these rights that are seemingly disconnected from the text itself.

At times, in order to justify its rulings striking down government acts, the Court has created elaborate rulings or tests that have not held up over time (see the Court's *Lochner* era decisions as one notable example). At times these decisions have been met with hostility and threats by other political actors (see FDR's proposed 'court packing' plan). While the Court has not suffered catastrophic harm from these decisions, collectively, they contribute to the perception that the Court engages in judicial activism.

In addition, the Court has either outright overruled itself or has 'readjusted' by relaxing the standards or tests it has established. Abortion is a good example. The Court has relaxed its standard for evaluating the constitutionality of government acts regulating abortion. The Court's initial decision in *Roe v Wade* was based on the 'right to privacy', a right not explicitly guaranteed by the Constitution, but one that the Court had earlier argued was protected 'by the 'penumbras and emanations' of a number of other guaranteed rights, such as a right to be free from unreasonable searches and seizures (*Grizwold v Connecticut 1965*). By 1992, the Supreme Court relaxed the more precise 'viability' standard it had established in *Roe,* replacing it with the broader 'undue burden' standard. Overall, the point here is that the absence of a specific and comprehensive list of rights contributes to the Court's relative weakness relative to the other high courts in this study.

In addition, the rights guaranteed in the US Constitution are 'negative' rights, with the exception of the 13th, 14th, and 15th amendments. Without the presence of such 'positive' guarantees or duties of the government, it is more difficult for the Court to issue decisions that dictate the action that the government must take in order to protect or enable specific rights. As one scholar notes, comparing the impact of these differences on decision-making by the US Supreme Court and the German Constitutional Court,

> The United States Constitution is more open ended than the German Constitution; unlike the latter, it does not purport to set forth the set of fundamental values that govern the legal order. The German Constitution attempts to identify both the fundamental rights and the legal interests that justify their limitation. The United States Constitution has not such comprehensive ambitions. Optional governmental policies in areas unaddressed by the constitutional text may figure as compelling interests that outweigh enumerated rights, and the Supreme Court's endorsement of government choices in upholding them against constitutional challenge does not commit the government to continuing those policies (Neuman 303).

Therefore, to summarize, the vague and limited nature of individual rights guarantees in the US, in conjunction with the absence of rules that obligate the government to protect or uphold particular rights, create conditions in which the US Supreme Court decisions are more likely to be limited and circumscribed than those of its German counterpart. In addition, the absence of 'positive' rights guarantees makes it more difficult for the Court to provide proscriptive decisions that instruct government actors as to what they must or should do, rather than merely what they cannot do.

GERMANY

Establishment of the Court

In contrast to both the Canadian and US Supreme Courts, which stand at the apex of the judicial system, the German Constitutional Court operates outside of the regular judiciary. The Constitutional Court is the "federal court of justice independent of all other constitutional organs," and it is equal in rank to other federal political institutions such as the Bundestag (Parliament) or the federal government (chancellor and cabinet) (Kommers 1997: 142). Echoing Article III of the US Constitution, Article 92, of the Basic Law states, "Judicial Power shall be vested in the Judges; it shall be exercised by the Federal Constitutional Court, by the federal courts provided for in this Basic Law and by the courts of the Länder."

As stated earlier, in contrast to the US Supreme Court or the Supreme Court of Canada, there is little contestation regarding the German Constitutional Court's use of judicial review since it is explicitly provided for in the Basic Law. Article 93 (1):1 states:

> The Federal Constitutional Court shall decide: 1. On the interpretation of this Basic Law in the event of disputes concerning the extent of rights and duties of a highest federal organ or of other parties concerned who have been vested with rights of their own by this Basic Law or by rules of procedure of a highest federal organ" and "in the event of disagreements or doubts respecting the formal or substantive compatibility of federal law or Land law with this Basic Law, or the compatibility of Land law with other federal law, on application of the Federal Government, of a Land government" (Law on the Federal Constitutional Court 66).

In addition, the Basic Law also outlines the composition of the Court, and explicitly states in Article 97 that, "Judges shall be independent and subject only to the law" and may be dismissed "only by virtue of judicial decision and only for the reasons and in the manner specified by the laws" (Ibid). Article 1(1) of the Law on the Federal Constitutional Court further enumerates the court capacities and functions, re-asserts this independence, "The Federal Constitutional Court shall be a federal court of justice independent of all other constitutional organs." The Law on the Federal Constitutional Court, while not a 'constitutional' document, expounds upon the powers of the Constitutional Court as stated in the Basic Law. Combined, the Constitutional Court's powers are more detailed and entrenched as compared to Canadian and US Supreme Courts. In addition, it is the only court that has a constitution that explicitly grants the power of judicial review, and establishes the court's independence from other political institutions.

Judicial Structure

As noted above, the Constitutional Court sits apart from the rest of the judicial system and compared to both Canada and the US. Federal law establishes the structure and organization of the federal courts. In contrast to the extensive role of the federal executive in Canada, the Länder select, employ and administer most of the lower judicial appointments in Germany (Schmidt 2003: 110). Lower courts and intermediate courts of appeal are under Lander jurisdiction, while courts of final appeal are federal courts. The hierarchical judicial system is organized by jurisdiction; in addition to lower criminal and civil courts there are administrative, finance, social and labor divisions (Ibid.). A high federal court, such as the Federal Court of Justice, which is the highest court of civil and criminal matters, tops each of these hierarchies. All but three Länder have high Land constitutional courts.

Unlike the US or Canada where lower courts may determine the constitutionality of governmental laws or actions, only the Constitutional Court is able to render decisions of constitutionality. If a lower German court finds that a law is in conflict with the constitution, the court is obliged to refer the case to the Constitutional Court (Kommers 1997: 13). The lower court must provide documentation to the Constitutional Court stating the legal question, the alleged violation of the Basic Law and the degree to which a ruling from the Constitutional Court is required to resolve the question at issue (Law on the Federal Constitutional Court Sect. 63-67). The Constitutional Court may decline to hear the case if it does not believe that the law in question was in possible violation of the Basic Law or if the case can be decided without addressing the law's constitutionality (Kommers 1997: 13).

Jurisdiction

In contrast to the two other courts, the German Constitutional Court's jurisdiction is limited almost exclusively to disputes over constitutional law. However, unlike the other two courts in this study, the German Constitutional Court has sole, original jurisdiction over constitutional questions. This is a significant distinction because having sole jurisdiction consolidates the German Court's power over constitutional issues, whereas in the US, all courts have authority to decide constitutional questions. This provides for numerous interpretations and constitutional policies on a given issue. In Germany, Article 93 explicitly delineates the court's jurisdiction. The Constitutional Court may determine the compatibility of the Basic Law with legislation, secondary statutory law, acts, and orders of federal and Land governments. It may also address questions of constitutionality regarding parliamentary elections and political parties, public international law, controversies between the Länder and Federal Government, and hear complaints from individual persons against governmental entities.[33]

One could argue that since the Constitutional Court's jurisdiction is limited to constitutional disputes, the German Constitutional Court's authority would be less influential relative to the United States Supreme Court or Canadian Supreme Court. This concern is mitigated by the fact that the Basic Law is much more comprehensive and detailed than either the Canadian Charter or the US Constitution. Therefore many more policy issues in Germany are likely to have a clearer connection to the constitution than in the US or Canada. As one German judicial scholar notes, "Taken together [the court's authority over interpreting the Basic Law and scope of the court's jurisdiction], these competencies amount to a general delegation of all constitutionally significant disputes to the Federal Constitutional Court, particularly since the Basic Law allows an extension [of court jurisdiction] by statutory law (Article 93 (2)); and corresponding delegations of power have actually taken place" (Magiera 91). Article 93 of the Basic Law permits the legislature *only to extend* the Court's jurisdiction and may not alter or remove any part of it. Such entrenched guarantees enable the Constitutional Court to exercise its authority securely since its jurisdiction may not be contracted by other political actors.

To summarize, the German Court, has a jurisdiction that is constitutionally explicit, comprehensive, and not subject to limitation by other political institutions. Both the Canadian and US Supreme

---

[33] See also Article 21 and 41 of the Basic Law and further exposition on these competencies in the Law on the Federal Constitutional Court, *Federal Law Gazette 1951.*

Courts are relatively weaker institutions on this dimension since their jurisdictions may be controlled or altered by other political actors. Legislative control over a court's jurisdiction may have the potential (and real effect) of limiting the court's opportunities to shape policy. Even if legislative action is more likely a threat than reality, the threat may be significant enough to restrain a court and temper its decision-making accordingly. Courts operating under such conditions may be less likely to exercise their power as authoritatively as courts that are not operating under these limitations.

Justiciability

Similar to Canada, in Germany there is neither an equivalent to the US Supreme Court "political question" doctrine, nor is there a 'case or controversy' requirement (Kokott 1998: 111). Given that the Constitutional Court may make 'a priori' decisions (abstract review) it seems logical that there would *not* be a comparable limitation. However, just like the other two courts, the German Constitutional Court refuses to address 'moot' questions, asserting that "there has to be a 'live' controversy or conflicts of opinions in cases brought to the court" (Kommers 1997: 50). In addition, the German Constitutional Court also does not accept cases not yet 'ripe' for review. For example, in the *Steam Boiler* case (1960), the Constitutional Court struck down federal legislation possibly obstructing state administration of a federal law, but did not outline specific conditions detailing what federal action would be constitutionally appropriate, since no harm had yet occurred (Kommers 1997: 50 citing case).

In regards to standing Article 93 of the Basic Law states that 'any person' who has a legal claim to rights may appeal cases. The German Court has interpreted this constitutional requirement to include individual persons, corporate entities, and other 'legal persons' holding rights under the law (Kommers 1997: 14, see *Mental Deficiency Case (1951), Bank Standing Case (1968), State Radio Cases (1971))*. Similar to the US and Canadian Supreme Courts, the German Court may choose whether or not to employ these justicability doctrines, and as Donald Kommers notes, "Yet here, as with much of its authority, the court's sense of self-restraint is the only check on the exercise of its power" (Kommers 1997: 51).

Nature and Timing of Judicial Review

The German Constitutional Court receives an average of about 9,000 pieces of correspondence per year from individuals requesting attention to their 'claim' (Kommers 1997: 26). Most of these filings come from 'constitutional complaints', which allows any person, if they have exhausted all other legal means, to petition the German Constitutional Court directly if they believe their fundamental rights have been violated by governmental action (Article 93, Basic Law, Law on the Federal Constitutional Court). However, this requirement of first seeking redress from other courts can be waived if the governmental act is likely to cause serious, irreversible harm to the complainant (Article 90 of the Law on the Federal Constitutional Court). There is no filing fee or formal process for these complaints and they are often handwritten submissions constructed without assistance from a lawyer (Kommers 1997: 15). The Court may impose minor fines for filing frivolous complaints, though this only occurs in a small fraction of complaints. These 'cases' are referred to the General Register's office, who responds to most constitutional complaints, informing 'petitioners' that the Court will be unable to address their claims. If such a petitioner is still not satisfied, the Register's office forwards the case files to the Court (Ibid. 27).[34]

Although the Court reviews the constitutionality of government actions allegedly perpetuated against the complainant, such review also includes review of the legislation that gave rise to the government action, not just the action itself (Ipsen 128). Article 93(1, 4a) of the Basic Law allows complaints (regarding a person's rights that have

---

[34] For those not familiar with the Court, is comprised of sixteen members, with eight members each serving on a Senate. The First Senate is chaired by the President, and the Second, by the Vice President. Both Senates review constitutional complains and statues. The Second Senate provides review over all other procedures. After the General Register's office has sorted through the complaints, each Senate, with a 'sub' senate (chamber) of three members, will determine whether a constitutional complaint is "patently well founded" and will hear the case. Senates issue rulings, and only if the Senates are in disagreement about a case will the entire plenary of sixteen judges decide a case. (German Constitutional Court, see http://www.bundesverfassungsgericht.de/en/organization/organization.html).

been violated by a "public authority") against not only governmental actions, but judicial decisions, administrative acts, and legislative acts (Kommers 1997: 15). Complaints must specifically identify the governmental action in question, the constitutional right that has been violated and the complaint must be presented within one month of the alleged governmental action or one year from the promulgation of the 'law' or "sovereign act against which action is not admissible" (Article 92-93 of Law on the Constitutional Court). Therefore there is a timeliness requirement built into the procedure. If a complaint is accepted, the Constitutional Court may have a full hearing and other governmental institutions are allowed to intervene in the case (Law on the Constitutional Court, Article 93a, 94).

Only little more than one percent of these complaints are accepted for a full review (Kommers 1997: 15). Therefore, while most do not usually result in major policy-making, the complaint is a potentially powerful institutional mechanism enabling presentation of particular controversies that the court otherwise might not be able to address (Blankenburg: 309). Many significant decisions of the Court have been the result of constitutional complaints and they comprise about little more than half of the court's published opinions (Kommers 1997: 15). For example, originating from a constitutional complaint, the Court addressed the constitutionality of legislation that would ratify the Treaty of Maastricht (enabling Germany's continuing integration into the European Union) in its controversial *Maastricht* (1993) decision (*89 Decisions of the Constitutional Court 155,* Ress 1994: 59). Overall, the Court addresses about 2500 cases a year, which includes abstract and concrete review cases, and constitutional complaints.

A Priori Review

Through abstract review the German Constitutional Court can determine the compatibility of a federal or Lander law with Basic Law, or a Land law with federal law (Ipsen 119). An abstract review appeal in Germany may occur *any time* after a statute's passage, but before it has been put in force or applied. However, abstract review is performed without the necessity of "adverse parties" (Kommers 1997: 13). The federal government, a Land government or one third of the members of the Bundestag may request an abstract review proceeding. A question regarding the constitutionality of the law must be presented in the request. In addition, the court may invite interested parties to present their positions and allow for expert testimony regarding the constitutionality of the governmental act in question (Ipsen 120).

Article 93 of the Law on the Constitutional Court outlines the competencies of the Constitutional Court in regards to abstract review in greater detail. It refers to safeguarding of 'rights', as opposed to 'laws' as defined in concrete review (a priori) (Article 100). This distinction between 'recht' (rights or law) and 'gesetz' (law or legislation) allows the court to address broader issues regarding the justice or fairness of the legislative process or supporting legislation. This distinction between rights and laws in abstract review allows the court to drill deep in its review in order to cover a comprehensive range of government acts including legislative statutes, as well as Federal and Land regulations, ordinances and executive orders (Ipsen 119). Given this emphasis on rights, "...the scope of [abstract] review is not limited to the applicant's assertions regarding what is at question.   Abstract judicial review, as an objective procedure to safeguard the constitution, authorizes the Bundesverfassungsgericht to review the law in every conceivable aspect" (Ipsen 122).

If the court chooses to declare a law or legislation completely incompatible with the constitution- 'unvereinbar und nichtig' (incompatible and void), then the decision binds all governmental organs and strikes the law from the statute books. The Court can also rule that the law or action is only incompatible (unvereinbar) with Basic Law, in which case the Court may order the legislative body to revise the law within a given time period (Ibid). In addition, the Court could also determine that a statute is unconstitutional only as it has been interpreted or applied, thereby imposing an 'interpretation in conformity with the constitution' (Ibid). Therefore, the Court's interpretation may limit the legislature's intent regarding the statute. Lastly, the Court may rule that a statute is unconstitutional, as it is applied in only particular situations. This variation in how the Court may express the 'finality' of its decision reveals how the Court may choose to be strategic in its decision-making; by softening the blow of a particular ruling, the Court allows for the opportunity for other political actors to respond and can also encourage compliance with its decision. This keeps the court in the game and preserve its position in the policy-making arena without having to make a far-reaching decision (or no decision at all) that may be strongly opposed by other political actors.

Abstract review, therefore, is a broad grant of authority, allowing the Court to determine the constitutionality of the legislation in its entirety. In addition to the broad nature of abstract review as stated above, it also enables a number of different actors access to the Court, which also distinguishes it from the reference procedure in Canada, which can only be initiated by the executive at either the federal or provincial level, reinforcing the notion of parliamentary sovereignty. In Germany, allowing one-third of the Bundestag to initiate review enables minority parties or even factions within majority parties, to utilize judicial review as a means to support their own interests and alter the terms of the debate over policy, making the Court a 'third legislative chamber' (see Stone-Sweet 1992, 2000). As chapter seven will discuss, the first two major abortion decisions came to the German Constitutional Court in this manner.

<u>A Posteriori review</u>

As noted previously in the section on judicial structure, lower courts must refer cases to the Constitutional Court when the constitutionality of the law or statute is in question (Article 100 Basic Law). The Court is not obliged to take these cases if it believes that the lower court has not shown that there is a constitutional question at issue.

Individual Rights Guarantees

Individual rights guarantees are primarily comprised of the first nineteen articles of the Basic Law plus a few others which have been added regarding rights of political participation and rights of criminal procedure. As shown in table four at the end of this chapter, the Basic Law of Germany provides the greatest breadth in the number of individual rights guarantees, and more of these rights are 'positive' guarantees as compared to United States' Bill of Rights and the Canadian Charter of Rights and Freedoms. Most notably, Article 1 guarantees that the government must protect human dignity and it is the responsibility of the state to ensure this right. The comprehensiveness of the Basic law facilitates the potential for the Constitutional Court to participate on many political questions. The impact of this presence is significant; "Consequently, almost every constitutionally significant issue--whether it be between the Federal and State governments, between different organs of the state or between citizens and the state--can be brought before the Federal Constitutional Court and ruled upon it" (Magiera 91).

Regarding these guarantees, the Basic Law categorizes particular rights to be fundamental and inviolable through Article 79, the 'eternal guarantee clause' (Ewigkeitklausel), which states that potential legislation or constitutional amendments may not be constitutional if it will abridge these rights (Mattli and Slaughter 1998: 274). More specifically, Article 79 (3) states that the basic principles of Article 1 and Article 20 (guarantee that Germany will remain "a democratic and social federal state") cannot be amended or changed. Article 19(2) also operates as a limit on the alteration of the essential content of rights provided in the Basic Law. Such rights may be altered in their wording but the underlying guarantee or freedom may not be removed or altered (Foster 144). If such fundamental rights/values are at issue in a case, the Constitutional Court has clear constitutional justification for nullifying legislative or constitutional acts, even if the procedure producing such acts was constitutional (Kokott 1996: 80). The Constitutional Court has also stated that there is a 'hierarchy' of rights within the Basic Law, meaning that the first right guaranteed in the Basic Law, that of human dignity, is the pre-eminent value protected by the document. This position has been buttressed by the constitutional guarantee that Article 1 may not be removed or significantly amended as stated by Article 79.

Apart from the above exceptions, similar to the Charter of Rights and Freedoms, the Basic Law (more narrowly) explicitly allows for the limiting of rights if they conflict with other constitutional values. Most notably, Article 2(1) states that free development of will is protected as long as the rights of others are not abridged. The Constitutional Court's justifications for striking down federal abortion laws rested on both Article 1 and Article 2 guarantees. In addition, the rights in the Basic Law have a 'double character' of subjective rights and objective guarantees. Subjective rights are the specific rights guaranteed to individuals; objective guarantees are those that limit the state authorities and are protected by the courts (Foster 155). Objective rights "...concern the general protection afforded by the basic rights...in the form of a set of guidelines for the authorities of the minimum standards to observe"(Ibid.). More specifically, they relate to the 'positive' rights of the Basic Law, such as the guarantees of public education, protection of marriage and family, etc. These positive guarantees enable the Court to make proscriptive decisions, by referencing the Basic Law and its requirements that the government provide and protect these rights.

CROSS CASE COMPARISON

In comparison, the US Supreme Court has relatively fewer institutional supports to help it withstand critiques and threatening actions by other political institutions than the German Constitutional Court. The Canadian Supreme Court has wide jurisdiction, yet little entrenched rules detailing its authority. The US Court has some entrenched rules but also faces entrenched limitations by other branches, whereas the German Constitutional Court is limited to hearing only constitutional questions, yet its authorities are the most detailed and entrenched. There are fewer clear constitutional means for the limitation or constriction of the German Court's authorities by other actors, for example, the Basic Law permits only the *expansion* of Constitutional Court's jurisdiction. The Basic Law reinforces the strong of role the Court in the political process, and to paraphrase Donald Kommers, the biggest constraint on the Court's exercise of power is its own sense of self-restraint (Kommers 1997: 51). In the Canadian context, the constitutional rules that establish the Canadian Supreme Court's authorities are limited or underspecified. In addition, rules that enable the Canadian Supreme Court to interact directly with other government actors (via the reference procedure) can only be employed by the federal executive or indirectly by the provincial executive. By not allowing a range of other actors such access, this limits the ability of the Court to intervene in the policy process as an 'independent' actor rather than one that is being 'used' by the executive to pursue its objectives.

Judicial Structure

The German Constitutional Court is a paradigmatic example of the unitary model. If constitutional questions arise in their cases, lower courts must forward them to the Constitutional Court. While the unitary system may limit the power of the entire judiciary to create constitutional policy, it strengthens the high (Constitutional) Court authority to make such policy. Both the judicial systems of Canada and the United States adhere to the 'all courts model', as the lower courts in both systems may render decisions on constitutional questions. The difference between the US and Canada is that the US judicial structure is more diffuse than the Canadian System. Although both reflect their federal design, in Canada, the higher provincial appeal courts are integrated into the federal system with the justices themselves appointed by the federal government. In addition, the fact that the criminal law is the province of the federal, not provincial governments provides a strong unifying element, as well as the fact that the Canadian Supreme Court is the final appellate court for all Canadian laws, federal or provincial.

In contrast, in the United States each state governs the selection and running of state courts. Additionally, the federal court system of the US is much more extensive than the Canadian system. Therefore, the US's extensive federal trial and appeals system of courts allows greater opportunities for variance in constitutional interpretation than either Canada or Germany. Coupled with the fact that the current United Supreme Court hears fewer than 100 cases a year, there are ample opportunities for lower court decisions to vary and contradict each other without being overruled by the Supreme Court. Given the variance in these judicial systems, Germany's adherence to the unitary constitutional model provides greater policy uniformity and lower court consistency which contributes to greater compliance with high court decisions, as opposed to the 'all courts' model of the United States and the integrated Canadian model. However, since the various features noted above make the Canadian judicial system more unified than the US, it is likely that the Canadian Supreme Court provides more consistency than the US Supreme Court.

Jurisdiction

In contrast to the Canadian and United States Supreme Courts, the German Constitutional Court's jurisdiction is limited almost exclusively to disputes over constitutional law. However, the German Constitutional Court also has sole, original jurisdiction over constitutional questions. This is a significant distinction because having sole jurisdiction consolidates the German Court's power over constitutional issues, whereas in the US, all courts have authority to decide constitutional questions, providing for numerous interpretations and constitutional policies on a given issue. Granted, the US Supreme Court has the 'final' say, but before such an issue can be definitively adjudicated by the US Supreme Court, government actors are obliged to follow the decisions of lower courts.

Table 3.1: Judicial Structure

	Canada	United States	Germany
Degree of Unification	Federally dominated; operates mainly as unitary system. All courts may rule on constitutional issues	Dual court system; all courts may rule on constitutional issues.	Land and federal courts are largely integrated and unified. Only Constitutional Court may rule on constitutional questions.
Position of Court in judicial system	Supreme Court –final appellate court for entire legal system including constitutional questions	Supreme Court is final appellate court for federal system and for federal constitutional questions. State supreme courts final appellate courts for state constitutional law.	Constitutional Court operates relatively independently from judicial structure. Lower courts must refer cases with constitutional questions to Constitutional Court.

One could say that since the German Constitutional Court's jurisdiction is primarily limited to constitutional law disputes, the German Constitutional Court's legal authority is less influential relative to the US or Canadian Supreme Court. This concern is mitigated by the fact that the Basic Law is much more comprehensive and detailed than either the Canadian Constitutional Act or the US Constitution. Therefore many more policy issues in Germany are likely to have a clearer connection to a constitutional issue than in the US or Canada. As one German judicial scholar notes, "Taken together [the court's authority over interpreting the Basic Law and scope of the court's jurisdiction], these competencies amount to a general delegation of all constitutionally significant disputes to the Federal Constitutional Court (Magiera 91). To summarize, with respect to jurisdiction, both the Canadian and US Supreme Courts are relatively weaker institutions than the German Constitutional Court.

Justicability

Since the US and Canadian Supreme Courts both have relatively weaker and underspecified authorities, relative to the German Court, it is not surprising that these two courts have established and employed internal rules in order to relieve political pressure and protect their legitimacy. However, if the Courts apply such rules inconsistently, it may hurt their ability to influence the policy process, diminishing their claims of authority and opening them up to critique. In addition, if these rules are constructed in order to limit access to the court, then the Court will be presented with fewer opportunities enabling court intervention. The German Constitutional Court, which faces fewer potential external pressures on its authority, has a number of independent powers grounded in the constitution, and has fewer internal rules limiting its jurisdiction, does *not* have as many justicablilty concerns. Therefore, given the absence of such limitations (external political pressure or intrinsic rules) the Constitutional Court is not likely to present arguments in its decisions justifying its role in (or choice to refrain from) the policy process, nor is it likely to defer policy questions to other branches of government.

Table 3.2: Justicability requirements

	Canada	United States	Germany
Case or Controversy		X	
Political question		X	
Standing	X	X	X
Mootness	X	X	
Ripeness	X	X	X

Judicial review

Using discrete terms for the moment, the Supreme Court of Canada and the German Constitutional Court employ both a priori (advisory and abstract review respectively) and a posteriori judicial review (concrete and concrete/abstract review respectively). In Germany, the Court's a priori review determinations are final and binding (Kommers 1997), whereas in Canada, court opinions are advisory, "but in practice they are treated as binding" (Russell, et. al. 1989: 23). The United States Supreme Court has only the power of a posteriori concrete review which "...occurs exclusively after the law or action has been promulgated or taken effect" (Tate 6). In addition, that review must be 'concrete', meaning that a specific 'harm' has resulted from government action.

Judicial review has no explicit constitutional foundation in either the US or Canada as opposed to Germany, where it is explicitly provided for in the Basic Law. The US Supreme Court is generally assumed to have the final say on constitutional questions, while all lower courts may also exercise the power of judicial review. The lack of any constitutional authority for judicial review in the American case contrasts with Germany, in which the Basic Law confers the sole authority of constitutional review to the Constitutional Court. In Canada, constitutional review, particularly in regards to rights, had not been particularly significant until 1982, when Canada ratified the Charter of Rights and Freedoms.

The *a priori* reference and abstract review procedures provide both the Supreme Court of Canada and the German Constitutional Court additional opportunities for political engagement and policy-making as opposed to the US Supreme Court. While a court's ability to exercise any review function depends upon other political institutions to 'appeal' or 'refer', these *a priori* procedures have been used with enough frequency to consider the impact of such review might have on policy deliberations and process. Such review facilitates inter-institutional interaction and coordination before policies are finalized. Alec Stone suggests that when a court has the power of a priori review, it may act as a 'third' legislative chamber (Sweet 1999, Stone-Sweet 2000). Even a threat of review can force political actors to anticipate a court's potential position on legislation, thereby influencing the direction of policy, particularly when varied actors (with competing interests) have access to such procedures (Landfried 1988, Stone 1992).

In contrast, the restriction of the US Supreme Court to 'a posteriori', concrete review delays the Court's entrance into the policy debate to after other political actors and institutions may have negotiated [and reconciled] their positions.

Therefore relative to the other two courts on this dimension, the US Supreme Court is in the weakest position, whereas the German Constitutional Court is in the strongest position. This is due to three factors: (1) the binding finality of abstract review, (2) the comprehensive nature of this review and (3) the greater number of actors who may initiate review. These factors provide greater potential for the Constitutional Court involvement in policymaking more so than the other two Courts. This constitutional arrangement also grounds the German Court as an equal player in the separation of powers game. Other actors cannot claim that the Court is overstepping its jurisdiction, since it is constitutionally required to respond to all appeals of abstract review and all governmental actors are bound to the court's ruling.

The binding nature of abstract review in Germany equalizes any power differential between the Constitutional Court and other political institutions which distinguishes it from the Supreme Court of Canada. In Canada, two factors mitigate the Court's equal player position in the policy process. First, the advisory nature of reference procedure, and second, references may only come from the standing government and not the opposition. Ward states this concern clearly,

> The advantages to a government of getting an advance opinion from a high court on a potentially controversial issue are obvious, but so are the dangers to the courts. The temptation for a government to bypass an awkward decision by referring the subject to the courts, thus using the judicial process for political purposes, is always present, and there can be no doubt that the abuse of references would threaten the courts' independence (Ward 258).

As seen in the Trudeau language rights example, the use of the reference procedure solely by the governing party can make the Court an instrument of the majority government's political machinations. Since the Court's decision is not formally binding, this leaves room for the government to dismiss the determination of the Court and bolster the perception that the Court must act as the executive's 'personal advisor'.

One might similarly argue that since the 'minority' in parliament can employ the abstract review procedure against the majority in the German system, it allows that minority to manipulate the Constitutional Court to their own political advantage, which is true. It is, however, one of a number of actors that can initiate abstract review and therefore the application of abstract review enhances the court's independence from other political actors. Again, the significant difference here between Germany and Canada is the binding nature of abstract review as opposed to the reference procedure. In Germany it is clear to all political players that once a review appeal is made to the Constitutional Court, its decision may be binding and final on all parties. Only the Court itself can blunt the force of its decision by determining how 'severe' imposition will be on political actors. This situation therefore raises the stakes higher for political actors in Germany than in Canada since it leaves less room for other political actors to deviate from the Constitutional Court's decision.

As will be discussed in chapter seven, in 1992, the governing majority in the German parliament, worked to come up with a compromise abortion policy that would be acceptable to all parties and adhere to the directives laid out by the Constitutional Court in their first *Abortion I* decision. That 'majority' legislation passed with support from members of all parties in Parliament. Nonetheless, a minority chose to bring an abstract review procedure to the Constitutional Court. The Court struck down most of the decision as being incompatible with the constitution and provided detailed and comprehensive abortion policy directives to parliament, which parliament enacted into law. While this tactic worked in the short term, in that this (extreme) conservative minority got the Court to issue a ruling that largely conformed to their policy views, not long after, the Court later rebuked this same minority when the Court ruled on a constitutional complaint regarding Bavarian implementation of the above federal revision on abortion.

Comparatively, the absence of such an institutional (and authoritative) process in the US system limits the US Supreme Court's influence on policy-making. Although both Congress and the Executive, (particularly the executive with the office of the solicitor general) have resources that provide advantages when appearing before the Court, both Congress and the Executive must make appeals to the court largely like 'ordinary' applicants. Without such direct access, these institutions attempt to access or influence the Court through other means and functions available to them. Therefore these 'indirect' means indicate the greater degree to which the US Supreme Court influence is interdependent on other institutions as compared to the German Constitutional Court. The 'politicization' of the US Supreme Court comes from 'within' the political system, rather than authorized from 'without' (Germany), and therefore the US Court is more vulnerable to critique and manipulation when it seeks to exercise judicial review. In contrast, the Canadian Supreme Court and the German Constitutional Court are provided with review functions that are more easily reconciled with the political process.

Lastly, one could also argue that the US Supreme Court's influence is not severely limited by the lack of a priori review because Congress may consider the constitutionality of a law prior to its enactment (Pickerill 2004 generally). I suggest that such legislative influence has less impact than a priori review for a number of reasons. First, while Congress may consider the constitutionality of a potential law during deliberations and drafting of legislation there is little immediate possibility that the Court itself can enter the legislative debate and alter the direction of policy. In Germany, the opposition may use the threat of abstract review to force amendments and alterations to the proposed law. In Canada, the standing government can use the reference to defer controversial issues to the Court, thereby using the reference to guide its strategy in proposing new legislation. In the US, even if there are complaints regarding the constitutionality of a bill prior to its enactment, those opposed must usually wait until the bill is passed and government action has been taken (see *Clinton v NY* re: line item veto as one example). This significantly increases the time between the promulgation of the law and adjudication. Using a median measure, one study notes it takes an average of ten years from legislative enactment to a Court ruling of unconstitutionality on said law (Pickerill 86). Second, with the exception of original jurisdiction, a case must first be heard by a lower court, increasing the time it takes for the Court to make a determination, as opposed to the direct appeal to the Constitutional Court afforded by abstract review.[35] Finally, the US Supreme Court may decline to hear the case, whereas the Constitutional

---

[35] In recent years Congress has included amendments requiring expeditious judicial review of the legislation itself.

Court is required to hear all abstract review appeals. A threat of review in Germany therefore may have a greater impact on the policy process due to the likelihood and immediacy of such review than in the US.

Table 3.3: Nature/Access to Judicial Review

		Canada	United States	Germany
Timing of review				
	Prior to construction	X		
	During debate/construction	X		
	Passed not promulgated	X		X
	Law implemented, 'concrete harm' from government action	X	X	X
Types of Review				
	Concrete	X	X	X
	Who can bring a case			
1.	*Individuals, corporations*	X	X	X
2.	*Government actors*	X	X	X
	Abstract	X		X
	Who can bring a case			
1.	*Sub-national government*	X		X
2.	*Federal Executive*	X		X
3.	*'minority' in federal legislature*			X
Constitutional Complaint				
Individuals, Corporations				X

These institutional linkages are significant when considering the roles of these courts within the general political process and in the development of abortion policy. The two major abortion cases in Germany arrived at the Constitutional Court via the abstract review procedure before the promulgation of the federal legislation. There was little controversy over the Court's intervention itself. The acceptance of the Constitutional Court's role within the policy process is particularly striking when compared to the US, where there has been significant critique of the US Supreme Court (even by its own members) regarding the legitimacy of the court's role in adjudicating the abortion issue in the first instance.

Rights Comparison

The United States Bill of Rights has fewer guarantees and is less specific in defining those guarantees as compared to the rights outlined in either the Canadian or German constitutions. In addition, both the Canadian and German constitutions outline limitations on such rights, implying that they are not absolute (with the Basic Law providing some exceptions). In Canada, those limitations are both in terms of how the Charter is to be interpreted (Section 1) and in implementation (notwithstanding clause).

In Germany, the Basic Law provides both positive and negative rights which are much more specific and detailed than in either the US or Canadian constitutions. With a greater number of rights present, this increases the likelihood that the Constitutional Court to will be able to intervene in the policy process. In addition, the specificity of said rights provides a stronger justification for Court interpretations. Lastly, the presence of both positive and negative guarantees also enables the Court to provide more proscriptive decisions, since positive rights are obligations upon the state. Therefore Court interpretations of these rights would more likely give rise to decisions in which the Court instructs government actors on what they must do in order to oblige these guarantees.

Table 3.4: Rights Guarantees

Canada	United States	Germany
		Human Dignity
"life, liberty and security of person"		Right to life
"..without discrimination based upon race, national and ethnic origin, colour religion, sex, age or mental or physical disability." *allows 'ameliorating of conditions of disadvantaged groups"	Equal protection under the law	Equality before the law
		Equal rights of Women and Men
"...conscience and religion"	Freedom of religion	Religious rights
Security of person*	Security from unwarranted searches and seizures	Privacy
		Personal Honor
"right to be secure against unreasonable search and seizure"	Security from unreasonable searches and seizure	Inviolability of Home and Person
'..right to enter, remain in, and leave Canada"		Movement and Travel
...expression including freedom of press and other media communication"	Freedom of speech	Spoken and written expression
		Marriage and Family
		Free development of personality

Table 3.4 (Continued): Rights Guarantees

Canada	United States	Germany
"Right to vote in election…and qualified for membership therein"	Election of President/Vice President/popular election of Senators	Vote and Run for elected office
	Petition	Petition
"freedom of thought, belief, opinion.."		Personal beliefs, ideology
		Resist political oppression
"peaceful assembly"	Freedom of assembly	Assembly
"freedom of association"		Association
		Private property
		Private Enterprise
"pursue the gaining of a livelihood in any province" (related to mobility rights)		Work
		Choose occupation
		Form and Join Labor Unions
		Strike
		Public Education
		Religious Education
		Teaching and research
		Private Schooling
Enforcement of by the courts/remedies ' may apply to a court of competent jurisdiction to obtain such remedy as the court considers appropriate and just in the circumstances."	Concrete review	Access to Courts/judicial protection 1. Concrete Review 2. Constitutional Complaint

Table 3.4 (Continued): Rights Guarantees

Canada	United States	Germany
		Immunity from retroactive application of laws
'validity of detention determined by habeas corpus.."	Habeas Corpus	Habeas Corpus
	Double jeopardy	Immunity from Double Jeopardy
	*no cruel and unusual punishment	No death penalty
		*Military service (duty of citizens)
		*Protect family and children (duty of state)
		*Provide public education (duty of state)
		*Guarantee media rights" (duty of state)
Language rights		
Language education		
Many more criminal procedural rights	Criminal Procedure rights- Due process, Trial by jury, confront witnesses, assistance of counsel, no excessive bail	Right of access to a judge; right to a legal hearing

CHAPTER 4

Comparing 'Extrinsic' Federal Design Features

INTRODUCTION

The *presence* and *nature* of a federal system provides particular avenues in which political actors may act. As chapter three addressed the 'intrinsic' features shaping the nature of court interventions in the policy process, this chapter examines and compares the federal systems of Canada, United States and Germany in order to determine which 'extrinsic' features of these political systems provide incentives or disincentives for legislative actors to comply with court directives, which thereby conditions the influence of the courts themselves. Each country's federal design has a different combination of these features providing different conditions in which this interaction takes place.

Defining Federalism

In basic terms, federalism is a means to order a political system (Meisel 341). William Riker, in his attempt to compare various federal systems, provided the following definition; "The essential institutions of federalism are, of course, a government of the federation and a set of governments of the member units, in which both kinds of governments rule over the same territory and people and each kind has the authority to make some decisions independently of the other" (Riker 1964: 5). Under Riker's definition, if entities fulfilled these conditions, then the country was a federal one. There are challenges, however, to systematically comparing federalist countries due to the variety of institutional arrangements employed in federal systems (Thorlakson 1). Under Riker's definition, Germany, Canada and the United States fulfill these basic requirements of a federal system, although the constitutional design and institutions of these countries reflect different approaches to federalism. These differences are, in part, what shape the varying policy responses by sub-state actors to national court decisions in these three countries.

CANADA

Establishment of the Federal System

Instead of being born out of revolution and conflict, as was the United States, the nation of Canada arose from compromise among the governing and commercial elites in the British North American colonies and a long sustained relationship with the British Empire (Watts 1987: 769).   The 1840 Act of the Union that had united the French speaking eastern Canadians (Quebec) and western Canada (Ontario) into one province could not be maintained.   Eastern Canadians wanted a complete separation between French and English speaking majorities. Western Canadians supported governmental representation based on population that would have put the French speakers at a clear disadvantage. In 1864 a coalition cabinet divided the province of Canada into two provinces of Ontario and Quebec, and allowed for expansion towards the west and the east. The details were approved, presented to the leaders of the two additional colonies (New Brunswick and Nova Scotia) and largely accepted by British Parliament in order to become the British North America Act (BNA Act) in 1867. This became the first 'constitutional' act of a nascent Canada. Since it was essentially an arrangement among business and political elites, there was little popular involvement in establishing the BNA Act.

Constitutional Framework

In contrast to the development of the US constitution, which forced states to relinquish substantial authority and consolidated power in the national government, the Canadian process included clear elements of both devolution and unification. The Canadian framers of the BNA Act had observed the evolution of American federalism and the bloody tensions that arose between the national and state governments. William Riker noted that the Canadian framers wanted 'watertight compartments', specifically delineating the specific powers of federal government and those of the provinces in order to avoid a crisis like the American Civil War (Riker 1964: 116).   These concerns of the Canadian framers are reflected in their construction of the BNA Act and subsequent constitutional acts (Ibid).

The BNA act emphasizes a 'layer cake' or dual sovereignty approach to federalism. It does so by outlining the exclusive policy jurisdiction of *both the federal and provincial governments*. This federal logic contrasts with Germany's more functional division of authority among the national government and the Länder in the Basic Law, and the US Constitution's emphasis on defining the powers of the national government as opposed to those of the states. While the US Constitution affirms that powers not granted to the national government are reserved to the states, the BNA Act guarantees the opposite. Authorities *not granted* to provinces by the BNA Act were to remain with the federal government. Any development of new jurisdictional areas was to be under federal government control and would likely strengthen the position of the federal government relative to those of the provinces. These expectations, however, did not develop as the Canadian framers intended.

As stated above, Canada's BNA Act explicitly grants jurisdictional areas to both the federal and provincial governments. Article 91, Section 2 grants the powers of trade, commerce, taxation, criminal law, national defense, currency and banking, and immigration exclusively to the federal government. Article 92 lists the powers assigned to the provinces, including property and civil rights (as established prior to the Charter of Rights and Freedoms), hospitals, public works, management and sale of public goods, administration of justice and the control and distribution of non-renewable resources. The provinces have control over 'direct taxation' to raise revenue, initially a little used power that has become a source of great provincial authority. In contrast, the United States Constitution assigns the federal government many concurrent powers under which federal authority would prevail if there were conflict between federal and state laws, thereby allowing the supremacy of federal laws over states regulation. The BNA Act, however, outlines only two areas under concurrent jurisdiction:

agriculture and immigration, in addition to pensions which was added in 1951 (Watts 1987: 785).

In a few instances, particular requirements found in early Canadian constitutional documents seemingly required the dominance of the national government over the provincial governments. The Crown (federal government) is to be represented in each province by the Lieutenant Governor, who is appointed by Ottawa (Section 56 of the BNA Act). Under this section, the Lieutenant may 'reserve' provincial legislation, meaning that he/she could withhold approval of such legislation until Crown examination could occur (Section 78 of the BNA Act) (Malcolmson & Myers 1996). This section also granted the national government the power of 'disallowance', enabling Ottawa to annul provincial legislation it does not approve of. Neither provision, however, has had any significant impact in modern provincial-federal relations.

In addition, the preamble of Section 91 of the BNA Act provided that the federal government was to make laws for the 'peace, order and good government' of Canada (POGG Clause). The POGG clause was likely intended to operate similarly to the 'necessary and proper' clause of the United States Constitution (Baier 25). However, while the US Supreme Court's early interpretations of the 'necessary and proper' clause enabled the development of the federal power, the Judicial Committee of the Privy Council limited expansion of the Canadian federal government's powers by narrowly interpreting the POGG clause (Ibid). Contravening the centralist intent of the Canadian framers, the Privy Council restricted the application of the POGG power to emergencies, and rarely upheld its use for addressing matters of national concern (Ibid). At the same time, many Council decisions upheld provincial authority over property and civil rights as outlined in Section 92, strengthening provincial authority at the expense of the federal government (Ibid).

Over time, both the federal and provincial governments have asserted authority over new policy areas through their existing constitutional jurisdiction. For example, the federal government, under its criminal law jurisdiction, has sought to regulate environmental pollution and labor practices (Ibid). Conversely, many of the provincial responsibilities, such as health care, natural resources and education, deemed insignificant at the time of the founding, have developed into important areas of provincial governmental power.

Increasing provincial autonomy and power led the call for

constitutional revision. While the Constitution Act of 1982 officially established Canada's separation from Britain and the historic Charter of Rights and Freedoms, it also included, at the insistence of the provinces, a right to override provisions of the Charter (the notwithstanding clause) and a provision ensuring continuing provincial control over natural resources (Ibid. 776). These inclusions to the Charter indicated that the provinces still retain significant power relative to the national government.

The Canadian constitutional demarcations of jurisdictional authority and subsequent interpretations of said authority have shaded Canadian intergovernmental relations with an adversarial tone. Jurisdictional rivalry and fiscal independence have led to confrontations and competition between the federal government and the provinces. In addition, federal and provincial governments' attempts to expand their respective constitutional jurisdictions over time have led to jurisdictional overlap (Bakvis 8). As Herman Bakvis and Grace Skogstag note, "The co-existence of jurisdictional overlap alongside the legal emphasis on jurisdictional exclusivity produces the first and preponderant element in Canadian federalism: the competitive dynamic" (Ibid.). Provincial-national confrontation and the competitive dynamic due to 'jurisdictional overlap' were evident in the Canadian debate over abortion policy. Both Alberta and Nova Scotia, in particular, objected to federal government attempts to implement the Canadian Health Act. In particular, the Alberta government claimed that it had the authority to 'de-insure' abortion procedures since the provinces had the authority over health care policy and began charging facility fees for abortions performed in private clinics. Nova Scotia refused to allow provincial health insurance to cover 'out-patient' abortions. The federal government retaliated by asserting that federal National Canadian Health Act prohibited provinces from unilaterally 'de-insuring' medical services, and subsequently withheld federal transfer payments in order to force provincial compliance with the Act.

Representation of Sub-National Interests in Federal Institutions

'Executive' institutions

Two features of Canada's federal design have concentrated power in the executive of both the federal and provincial governments. The first is a parliamentary system enabling the calling of elections and dissolution of legislatures and the second is the lack of a strong second legislative chamber in the federal legislature. Due to these features, intergovernmental relations have taken on a "quasi-diplomatic character resembling those between sovereign powers" (Watts 1987: 782). Many Canadian federal scholars have named these relations as 'executive federalism', indicated by the significant role of first ministers' conferences which has become necessary in order to facilitate agreements among the federal government and the provinces on various policy issues (Watts 1987, Smiley 1980, Smiley and Watts 1985 generally).

Canada is a parliamentary democracy in which the 'executive' branch serves at the discretion of the parliament and therefore both the executive and the legislative roles are fused. More specifically, Canada has a 'Westminster' style system in which the party winning the majority of seats in Parliament establishes a cabinet and prime minister. The legislature is bi-cameral, with a lower House of Commons and a Senate. The 'Government' is in power as long as it holds the confidence (majority or plurality of votes) in the House of Commons. If a vote is lost, Parliament must dissolve the cabinet, and new elections must occur with the majority party creating a new government with a new Prime Minister, who appoints a new cabinet. This procedure contrasts with the United States' separated system, in which the President and Congress do not formally rely on each other in order remain in office.

Regarding cabinet formation, the Canadian Constitution Acts provide little formal foundation for provincial representation in national institutions. Some scholars assert that the Canadian framers did not formally address such concerns because they assumed the central government would include provincial representation (Tuohy 29). In the absence of such formal procedures, an informal norm has developed in which the Prime Minister selects as regionally representative of a cabinet as possible (Ibid.). Depending upon the size of her party's majority in Parliament, this can be either an easy or a difficult task for the Prime Minister.

Lacking a formal mechanism providing regional/provincial representation in the federal government has facilitated a consolidation of power in the executive branch at both levels of government (Ibid.). This centralization is due in part because of the Canadian framers' assumed that the cabinet would provide territorial representation in the federal government (Sutherland and Doern 1985: 26-7). Adhering to this principle has "strengthen[ed] the cabinet's authority at the same time as it complicates the process of cabinet building" (Tuohy 30). This norm has contributed to the development and significance of the 1st minister's conference in Canadian policymaking.

In these conferences, the Prime Minister meets with provincial premiers to negotiate new federal policies overlapping with or relating to provincial jurisdiction. The Prime Minister and provincial premiers often must obtain the formal approval of the agreements made in these meetings by their respective parliaments (Olson & Franks 19). The success of these bargains is dependent upon disciplined party majorities and whether or not the provinces have the constitutional authority and/or political will to "withhold consent to the policies of the national government "(Olson 19). These conferences are conducted not only among the Prime Minister and Premiers, but also conferences among ministers of various departments, such as finance or health (Tuohy 30). Without a formal mechanism to coordinate policy among the federal and provincial governments, these conferences are the main arena in which policy coordination and resolution of national-provincial concerns occur. As will be discussed in the next chapter, this procedure was used to help resolve conflicts between the federal government and the provinces over abortion policy.

Federal Senate

Similar to the deliberations regarding the design of the US Congress, the Canadian Senate was established due to compromise among the Canadian provinces. The Canadian Senate was to provide a 'second opinion' on the legislation pursued by the House of Commons. The Senate was intended to be independent of both the electorate and the party machinations of the House of Commons (Ward 1987: 153). This independence was to be achieved through lifetime appointment by the crown (the reigning government). The Senate was also expected to protect regional, not provincial, interests. Ontario, Quebec and the Maritimes, have 24 Senate seats combined as compared to the Western provinces which share 24 seats among 4 provinces (Ward 1987: 167). This division reflects and reinforces the division between 'Eastern' Canada and 'the rest of Canada'. Therefore, the Senate has never been understood as to represent provincial interests in the federal government (Riker 1964: 117).

In addition, the BNA Act required Senators, beyond their liabilities, to own assets of $4,000 or more. While this requirement seems paltry now, in the 19th century, this represented a significant amount of wealth that few Canadians had at that time. This requirement was to insure that the Senate represented the property interests of wealthy Canadians (Malcolmson & Myers 140). Attempting to avoid the mistakes of the US framers, the Canadian framers took additional measures to secure that the national institutions they proposed were to protect propertied interests.

Regardless of these requirements, the lack of democratic accountability has eroded the Senate's authority and influence in government. Senatorial appointments became an effective means of patronage for the standing party in government, eroding the political legitimacy of the Senate (Malcolmson and Myers: 141 and Ward: 156). Over time, a norm developed dictating that the Senate should not oppose a bill that had the support of the House of Commons (Malcolmson and Myers: 141). The Senate has generally adhered to this norm because the Liberals had control of the federal government for long periods of time, enabling them to have a longstanding majority in the Senate, thereby posing no partisan conflict between the House and the Senate (Ibid.). In recent years, however, particularly under conservative governments, the Senate has attempted to block government bills and force general elections due to the dominance of the Liberal party in the Senate (Ibid.).

Throughout modern Canadian history, there have been periodic calls to reform the Senate due to these concerns. Reflecting the influence of the United States, most reform proposals advocate for the Canadian Senate to resemble the US Senate by providing for equal provincial representation and direct accountability through elections (Ibid. 143). Other supporters of reform have supported changes emulating the German model, in which a provincial government would select half of its delegation to the Senate with the other half chosen by House of Commons (Ward 169). Some have advocated the complete abolishment of the institution. Still, given all the talk, little has actually been done. Only two reforms have been instituted; replacing life terms with a mandatory retirement age of 75, and an imposition of a 180 day limit on the Senate's ability to obstruct or delay votes on constitutional amendments that have the support of the House of Commons (Ward 155).

Supreme Court Federalism Jurisprudence

While the constitutional demarcations of both provincial and federal authority were made clear by the BNA act, early decisions of the Judicial Committee of the Privy Council established a number of precedents strengthening the powers of the provinces relative to the federal government (Hogg 119). Therefore, the history of judicial interpretation of Canadian federalism began with showing greater deference to Canadian provinces and limiting the federal government's powers, an orientation that was relatively inconsistent with intention of the framers. According to Section 91 of the BNA Act, Parliament has power to make laws for the 'peace, order and good government' (POGG) of Canada. At the time Canada was confederated, it was believed that this was a grant of general residual plenary power, another means to insure the centralization of power in the federal government (Baier 25). Several Council decisions narrowed the powers of the federal government particularly in areas of residual, trade and commerce powers, while broadly interpreting provincial powers (R. Watts 1987: 789). Scholars of Canadian constitutional history believe that these early decisions were consistent with the political views of the time. For example, in the early 1900's, the Liberal majority in Parliament depended upon the support of French Canadians, who supported greater provincial autonomy and power (Hogg 119). These interpretations are consistent with American judicial scholars' assertions that high court exercises of judicial review support or reinforce the interests for existing governing coalitions (Dahl, Whittington, generally). However, I would add that since the Privy Council was a British institution, the Privy Council interests were also to insure that the Canadian federal government did not get too powerful. Therefore, by reaffirming the authorities of the provinces, decisions of the Privy Council were a means to keep Canada as a whole from seeking independence from the Commonwealth (which eventually occurred).

When the Canadian Supreme Court was established, critics of the Privy Council were hopeful that the new Court would not interpret the POGG power narrowly, and the early decisions of the Supreme Court of Canada confirmed this hope (Baier 26).   Starting in 1949, the Supreme Court of Canada began to issue rulings that expanded the federal government's jurisdiction under the POGG clause (Baier 26). Building upon one of the last decisions of the Privy Council, which alluded to the possibility that the POGG power could be more broadly applied to national issues, the Supreme Court granted the federal government authority over aeronautics, atomic energy, and seabed natural resources (Ibid.). Yet, in the 1970's the Court began to interpret federal authority more narrowly, as evidenced most notably by the *Anti-Inflation Reference* of 1976 (Ibid.). Asked by the Prime Minister to evaluate the constitutionality of the federal government's inflation control regulation, the Court offered a muddled decision providing little clear support for the federal use of POGG power for matters of national concern (Ibid.).   This case led the way for a new era in federalism jurisprudence, as the Court began to 'balance' the interests of the provinces and the federal government, providing no consistent support for one side or the other (Ibid.).

Since 1976, the Court has attempted to utilize clearer tests in order to determine the appropriate boundary between provincial and federal authority with varying degrees of success (Baier 26).   In the case, *R.v Crown Zellerbach* (1988), a wood products company was found to be dumping waste products in the open sea beyond provincial marine waters.   The Court had to decide whether such marine pollution was subject to federal jurisdiction. The Court established a four part test, determining whether (1) an issue was an emergency or permanent nature, (2) a new or old issue, and if old, now taking on national dimensions, (3) the issue was concrete and distinct, thereby not an collection of previously provincial responsibilities, (4) and the prior (3) could be tested by 'provincial inability' (Ibid.). "[P]rovincial inability exists when one province alone cannot ensure that a subject matter of concern can be properly regulated or controlled--often because the specific conditions involved do not respect provincial borders"(Ibid. 27).

Although the *Crown-Zellerbach* test was intended to limit the range of federal authority, it did not have this effect in subsequent cases, and the Court has largely moved away from POGG justifications to more specific areas of constitutional justification (Ibid.). The Court has particularly emphasized the federal government's authority under criminal law as justification for federal action (Ibid.). For example, the

Court found that the Canadian Environmental Protection Act was a legitimate exercise of criminal law, under which Hydro-Quebec was charged for dumping PCB waste (Ibid.). Some Court commentators worry about this over-reliance on the federal government's jurisdiction over criminal law. They believe it may become a new source of federal plenary power, meaning that "[a]s long as criminal sanctions are attached to a regulation, the Court seems willing to justify the legislation as a matter of criminal law" (Ibid.). This approach of justifying federal action by incorporating some form of criminal sanction is analogous to the US Supreme Court's long standing approach to interpreting congressional power under the commerce clause. Until recently, the US Supreme Court has allowed Congress to regulate various areas, including civil rights, due to an arguably tenuous relationship to the commerce power.

This 'new' approach of the Canadian Supreme Court has not gone unnoticed by the provinces. Recently, provincial governments challenged federal gun control legislation as being *ultra vires* [beyond the authority of] of Parliament (Baier 27). The provinces and gun control lobby argued that such regulation was under the provincial authority over property and civil rights, and not justified by either POGG or the federal criminal law. The Court unanimously rejected this claim, stating that the federal law may regulate any kind of firearm as a matter of public safety (Ibid.). It is unclear to what degree the federal criminal law will be used to justify further federal actions, but its requirement of criminal sanction and stated criminal law purpose make it a more limited means than the POGG power as a source of federal plenary authority (Ibid.). In addition the Court has ruled against provinces that have attempted to encroach on the federal authority over criminal law. In *R v Morgentaler* (1993), the Supreme Court found Nova Scotia's inclusion of a criminal sanction in its legislation banning private abortion clinics *ultra vires*, arguing that since the establishment of criminal law is the sole authority of the federal government, the province could not include criminal sanctions in its regulations of private abortion clinics.

In addition to using this approach to determine federal-provincial authorities, the Court has used federalism concerns to limit government intrusion upon individual rights. Long before the Charter, in *Saumur c Quebec City* (1953), the Court found that a Quebec municipal bylaw prohibiting the distribution of religious pamphlets infringed upon

Parliament's authority over the criminal law. By striking down the prohibition, the court's decision implicitly supported an individual's right to 'freedom of religion' (Des Rosiers 67). One might argue that the Supreme Court's decision in *Morgentaler III*, also implicitly supported a women's right to access abortion, since it limited the ways in which provinces can regulate abortion policy.

One other recent Supreme Court case focused on issues of executive or co-operative federalism as opposed to jurisdictional concerns. In the *Canada Assistance Plan* (CAP) *Reference* (1990), the Court had to determine whether the federal government could limit federal transfers to the provinces when it sought to decrease and cap the growth of federal contributions to the 'wealthier' provinces, including Alberta, Ontario and British Columbia (Ibid). The British Columbia Supreme Court heard the case, on reference from the BC government, and ruled that Parliament did not have the right to make unilateral changes to the CAP agreement without provincial consent (Ibid.). On appeal, the Supreme Court of Canada disagreed, supporting the federal government's authority over its spending power (Ibid.). The Court justified its decision by stating that exercises in 'executive federalism' could not bind future governments should they seek to change federal statutory provisions such as CAP (Ibid.). In addition, the Court asserted Parliament cannot be tied down by the mere expectation of funds, which would override parliamentary authority over the spending power (Ibid.). The general federal-provincial conflict over federal transfers also shaped the debate over abortion policy as some provincial governments argued that decreases in federal health transfers forced them to cut costs by 'de-insuring' medical procedures including elective abortions.

Summary Evaluation of the Canadian Federal Design

While the Canadian Framers had hoped to clearly distribute jurisdictional areas to both the federal government and the provinces in order to avert possible conflicts and avoid a crisis like the American Civil War, Canadian federalism has developed into a competitive dynamic between the federal government and the provinces. Even with the nationalizing force of creating a constitutional Charter of Rights, the provinces still have, under certain conditions, the right to opt out of adhering to Charter principles. No constitutional mechanisms have been established to enable cooperation among the two levels of government and the informal mechanism of the first ministers' conference has been the primary outlet for resolving tensions between the two levels of government. In regards to the Canadian Supreme Court's role in shaping the direction of Canadian federalism, it seems that the Court is likely to determine questions of federalism on a case by case basis which will likely lead to more limitations on its role in determining questions of federalism as more acts of informal intergovernmental relations will (and continue to) dominate Canadian politics.

UNITED STATES

Establishment of the Federal System

America was born out of a collection of territorial and political entities, which preceded the formation of a national government, somewhat similar to Canada and Germany. Canada and Germany, however, had the opportunity to learn from the United States experience in developing a viable federal design. Briefly reviewing the historical origins of this design, the American colonists, after a series of reprisals from the British government in which the British enacted harsh restrictions and penalties on the American Colonies, violently paid for their freedom through winning the American Revolution. In 1776, delegates from the colonies came together in the 2nd Continental Congress and formally declared independence from British rule.

Having established the Declaration of Independence, the colonies attempted to forge a new central government. Ratified in 1781, the Articles of Confederation provided for a national government. The Articles instituted a limited central government with no executive or judicial authority. Congress was the sole national political institution, leaving the execution of laws to the states. State legislatures effectively controlled their members of Congress, who were subject to recall. Congress could neither regulate commerce among the states or with foreign entities nor could it levy taxes. States retained almost all power and jurisdictional authority. The limited authority of the federal government in governing and the increasing restlessness and increasing power of radical factions of colonists led to a reconsideration of the Articles of Confederation. Convening in Philadelphia in 1787, delegates from the 13 states, excluding Rhode Island, met in secret to fix the weaknesses of the Articles of Confederation, leading to creation of the US Constitution.

The Constitution, emerging out of compromise and debate, established a stronger central government based on federalism, separation of powers, and checks and balances. The new bicameral Congress had a 'lower' house with seats apportioned based upon state population. The population of slave states was determined by the 'Three-Fifths Compromise', allowing slave states to count five slaves as representing three persons for purposes of establishing population. Representatives were directly elected to two-year terms. The 'upper' house represented the states equally. The Senate was comprised of two representatives from each state regardless of population and appointed by state legislatures for six-year terms. A separate and independently elected executive branch was established in order to check the powers of Congress through veto power, convening special sessions of Congress and negotiating treaties. The Constitution also incorporated the Judicial Branch and the Supreme Court, which had the power to resolve disputes between federal and state governments and to determine the proper authority of each government.

Constitutional Framework

The US Constitution focuses almost entirely on the responsibilities and competencies of the federal government as opposed to those of the states. It provides few details regarding the powers or authority of the states. Although the Constitution mentions the supremacy of the laws of the national government over the states, there is little explication of the nature of the union between the states and the national government. The Constitution outlines what the national government can do, but provides little guidance concerning the dimensions of the states' responsibilities. Article 1, Section 8 lists the specific enumerated powers of Congress, rectifying the limitations of the Articles of Confederation. The Constitution allocates specific authority of the national government to deal with issues of national defense, international affairs, money, and interstate and foreign commerce. In addition to these enumerated powers, Congress has seen its powers and authority expand through the necessary and proper clause, which has been interpreted by the Supreme Court to allow Congress to pass laws 'necessary and proper' to effectuate the execution of its enumerated powers.

The Constitution does make some guarantees to the states, regarding what the national government will do to protect the states (e.g.: Protection against invasion (Article IV, sect. 2)). It also outlines limitations on state authority (States may not enter treaties, alliances or confederations (Article I, Sect. 10)). States are bound to the authority of the constitution and all the laws made under it are to be the supreme law of the land (Article IV and VI). However, the Constitution provides little elaboration on what are the explicit jurisdiction and powers of the states. Only the 10th amendment of the Bill of Rights guarantees that powers not "delegated to the US by the Constitution, or prohibited by it to the states, are reserved to the states". The Constitution does not require the states to administer federal laws. Concerned with crafting the institutions and (limited) authority of the national government, it is likely that the framers assumed it was unnecessary to list or grant powers to the states in the Constitution, since the states existed as autonomous entities for years prior to the Constitution.

Representation of Sub-National Interests in Federal Institutions -- United States Senate

At the Philadelphia constitutional convention, the 'great compromise' created the Senate, a second legislative chamber addressing the concerns of the small states and enabling continued state participation in national lawmaking that had occurred under the Articles of Confederation. Under the Articles, state governments effectively controlled and directed their Congressional legislators so that "laws were actually approved not at Philadelphia where Congress sat, but at each of the state capitols" (Riker 1964: 88). Congressmen (and they were men) were beholden to the states because state legislatures elected them, instructed their voting and could recall them. When the Constitution replaced the Articles, these specific instructions and recall provisions were omitted. It is likely that the framers intended to institutionalize this role of the states through the creation of the Senate. Some scholars believe that the Framers likely assumed that constitutionally requiring the election of Senators by state legislatures would be sufficient to ensure the representation of state interests (Ibid.).

By failing to include specific instructions and recall provisions for Senators, however, the Framers "rendered state legislative control quite tenuous and ultimately non-existent" (Ibid. 89). Whether this omission was intentional or accidental, later amendment attempts to include instruction and the recall of Senators failed (Ibid.). Without such controls, the Constitution effectively insulated Senators from their state governments. Even the threat of elections was not sufficient to keep Senators in line with the interests of their home state. If Senators deviated in their voting from the state's instructions, they could hope that a new change in state leadership would be more favorable to them when election time came around (Riker 1964: 89).

The final bulwark against state control over the Senate was the passage of the seventeenth amendment providing for the direct elections of Senators by the people. The amendment formalized what had already been occurring within the states. In the 19th century, Senate candidates would 'campaign' on the behalf of candidates for the state legislature, who in turn pledged support for the Senate candidate. The rise of these senatorial 'campaigns' led to the state legislator owing his political existence to 'popular appeal of the Senatorial candidate'. This practice effectively cut the ties between the state's interests and the Senator's carrying out those interests in Washington (Riker 1964: 91). The seventeenth amendment effectively severed the one institutional means to effect state representation of interests in the federal government. Without any significant means of integrating of state interests into federal policy-making, the US system is distinct from Canada, which has developed the first minister's conferences and Germany, which constitutionally enshrines Land and federal cooperation through the second legislative chamber of the Bundesrat.

Supreme Court Federalism Jurisprudence

Throughout its existence, the United States Supreme Court has played a significant role in shaping the course of federalism in the United States. This role is primarily due to the Court's interpretation of the scope of Congress's powers under commerce clause, and recent 're-examinations' of the 10th and 11th amendments of the Constitution as a basis for determining boundaries between states and the federal government.[36]

One of the Court's earliest and most significant decisions regarding the division of power among the states and the federal government was *McCulloch v Maryland* (1819), in which the Court determined whether or not the federal government had the power to create a national bank via the 'necessary and proper' clause. The state of Maryland imposed a harsh tax on the bank in order to put it out of business and out of competition with the state's bank. Chief Justice Marshall argued that the 'power to tax constituted the power to destroy' referring to Maryland's attempt to impose the tax. The Court ruled that since Congress had the 'enumerated' power 'to tax and establish a currency', it also had the constitutional authority to create a bank in order to achieve these goals. Other early cases such as *Gibbons v Ogden* (1824), asserted the national government's authority to regulate interstate commerce. In *Barron v Baltimore (1833)*, the Courts asserted that local policy disputes cannot be addressed under the constitution. These early cases helped support national power at the expense of state authority. As Keith Whittington and other have noted, at various times in history national government actors, when it has suited their interests, have supported the Court "interposing the national will against the states" (Whittington 2005: 587).

Yet, also during the early period of industrialization and expansion in the United States, the Court sought to protect states powers, particularly when it came to commerce. In doing so it tried to maintain a clear distinction between the powers of the states and the federal government. A significant number of Supreme Court cases decided between 1835-1937 centered around the issue of whether 'commerce' or commercial activity was primarily inter- or intra-state. For example, the Court made distinctions between manufacturing (the making of goods) and commerce (selling of goods across state lines). More often than not, the Court interpreted what constituted interstate commerce narrowly, resulting in decisions that limited Congressional power to regulate commerce, effectively giving states more power to regulate

---

[36] The 10th amendment establishes state sovereignty, and the 11th provides sovereign immunity guarantee, which restricts the power of federal courts to hear claims brought against states by individuals.

commerce. With some exceptions (see *Muller v Oregon 1908)*, the Court's dual federalism approach to regulating commerce was evident in a number of cases at this time, (e.g., see *Adair v US* (1908), *Coppage v Kansas* (1915), *Adkins v Children's Hospital* (1923). Between the years of 1897 and 1937, the Court struck down over 200 state and federal laws.

The justifications for these decisions limiting government authority were largely based on the economic theory of 'laissez faire' capitalism. *Lochner v New York* (1905) is often cited as the high water mark for the Court's attempts to prohibit government regulation. In the case the Court struck down New York state legislation regulating the conditions and limiting the number of hours bakers could work. The Court majority asserted that the legislation infringed upon the 14th amendment due process liberties of the bakers to 'contract'. The Court's broad interpretation of liberty to justify its decision was controversial and future attempts at limiting regulatory behavior would soon come to a halt. External events, such as the Depression and the national government's response to it via the New Deal, forced the court to change course on its interpretation of the commerce clause.

After striking down a number of popular New Deal programs attempting to pull the country out of the depression, the Court faced a confrontation with President Franklin Roosevelt. In a controversial move, the President threatened to raise the number of seats on the Court from 9 to 15 in a blatant effort to appoint judges more sympathetic to New Deal policies. With this challenge to the Court's independence, the Court changed direction beginning with *NLRB v Jones* (1937). This case is seen as the 'switch in time that saved nine'; one justice switched his vote, swinging the Court in favor of the federal government's establishment of the National Labor Relations Board. Other decisions quickly followed, in which the Court supported the establishment of state wage and hour regulations (*West Coast Hotel v Parrish (1937)* overturning *Adkins*). From 1937 up to the early 1990's, the Court overturned only one federal statute, in *National League of Cities v Ursery (1976,)* on the basis of the 10th amendment and that Congress had exceeded its authority under the commerce clause (which was eventually overturned, *see and Garcia v San Antonio (1985))*.

Although *Garcia* overturned the *National League of Cities* decision, which had struck down Congress's attempt to expand federal minimum wage provisions to state and local government employees, in hindsight, *National League of Cities* signaled a new shift in the Court's federalism jurisprudence. This shift revived the 10th amendment limitations on Congress's legislative authority and supported state sovereignty. The Court's decision in *US v Lopez* (1995) ushered in this shift, a case in which the Court ruled that Congress' passage of the *Gun Free School Zones Act* exceeded its regulatory power over interstate commerce. The legislation had made it a federal crime for a person to possess a firearm within 1000 feet of a school zone. Articulated by Chief Justice Rehnquist, the majority based its decision on the federal division of authority and the limited nature of Congress's enumerated powers as mandated by the Constitution. The 1990's saw additional cases detailing the Court's renewed support for the federalism principle, including *Printz v US (*1997), *New York v US* (1992), and *US Term Limits v Thorson* (1995), and 2000's *Morrison v US*.

One could argue that other 'non-federalism' cases decided during this period reflected the Court's increasing support of state sovereignty and authority. For example, prior to *Webster v Reproductive Health Services* in 1989, the Supreme Court had routinely struck down most state abortion regulations; yet in *Webster* it began to reverse course and upheld state regulations previously struck down and virtually invited states to enact restrictive abortion legislation. The Court's support of state legislative authority was evident in other 'non-federalism' cases, even when finding state legislative acts unconstitutional, such as *Washington v Glucksberg* (1997). The Court stated in *Glucksberg* that while there was no federal constitutional 'right to die' this did not necessarily prohibit the states from in establishing future policy on physician assisted suicide.

During this federalism 'revival' period the Supreme Court also issued decisions reviewing the sovereign immunity guarantee of the 11th amendment, which limits federal courts on hearing claims brought against states by individuals. The first most notable decision in this area came one year after *Lopez,* in *Seminole Tribe of Florida v Florida* (1996). The Supreme Court ruled that state sovereign immunity protected states from being sued by native Indian tribes. The Tribes had sued the state of Florida to force negotiation of gaming contracts and Congress had legislatively authorized such suits based on its legislative authority over Indian reservations. The Court ruled that Congress could not limit a state's sovereign immunity through its other constitutionally recognized powers. A number of other decisions, such as *Alden v Maine* (1999) and *Kimmel v Board of Regents* (2000) provided further evidence of the Court's support of state sovereign immunity by rejecting attempts by individuals to compel state compliance with federal regulations via litigation.

Taking view of these recent cases, it would seem that the Court is forging a new path of reestablishing the dividing line between the states and Congress, thereby supporting state authority to legislate and reigning in Congress's ability to encroach on such state powers. However, one could also argue that through these decisions the Court was implicitly asserting its authority to interpret Constitutional guarantees (instead of Congress or state legislatures); (see Keck 2004). In 2000, in addition to *US v Morrison (2000)* and *Kimmel,* the Court also gave us *Bush v Gore,* in which Court intervened into when and how the recount of ballots should occur in Florida during the contested 2000 presidential election. In light of state and federal constitutional guarantees, and its interpretation of the state's elections law, the Florida Supreme Court ordered suspended ballot recounts to continue. This case was challenged by (then) candidate George Bush (who arguably had 'standing' to sue) and appealed to the US Supreme Court. The US Supreme Court, in a fractured decision, ruled there was not a constitutionally acceptable means to finish a recount by the deadline for selecting presidential electors for the Electoral College. By halting the recounts, the US Supreme Court's decision therefore allowed the previous tallies to stand in Florida, thereby making Bush the winner in Florida and in the presidential election with a majority of electoral votes.

As Keck argues, one can take the view that underlying the Court's recent revitalization of federalism jurisprudence is the Court's imperialism in interpreting the Constitution regarding Congress' legislative authority vis a vis the states rather than a principled adherence to determining federalism's proper balance. In fact the Court directly asserted this position in *City of Boerne v Flores* (1997). In the case, the Court rebuked Congress' attempt to protect religious freedom via its enforcement powers under the 14th amendment. The Court ruled that Congress had only the power to enforce provisions of the article, not determine what constitutes a constitutional violation. Determining what constitutes a violation of the 1st amendment amounts to constitutional interpretation which is not an 'enforcement' power as guaranteed by the 14th amendment. Therefore, Congress cannot expand its own powers through its own interpretation of the 14th amendment. By rejecting Congress's authority, the Court reasserted its own: "The ultimate interpretation and determination of the Fourteenth Amendment's substantive meaning remains the province of the judicial branch" (*City of Boerne v Flores* (1997) at 536). This statement supports arguments that the US Supreme Court's jurisprudential shift in federalism cases also highlights the Court's reassertion of its (sole) authority over constitutional interpretation.

Collectively, these developments in federal jurisprudence indicate that the United States Supreme Court's priority is in consolidating its own authority over constitutional interpretation and limiting the ability of elected officials to interpret the Constitution. In addition, one can also view the Court's abortion decisions as re-affirming the Court's authority to interpret the Constitution and therefore determine the course abortion policy in the US, rather than simply resurrecting the power of states to regulate said policy. *Planned Parenthood v Casey* (1992) exemplifies how the court chooses to reaffirm its own precedent (however tenuously) and thereby its own judicial power in the policy process (see Keck as well for supporting this view). If empowering states were really the primary focus of such efforts, then states like Utah, whose legislature attempted to limit abortion policy (because they believed that *Webster* and *Casey* signaled to the states that the Court would uphold further state authority over abortion policy) should have had more success when their legislation was challenged in the federal courts. However, due to the fragmented nature of the federal system, and the slowness inherent in the judicial appeals process, for seven years the state was able to evade sanction for passing unconstitutional legislation. The standstill ended when the Supreme Court rejected Utah's appeal on the merits and the case was remanded to the 10th Circuit Court of Appeals who struck down the legislation as unconstitutional.

Summary Evaluation of the United States Federal Design

The US separated federal system provides few institutional mechanisms facilitating integration or cooperation among the states and federal government. First, while the federal government may attempt to coerce state compliance with federal directives through the withholding of funds, there are no significant constitutional or institutional requirements for such compliance. Second, since the passage of the 17th amendment and popular election of US Senators, there is no formal federal institution representing state interests. Third, Supreme Court jurisprudence has done little to integrate or balance power between the states and federal government. The Supreme Court has tended to interpret the federal principle to favor either the federal government or the states at different points in time, while asserting its authority over Constitutional interpretation vis a vis other political actors. Overall, the nature and development of the federal logic has provided few consistent or institutional linkages between the states and the federal government. Subsequently this fragmented federalism has facilitated the ability of states to determine their own direction on abortion policy.

GERMANY

Establishment of the Federal System

Pre-1945 Germany was an aggregation of various units that shaped the development of the post-war state. After WWII, many distinct regions of Western Germany were established officially as Länder (Nicholls 35). Bavaria was left almost entirely intact, while Württemberg and Baden were combined to become Baden-Württemberg (Ibid). The formerly Prussian province of Hesse-Nassau became Hesse. In addition, brand new regional territories were created by the occupational forces, such as Lower Saxony, Hamburg and Schleswig-Holstein and North-Rhine Westphalia (Ibid). Under American, British and French occupation rule, the institutions and the Basic Law eventually created in West Germany reflected those countries' experiences with democracy and federalism.

Allied forces still occupied Germany when the first national political body, the Parliamentary Council, was established in order to create a constitution and a new governing structure. Germans were concerned with the Allies' demand for a new constitution, because they felt this would restrict the possibility of a reunification with East Germany (Nicholls 75). The term 'Basic Law' was used to signify the provisional nature of the governing document until such time reunification could occur, not knowing that reunification would come many decades later than the Council anticipated (Ibid).

The sixty-five members of the Parliamentary Council did the actual work of creating government institutions. The Council was comprised of sixty-five delegates from Land parliaments and representatives from the Berlin Party. Delegates were selected proportionally according to party success in the recent Land elections. The two largest parties, the Social Democrats (SPD) and the Christian Democrats (CDU) were equally represented, in addition to representatives from the Free Democratic Party, German Party and the Communist Party (Schmidt 10-11). This balance among the major parties required compromise and negotiation in order to create the new constitution.

The main Council debates centered on what kind of federal state Germany should become. Northern Germans advocated for an American-like Senate with popularly elected representatives. This proposal would have left little room for Lander representation in the federal government, but would have allowed Länder to operate more independently by completely separating their resources and administrative functions from the federal government (Nicholls 77). SPD leaders did not welcome this approach as they believed in a strong central government and socialization measures. Instead, the Bundesrat was established, representing Land governments rather than populations (Ibid.). This institution reflected prior German political institutions, as a similar chamber existed under Bismarck from 1866-1871 (Ibid.). The new Parliament included the Bundestag, elected democratically by all eligible German adults, and the Bundesrat, comprised of 41 members selected by Land governments. Bundesrat seats were delegated to Länder according to population (Ibid.).

Wary of the power of a federal president, the Parliamentary Council reduced the powers of this position to mostly ceremonial functions, and required indirect election by members of Parliament (Nicholls 80). To fill this power vacuum, the role of the Federal Chancellor was expanded. The Chancellor was to be elected at each four year legislative period. As in most parliamentary systems, the Chancellor was to be responsible to the Parliament, and could not be forced to resign unless Parliament had chosen a successor in a 'constructive vote of no confidence' (Nicholls 1997: 81).

In attempt to blunt the potential governing instability of a proportional representational system, a split ticket system was established for parliamentary elections. Each elector had two votes, one to vote for a specific candidate in his own district, the other for a Land party list. Candidate votes would lead to a simple plurality winner, and list candidates would be elected by proportional representation, dependent upon the entire votes cast for each of the political parties (Ibid.). The number of directly elected candidates would be subtracted from each party's assignment of seats according to the list votes. The Parliamentary Council passed the Basic Law in 1949. All Lander governments ratified the Basic Law with the two-thirds majority required except for Bavaria and the Allied forces also consented (Ibid.). The Basic Law has remained in force ever since. While this election system has been relatively stable, it has allowed smaller parties to wield (some might say disproportionate) significant influence in federal politics and muting the rule of the majority party. In recent decades, both the two major parties have governed in coalition with minor parties (see the CDU-FDP coalition in the 80's and within the last decade, a SPD-Greens coalition).

Constitutional Framework

The Basic law provides numerous detailed articles describing the nature of German federalism. Article 20 (1) and Article 79 (3) guarantee that provisions establishing the federal design and the Länder's role in the legislative process may not be altered. It has been somewhat more accepted in Germany than in the United States that the federal government and the Länder should have a 'separate but equal' relationship (Leonardy 53). Two articles of the Basic Law reflect this approach. First, Article 29 states that in both the political and economic realms, "the Länder by their size and capacity are able effectively to fulfill the functions incumbent upon them". Second, Article 106, Section 3.2 of the Basic Law requires the entire political system to guarantee a 'uniformity of living standards across the country' (Ibid). These two articles provide a foundation for the Länder to fulfill their duties *and* to work with the federal government to insure the requirement of uniform living standards. In addition to these two Articles, the notion of 'proportionality' has been inherent in the execution of German federalism. This 'transcending constitutional principle' is applicable to all state actions (Wuertenberger 77). In essence, proportionality requires that governments and agencies must take legitimate actions that are the least intrusive or limiting upon a citizen's basic rights. The 'proportionality' principle is somewhat comparable to that of the US Supreme Court's jurisprudence balancing 'state interests' with individual rights guarantees. Proportionality is also related to the concept of subsidiarity, which is commonly referred to but does not have a specific place in the Basic Law, except in Article 23, which deals with Germany's role and participation in the European Union. Broadly speaking, subsidiarity is the idea that decision-making should be as close to the individual citizen as possible. Therefore, decision-making and implementation should be the responsibility of the lowest capable level of government.

Despite these equalizing principles, the powers of the German federal government are much broader than these Articles suggest, particularly since the Basic Law also provides for extensive concurrent and joint powers for both the Länder and federal government. The Basic Law outlines the specific competencies of the federal government, similar to Article I, Sect. 8 of the American Constitution. Articles 72 and 74 outline the concurrent powers under which both Länder and the federal government may legislate. The Länder are required to administer and implement federal laws, except where the Basic Law provides otherwise (Articles 83-5). In addition, the Länder formally participate in federal politics through the Bundesrat, whose function and orientation is outlined in Articles 50-53.

The distribution of legislative jurisdiction between the federation and Land governments

Articles 70-105 of the Basic Law distribute the legislative powers among the different levels of government in Germany. Article 70 states that as long as the Basic Law does not grant otherwise, the Länder have the right to pass legislation, somewhat akin to the 10th Amendment guarantee of the US Constitution. Article 73 of the Basic Law lists the federal government's exclusive powers, which include issues such as foreign affairs and citizenship. Article 72 and 74 address the concurrent legislative powers of the federal government and the Länder. The list of concurrent powers is extensive and any Land legislation may be preempted by federal action over concurrent powers. Concurrent matters most notably include criminal and civil law matters, which usually require uniform regulation (Wuertenberger 74). Since the federal government has passed legislation on most of the matters listed in the Articles, there little real 'dual authority' regarding concurrent powers (Gunlicks: 187). The German Constitutional Court has ruled that Land legislation is preempted even when the federal parliament has explicitly decided *not to legislate* in a particular area.

In addition to concurrent and exclusive powers, Article 75 allows framework legislation, which enables the federal government to pass regulations that Land governments are obliged to support with supplemental Land legislation. The federal government is supposed to pass framework legislation only when uniform regulation across Länder is necessary, such as regulations of uniform or minimum living conditions (Article 75, 1). The Federal Constitutional Court has ruled that the federal government has the responsibility to determine whether framework legislation is necessary (Wuertenberger 75). These types of legislation have included joint financing of public works and the legal status of persons in public service (Ibid and Gunlicks 187). Given these powers, some legislative tasks between the Länder and the Federal Government are still shared.   Such tasks include foreign affairs, particularly issues related to the European Union, and the distribution of revenue (Art. 24 para 1a, Art 32, para 3, and Article 104). Nonetheless, over the years, amendments to the Basic law have steadily increased the powers of the federal government (Wuertenberger 74). This overall distribution of legislative authority has favored the federal government. The remaining areas over which the Länder have sole legislative jurisdiction are education, culture and general police powers (Ibid.).   As chapter seven shows, most of the legislative activity on abortion was completed at the federal level, while the Länder were mostly responsible for passing abortion counseling regulations implementing the federal abortion laws.

The distribution of administrative authority between the federation and Land governments

Though the federal government holds the majority of substantive legislative authority in Germany, the Länder are largely responsible for the administration and implementation of federal legislation. Article 83 states that the Länder are to "execute federal statutes as matter of their own concern in so far as this Basic Law does not or otherwise provide or permit" (Leonardy 42). The federal administrative powers listed in Articles 97-90 are limited and understood to be exceptions to the general authority of the Länder (Ibid). This understanding is somewhat reminiscent of 'dual federalism' where each level of government operates autonomously from the other within its own sphere of authority (Gunlicks 187). However, when federal legislation outlines administrative procedures regarding how a particular policy should be carried out, these laws may interfere with the Länders' powers of independent execution.

Nevertheless, the second legislative chamber, the Bundesrat, which represents Land interests, must first approve such legislation outlining any administrative rules, effectively limiting such conflicts (Wuertenberger 75). In the US, the executive is primarily responsible for the administration and execution of federal laws, whereas given that the Länder are largely responsible for implementing federal legislation. The Bundesrat " 'consider[s] itself the controller of the technical-administrative quality of federal statutes' " (Wuertenberger 83 quoting Scharpf). Therefore, as discussed in greater detail below, "[i]t is this fact then, which explains that in spite of the diminishing role of the Länder in the passing of legislation as such, their impact in the process of preparing federal legislation has constantly expanded rather than receded. Moreover, this fact…is the underlying reason why the Bundesrat has always been an intergovernmental organ" (Leonardy 42). Compared to the limited role states or provincial interests may directly impact federal legislation in the United States and Canada respectively, the Länder have much greater constitutional authority and involvement in federal institutions, due to the presence of the Bundesrat.

Representation of Sub-National Interests in Federal   Institutions-The Bundesrat

As compared to the US and Canadian institutions, Germany's Bundesrat is the only federal institution formally representing the interests of sub-national governments. Land governments may appoint and recall members to the Bundesrat (Schmidt 57). With the federal parliament (Bundestag) responsible for passing most substantive legislation and the Länder responsible for implementing or administering those policies, the Bundesrat effectively functions as a mediator between the federal and Land governments, rather than a solely legislative institution (Watts 31-32).

In contrast to the Canadian and United States upper houses, a Land can only cast its votes as a block in the Bundesrat. A Land's votes are invalid if they are not unanimous (Schmidt 57). Under the Basic Law, each Land receives a minimum of three votes. Länder with more than two million inhabitants have four votes, and those with more than six million have five votes. Since 1990, Länder with more than seven million residents have six votes. This change was due to the fact that the larger Länder were providing most of the fiscal redistribution to poorer Länder and demanded more representation in the Bundesrat. This shift allows the larger Länder to have a blocking minority in the Bundesrat, since two-thirds majority is required to amend the Basic Law in both the Bundesrat and the Bundestag (Schmidt 58). Similar to the United States Senate, citizens of the smaller Länder are over-represented in the Bundesrat. With a population over 18 million, North Rhine-Westphalia only has six votes in the Bundesrat, as compared to Bremen, with three votes and population of about 660,000 (Ibid.).

The Bundesrat plays a central role in the policy process because of the constitutional guarantees to Länder and the necessity of the Bundesrat approval for federal legislation. Besides the exclusive areas of foreign policy and the protection of the constitutional democracy, most federal legislation must have the consent of the Bundesrat since it is likely to affect the interests of the Länder. Since the 1950's, about half of all proposed federal legislation and almost all domestic legislation have required the vote of the Bundesrat (Schmidt 58). The Bundesrat often will pursue a reconciliation procedure on controversial legislation, attempting to work with Bundestag on a compromise bill through a committee for joint consideration (Wuertenberger 82). If a federal bill requires the consent of the Bundesrat, then the legislation will die if no consent is given. The Bundesrat must provide consent to any federal legislation regarding administrative law, budget and distributive financial policies (Articles 84, 85, 87, 109, 107 respectively).

Due to these requirements, German legislative scholars have characterized German federalism as 'co-operative federalism' or politikverflechtung--interlink/interlocking politics, or the 'joint decision trap' (Scharpf 1988). The institutional interdependence and constitutional guarantees enable the Länder to assert their interests against those of the federation from within rather than from without. However, Land delegations do not always protect or serve the interests of the Land governments in the Bundesrat or of the higher constitutional order. Because there is a strong relationship between national and Lander parties, party competition may often influence decision-making Bundesrat. Similar to United States where divided party control of Congress can lead to legislative gridlock, control of the Bundestag and the Bundesrat by opposing parties can lead to policy-making stalemate in Germany. During the passage of the 1992 federal abortion regulations and corresponding support acts, 2/3rds of Bundesrat approved the legislation, while the other $1/3^{rd}$ opposed represented Länder with elected coalition governments of the CDU and other parties (SPD, FDP) that had supported the federal legislation in the Bundestag but could not provide unanimous votes in the Bundestag.

Constitutional Court Federalism Jurisprudence

As compared to the United States Supreme Court or the Canadian Supreme Court, the German Constitutional Court has addressed fewer 'pure' federalism cases without 'party-political' dimensions, and only a handful of quasi-federal cases (Blair and Cullen 121). Cases with 'party-political dimensions' are those where ruling parties in federal government have used abstract review procedures to contest actions taken by opposing party *Land governments* which appear to be a Lander-Federal disputes but are disputes between parties (Blair and Cullen 121). This category also includes cases where Land governments have taken the same approach; filing an abstract review appeal in order to oppose federal policy created by the ruling party (Ibid.).

In a handful of cases the Constitutional Court has addressed Article 20's declaration of Germany as a federal state. Most of these decisions focused on the issue of federal comity between the federal government and the Länder (133). In some of its earlier decisions, the Court asserted that the federal principle or comity requires both the federal government and the Länder to mutually support each other, and for the stronger Länder to support the weaker (Ibid 132.). A significant example of the Court's approach to this matter was in the *Concordat* case of 1957, where the Court examined a 1933 German treaty guaranteeing Roman Catholic control over separate schools for all Catholic children. Lower Saxony had abolished all such education, and the federal government brought the abstract review appeal against the

Land, asserting the federal authority over treaties superseded the Land's authority (Ibid.). While acknowledging that the treaty was valid and binding, the Court stated that education, as stipulated by the Basic Law, was clearly under the Land's authority. The Court referred to the federal comity concern, and stated that, "'In the case of tension between Federal and Land interests, it must be left to an accommodation between Bund and Länder on a basis of equality to reach an acceptable settlement' "(Ibid. 134, citing the decision). Soon after the decision, the federal government and the Länder reached an agreement. The 'Lindau' agreement stated that when international contractual obligations of the Federal government impinge upon Land authority, such obligations are provisional until Land assent is given (Ibid.).

One of the most notable and controversial federalism decisions by the German Constitutional Court was the "*Television Case*" (1961), addressing the issue of federal intervention into Land competencies. At issue was whether the Adenauer government had the authority to establish a second television network under its federal competence. The SPD led Land governments challenged this action as infringing upon their constitutional authority over cultural affairs and violating the comity principle (Cole 148). The Court asserted that the Federal government's authority for 'post and communications' under Article 87 (areas of direct federal administration), included only the technical aspects of transmission and did not cover broadcasting in its entirety (Blair and Cullen 135). The Court criticized the Federal government for attempting to 'divide and conquer' because it sought agreements only with Land governments politically amendable to the federal government's plan, thereby forcing other Land governments to accept what was given to them (Ibid.). While some observers saw the Court's rebuke of the federal government's actions as excessive and overstepping the court's authority, the decision has stood as a protection of Land authority over broadcasting and television (Cole 149).

Since the "*Television Case*", the Court has limited its application of the comity principle to federal government and Land relations, although it has interpreted this principle in recent questions regarding Land authority and German relations with the European Community (Blair and Cullen 136). In a case brought by the Bavarian government in 1989, the Court found that the federal government failed to fully inform and accommodate Land interests regarding German assent to quota provisions in a European Community directive over broadcasting (Ibid.). The Court supported the involvement of Land governments in approving European Community directives and legislation, particularly when the European Community was to adopt regulations impinging upon exclusive Land authorities. This approach is consistent with the Court's ruling in the *Concordat* case.

Beyond defining the basic nature of federalism, the issue most frequently addressed by the Constitutional Court through its federalism decisions has been determining the parameters of the federal government's legislative powers vis a vis the Länder. Given the specificity of the Basic Law, Constitutional Court has been fairly consistent in supporting the general authority of the Länder in its interpretations of Article 70 (legislative jurisdiction- the Lander right to legislate as long as the Basic Law specifically does not grant such authority to the federal government) and Article 83 (the execution of Federal Laws) (Blair and Cullen 123).

However, there have been some exceptions in which the Court has expansively interpreted the role of the federal government, particularly in economic matters (Ibid.). For example, the Court has broadly interpreted the federal government's power authority over 'trade' issues to allow federal government regulations over safe building procedures, rather than finding that such regulations fall under the Land responsibilities of public safety and order (Ibid.). One might compare such interpretation of federal legislative authority to the US Supreme Court interpretations of federal authority via 'necessary and proper' clause. Relatively speaking, the Constitutional Court has done little to expand the 'implied powers' of the German federal government (Ibid.). However, as Chapter seven will show, in its third major abortion decision reviewing the constitutionality of Bavarian abortion implementation regulations, the Court ruled that since the federal government had 'conclusively' decided *not to regulate* abortion in particular ways, Bavaria was precluded from providing its own regulations on these issues. While this was not a major focus of the decision, this interpretation of the division of legislative authority between the federal government and the Länder clearly seems to be an 'expansive' view of the federal authority and limits what Article 70 actually guarantees.

In regards to Court decisions regarding the expansion of Land competencies, the Court has addressed this issue indirectly through examination of the Bundesrat's veto power (Blair and Cullen 130). In its early history, the Bundesrat pushed for broadening the category of federal legislation requiring Bundesrat consent in order to become law (Ibid. 130). The Court supported the Bundesrat's claims and the federal government responded by providing for more negotiation between the Bundestag and the Bundesrat on various issues (130). The politics of accommodation became more difficult after 1968, when party political conflict arose between the federal government and the Länder governments (Ibid.). The CDU/CSU Land governments used the 'veto power' of the Bundesrat to oppose policies of SPD/FDP federal government. The Constitutional Court provided some relief over this conflict in a dispute over the Fourth Pensions Insurance Amendment Act, which the CDU/CSU governments of Rhineland-Palatinate and Bavaria claimed was passed without the necessary consent of the Bundesrat (Ibid.). The Court ruled in favor of the federal government by limiting the Bundestag veto to "amendments of provisions which themselves required consent: if a latter amendment made no new inroad into the field of Länder powers, then it did not need to be 'sanctioned' anew by Bundesrat consent" (Ibid. 131).

This approach has generally sufficed and such Bundestag-Bundesrat conflict subsequently subsided up through the 80's largely due to the CDU/CSU-FDP dominance in both the Bundestag and in the Bundesrat. Conflicts between the federal government and the Länder reappeared in the 1990's due to the SPD holding a majority of Land governments in the Bundesrat (Ibid.). Rather than resorting to Court intervention, most conflicts were sorted out in Parliament through the Joint Bundestag-Bundesrat Mediation Committee (Ibid. 132). This approach could be loosely compared to the use of First Ministers' conference in the Canadian case, in order to negotiate compromise between the federal government and the Länder. However, as will be seen, even with a coalition of members across party lines supporting the revised federal abortion law (as well as a majority of the public), a number of CDU/CSU members of the Bundestag and the Bavarian government brought an abstract review appeal against the legislation.

Summary Evaluation of the German Federal Design

While some Constitutional Court cases have been significant in shaping Land-federal relations, overall Constitutional Court jurisprudence has not played as significant a role in shaping the nature of German federalism as compared to the other courts in this study. First, the comprehensive and detailed nature of the Basic law outlining the competencies and jurisdiction of the two levels of government and the relative ease in amending the Constitution has enabled legislative actors to shape the contours of federalism in Germany (Blair and Cullen 141). For example, recent constitutional amendments have smoothed Germany's entry into the European Community, while protecting the competencies of the Länder in European relations. Second, the Bundesrat's role in federal policymaking, acting as a intergovernmental institution negotiating federal government and the Länder interests has often mitigated the need for the Court to operate as a third party arbitrator between the two levels of government. Third, in addition to the Bundesrat, the distribution of jurisdictional and administrative legislative competencies between the federal government and the Länder has facilitated the 'interlocking' nature of German federalism. Lastly, these institutional federal-Land linkages have provided incentives for federal and Land political parties to integrate as well. Therefore, parties who are unsuccessful enacting their preferred policies at one level may seek to use federalism claims to advance their interests.

CROSS CASE COMPARISON

From the above discussion, we can see how the federal structure establishes the relationship between federal and sub-national governments. The particular features of a country's federal design condition the influence of court interventions in the policy process as well as shape sub-national responses to high court decisions.

Canada's attempt to adhere to a formal jurisdictional division of authority has led to an 'executive' or 'competitive' dynamic between the federal government and the provinces. Canada's founding and constitutional origins allocated authority between the federal and provincial governments on jurisdictional basis. Over time, as the separate levels of government expanded their constitutional grant of authority, this led to jurisdictional overlap and competition between the federal government and the provinces. Lacking strong intergovernmental institutions facilitating negotiation between the two levels of government within its parliamentary system, Canada developed the 'first ministers' conference'. This extra-constitutional institutional norm has provided a means for intergovernmental interaction between the governments, even though it has no constitutional authority. In addition, with the Federal Senate providing little means for representing provincial interests, there is little institutional incentive for integration between provincial and federal parties, and the domination of one-party federal governments has also fueled the competitive dynamic between the two levels of government. Provincial and national politics also operate autonomously from each other both in terms of finances and recruitment (Watts 1987: 783). Therefore, provinces that are politically opposed (in opposition) to federal government policies may be less likely to support and/comply with Canadian Supreme Court decisions that support federal authority. Chapter five shows how, with the Canadian Supreme Court failing to provide little direction beyond asserting the federal government's responsibility to establish a federal criminal law on abortion, the abortion controversy morphed into a debate between the provinces and the federal government regarding the jurisdictional overlap between criminal law (responsibility of the federal government) and health policy (responsibility of the provinces).

In comparison to Canada, the United States system has developed into a diffuse federal system with a strong central government. Like Canada, the United States' federalism divides jurisdictional authority between the states and the federal government. The US Constitution, however, provides little detail regarding the competencies of state governments relative to the federal government. This lack of clarity has meant that the federal government has little formal authority to compel states when states operate within their own jurisdiction. By detailing only the authorities of the federal government, this has enabled the federal government (with help from the Supreme Court) to enlarge its powers, since the Constitution does not outline the specific competencies of the states.

As compared to the German Constitutional Court, the Supreme Court has played a larger role in determining the contours of American federalism. Also, without the Senate playing a significant role in articulating state interests at the federal level and no other intergovernmental institutions or norms facilitating federal and state relationships there is no institutional mechanism facilitating federal-state interactions. Not surprisingly, party politics are also bifurcated, and there is fewer collaborations between federal and state parties (and politicians) than in Germany. The fragmentation or diffuseness of the American federal system allows states to operate relatively independently from the federal government regarding abortion policy, particularly when the federal government chooses not to act. With the federal government making few attempts to regulate abortion at the federal level, the states were largely left to construct their own policies without federal interference or intervention, beyond the Supreme Court providing potential oversight through its decisions. During the time period examined, the most significant action the federal government takes to influence state abortion policy is to prohibit the use of federal Medicare monies to fund abortion procedures.

Lastly, in contrast to the United States and Canada, through the operation of the Bundesrat as an intergovernmental institution, and the Basic Law distributing the substantive and administrative legislative competencies between the federal government and the Länder, the German approach to federalism has been one of interlocking the federal and state governments. These institutional arrangements have also supported integrated party relations in Germany. This contrasts with the more separated dual party systems in Canada and the United States. Federal parties in Germany are involved and invested in Land elections since it is Land governments who will determine the composition of the Bundesrat and therefore may influence the direction of federal legislation (Blair and Cullen 141).

Moving from the other direction, given the substantial role Land governments play within the national legislative body, Land governments also have a stake in national issues (Ibid.). This interlocking politics has meant that Land-Federal relations have often been the site of policy conflict between political parties, rather than conflict over the appropriate distribution of Federal-Land competencies. Asserting 'Land' interests against the Federal government (or vice versa) has been a means to achieve policy objectives that were not achieved through the national legislative process. However, since most of the substantive legislative competencies reside with the federal government, Land governments are relatively limited in their ability to deviate from federal policies they disagree with, as compared to provinces in Canada. As chapter seven illustrates, Bavaria could attempt to impose its 'policy view' legislatively through its counseling regulations implementing the federal law. Given that the federal legislation was comprehensive (as dictated by the Constitutional Court) there was relatively little policy room left upon which Bavaria could legislate.

Table 4.1: Dimensions of the Federal Logic

	United States	**Canada**	**Germany**
Constitutional Framework	Details federal authority, little mention of sub-national authority	Delineates among the jurisdictional authorities of provinces and those of the federal government	Highly detailed; outlines federal/concurrent/Land jurisdictional and administrative competencies
Institutional linkages-- Representation of sub-national interests in federal institutions	Senate used represent state interests, changed in 19th century to popular representation	Executive Federalism-1st ministers conference— extra-institutional process to reconcile federal and provincial interests	Bundesrat— specific federal institution representing Land interests. Bundesrat may veto federal legislation
High Court Federalism Jurisprudence	Court decisions have shaped direction of federalism over time; certain periods favored states over the federal government and vice versa; 80's onward has seen balance tip towards state authority	Early decisions deferred to provincial authority; yet in recent times have ruled with federal government. Attempting to find balance of power among provinces and federal government.	Few significant decisions; Court has often sought a balance of power among Lander and federal government.

CHAPTER 5

Canada

INTRODUCTION

This chapter examines the development of abortion policy in Canada and particular the role of the Canadian Supreme Court both 'in time' and 'through time' revealing how the institutional and federal arrangements present in the Canadian political system structure the interaction between political actors and shape particular outcomes. This chapter shows how the presence and nature of particular institutional features of the Canadian system have consequences both for shaping court policy outcomes and for the compliance with those outcomes by other political elites.

The historical and legal analysis presented below leads to a number of conclusions regarding how the presence or use of institutional rules shaped the development of abortion policy in Canada. First, the presence of the Canadian Charter of Rights and Freedoms does provide the necessary institutional support for the Canadian Supreme Court to review and overturn the federal criminal law on abortion (S.251). However, without other significant institutional guarantees such as a clear authority to judicial review, or a strong 'reference procedure', the Court repeatedly fails to provide clear instructions regarding what would constitute constitutionally permissible abortion policy and repeatedly defers to the legislature for determining a new abortion policy. In addition, the rights guaranteed in the Charter provide neither the specificity needed in order for the Court to craft clear rights limitations on government action, nor the 'positive' responsibilities for government actors to ensure rights are protected.

Second, while the Court is unwilling to significantly challenge the authority of the federal legislature, the Court is more willing to exercise its authority by employing judicial 'rules' such 'standing' or 'mootness' and overturning lower court interpretations of common law and provincial bill of rights. Third, even with a majority government in a parliamentary system, the federal government fails to pass a new federal law on abortion. The government first uses a 'free' vote instead of imposing party discipline, and does not ask for a 'reference' to the Supreme Court, which would have required the Court to provide an opinion regarding the constitutionality of a proposed new abortion policy.

Lastly, with the absence of any federal criminal law on abortion, the 'competitive' dynamic of Canadian federalism between the federal government and the provinces shapes the subsequent policy activities on abortion. Provincial authority to administer health insurance provides the opportunity for provinces to either limit or enable access to abortion. The federal government attempts to coerce provinces to provide abortion services by withholding transfer payments to provinces who fail to comply with the Federal Health Act.

Historical background

Abortion was criminalized in early 19th century in Canada, and those performing abortions could receive life in prison, while women would receive seven years in prison. In *Bourne,* a 1939 British House of Lords decision, the Lords ruled that an abortion performed on a 14-year-old girl was "medically necessary" to the girl's mental health. Subsequently, if a doctor could justify that an abortion was "medically necessary", then it was likely he or she would not be prosecuted in Canada (Farid 122). While for most of Canada's history the Federal Criminal Code generally banned abortion, the liberalization of the Criminal Code in 1969 permitted medical or therapeutic abortions under certain conditions (Farid 122).

The debate leading up to creation of the 1969 provision in the criminal code was not instigated primarily by women or activists, but by doctors performing abortion procedures who were concerned about prosecution, despite the *Borurne* exception (Jenson 1994: 125, Farid 122). In 1969, section 251 Criminal Code of Canada was amended to reflect this limited access to abortion. As stated in the Federal Criminal

Code " ...(i) the abortion had to take place in an approved or accredited hospital; (ii) the hospital's therapeutic abortion committee (TAC) comprised of at least three qualified medical practitioners, had to opine that the continuation of the pregnancy would or would likely endanger the life or health of the pregnant woman; and (iii) the abortion had to be performed by a qualified medical practitioner who was not a member of the TAC"(122) (Criminal Code, RSC 1970, c C-34, s.251). The law effectively codified existing hospital practices across the country (Jenson 1994: 126). Although the federal government was responsible for establishing the criminal law, the constitutional division of powers between the federal government and the provinces allowed provinces to control the delivery of health services. Even though the federal abortion law required legal abortions to take place in 'accredited facilities' or hospitals with Therapeutic Abortion Committees (TACs), the law neither required hospitals to establish such committees, nor was it specific on the meaning of health, both issues crucial for policy implementation. These two issues put women who wanted to obtain abortions at the mercy of the provincial governments. Provincial governments determined what constituted an 'accredited facility' and whether or not it could provide abortions (Kellough 1996: 186). By restricting accreditation, provinces could effectively limit access to abortions. In addition, the law did not compel hospitals to set up TACs and many refused to do so. Hospitals with TACs often staffed them with doctors opposed to abortion. The federal abortion law failed to provide uniform direction to the provinces; from province to province there was a wide variance in ability of women to have access to abortions.

Soon after the 1969 criminal reform was passed, feminists and nascent women's organizations criticized the law by stating it gave too much power to doctors and that the Criminal Code should not provide regulations of medical procedures (Jenson 1994: 126). As in the United States, the emerging women's movement at this time fostered greater interest in the issue. Various interest groups staged protests across Canada to support decriminalization (Ibid). The developments across the border, particularly in 1973, when the US Supreme Court decided *Roe v Wade* bolstered the efforts of these groups in Canada.

However, the Canadian government had legally framed Section 251 of the Criminal Code as a technical medical regulatory regime; the abortion debate was not politicized as *one of individual choice* as in the

US, but as *one of access* to necessary health services for women. In the following years, most of the Canadian Supreme Court decisions on abortion and much of the abortion debate generally focused on the actions of one individual, Henry Morgentaler. A Montreal doctor, Morgentaler was one of the first advocates of abortion on demand. In clear violation of the federal law, he opened an abortion clinic in Montreal soon after the reform was passed, and asserted that Section 251 prevented women from receiving necessary care from their doctor.

Throughout the 1970's and 80's Morgentaler was repeatedly charged with violating the law, and twice juries acquitted him. His first case reached the Canadian Supreme Court in 1975 and was decided on technical legal issues; however, his second case resulted in the seminal case *Morgentaler v the Queen II* (1988), in which the Supreme Court struck down S. 251 in its entirety. Over almost two decades, the federal government took little legislative action on abortion, likely hoping the Supreme Court would provide direction and political cover for the Conservative government. However, after the Court's 1988 decision, the federal government made two failed attempts in the late 1980's and early 1990's to revise S.251. With the absence of any federal law, provinces largely were left to their own devices in how to regulate abortion. Even when the Liberals assumed control of the federal government there was no attempt to pass a new S.251. However, the federal government did attempt to use the Canadian Health Act and federal transfer payments to ensure that provinces provided access to abortion. The last significant Supreme Court decision on abortion during the time period examined again involved Mr. Morgentaler. In *Morgentaler v the Queen III (1992)*, Morgentaler, opened a free standing abortion clinic in Halifax and was charged with violating the Medical Services Act, a regulation passed by the Nova Scotia provincial government prohibiting the establishment of free standing medical clinics. The Court stated that the Nova Scotia government had violated the principle of 'ultra vires' with the passage of the Medical Services Act, and asserted that by including a criminal sanction in the law, the provincial government had overstepped its legal authority since only the federal government has the authority to establish criminal regulations.

Brief summary of the Supreme Court's major abortion decisions

The first major abortion case arrived at the Canadian Supreme Court by way of a procedural issue. In *Morgentaler v the Queen,* in March 1974, the Canadian Supreme Court reviewed a Quebec Court of Appeal decision which had overturned Dr. Henry Morgentaler's jury acquittal of violating section 251 and replaced it with a guilty verdict.

As noted above, after the 1969 federal law was passed, Henry Morgentaler opened a free standing abortion clinic in Montreal, Quebec. Montreal police arrested him under the federal law for performing 'non-therapeutic' abortions. Three years after the charges had been filed, Morgentaler appeared in trial court and based his defense on Section 45 of the Federal Criminal Code, allowing protection from criminal liability if acts were committed out of 'necessity' to protect the health of the patient (Bourne Defense). Morgentaler was acquitted by a jury, and on appeal, the Quebec Court of Appeal overturned the trial court verdict, asserting that there was insufficient evidence to support and allow a defense of necessity (Bourne defense) (Campbell & Pal, 1991: 17). While waiting for the Supreme Court of Canada to hear his case on appeal, Morgentaler spent 18 months in prison (Collins 1982: 12). On appeal the Supreme Court was presented with two issues; one was to decide was whether or not to uphold the Appellate Court's decision, the other was whether Section 251 violated rights guaranteed by the 1960 Bill of Rights.

The Supreme Court only addressed the criminal procedural issues the case presented and avoided determining whether the federal law violated the Bill of Rights. The Court ruled that the Criminal Code statutes permitted the Court of Appeals' decision overturning the jury acquittal, although it also asserted that the lower court's action was inconsistent with the conventions of English common law. The Court did acknowledge upfront what their decision was *not addressing* - the constitutionality of abortion. As Justice Dickson stated for the majority, "It seems to me to be of importance, at the outset, to indicate what the Court is called upon to decide in this appeal and, equally important what it has not been called upon to decide. It has not been called upon to decide, or even to enter, the loud and continuous public debate on abortion which has been going on in this country..." (*Morgentaler v the Queen (1975) 20 CCC 2nd 449, 491*).

In addressing the Court of Appeals decision to overturn the jury acquittal, the Court found that while the Quebec court's action significantly departed from conventional principles of English criminal law, it was within the legal parameter set out by Parliament in section 613(4)(b)(I) of the Criminal Code, which allowed appellate courts to "enter a verdict of guilty with respect to the offence of which, in its opinion the accused should have been found guilty, but for error in the law....".(*Morgentaler v the Queen (1975) 20 CCC 2nd 449, 491*).

Chief Justice Laskin dissented from the majority opinion, believing the federal statue was unconstitutional as were the actions by the Quebec court. He asserted that it contravened traditional notions of justice and the right to be tried by a jury of one's peers. To support his position, he found no other examples where an appellate court had overturned a jury decision (Morton 1992: 79). More significantly, Laskin chose to explain why the Court did not address the second issue raised in the case; whether the federal law contravened the guarantees in the legislatively enacted Canadian Bill of Rights in regards to abortion.

With the notoriety of the US Supreme Court's decision of *Roe v Wade* lingering in the air, Chief Justice Laskin compared the differences between the two countries, the two courts and the two different decisions. First, he noted that the historical and constitutional origins of judicial review in the US contrasted with Canada's regime of parliamentary supremacy and the limited application of judicial review (Morton 1992: 79). Second, he asserted that unlike the constitutionally entrenched American version, the Canadian Bill of Rights was a legislative document, which limited its influence. "It cannot be forgotten that it is a statutory instrument, illustrative of Parliament's primacy within the limits of its assigned legislative authority, and this is a relative consideration in determining how far the language of the Canadian Bill of Rights should be taken in assessing the quality of federal enactments which are challenged under s.1(a)" (*Morgentaler v the Queen (1975) 20 CCC 2nd 449, 491*). Therefore, while Laskin did not state it explicitly, the conclusion to be drawn was that the Canadian Supreme Court had neither as expansive judicial review authority as the US Supreme Court nor could draw upon a constitutional document expressly detailing the freedoms and liberties of its citizens. As F.L. Morton, a prominent Canadian Supreme Court scholar noted, "The difference between the outcome of *Roe v Wade* and *Morgentaler v the*

Queen, it seemed, simply reflected the difference in status between the American and the Canadian Bill of Rights" (Morton 1992:80). Laskin's statement case demonstrates how the Court was unwilling to challenge parliamentary authority without the institutional support of a constitutional bill of rights.

While in dissent and therefore not binding, Laskin's words, nevertheless, were prophetic. Seven years later, Canada replaced the Bill of Rights with the constitutional Charter of Rights and Freedoms. This institutional change provided the basis for Henry Morgentaler's second and eventually successful challenge to Sect. 251 in *Morgentaler v the Queen II,* on January 28, 1988, striking down S. 251 in its entirety.

Morgentaler v Queen (II), stemmed from similar circumstances as *Morgentaler* (I). The Ontario Court of Appeal had overturned a Toronto jury decision acquitting Morgentaler of violating S.251 by performing abortions in his Toronto clinic. In a fractured 5-2 decision, the Supreme Court of Canada struck down S.251 in its entirety, asserting it contravened the Charter's section 7 guarantee of 'security of person'. While the Court majority agreed on outcome, three different opinions presented arguments as to *why* the federal law was invalid. Of those opinions, only Bertha Wilson, the lone woman on the Court at the time, explicitly argued for a *Roe*-like substantive constitutional right to abortion. The two other majority opinions presented narrower reasons for striking down S251, asserting that S.251 violated only a *procedural* guarantee of fairness as protected by section 7 of the Charter. With the Charter present, the Court was willing to strike down the federal law *in Morgentaler* II, but without a strong institutional guarantee and the limited nature of rights guarantees in the Charter, it was unwilling to provide specific directives to the legislature as to what constituted constitutionally justifiable policy.

In two separate cases the Supreme Court addressed abortion issues prior to its last major decision involving Morgentaler. In *Borowski v the Queen,* Joe Borowski, an anti-abortion activist, sought to overturn S. 251, arguing that it contravened the Charter and did not provide sufficient protections for the fetus. While the Court allowed Borowski to have standing to make this legal charge, the Court did not address the case on its merits, stating that *Morgentaler II,* effectively made his case moot. In *Tremblay v Daigle (1989),* Guy Tremblay brought an injunction in a Quebec court against his girlfriend, Chantal Daigle, who was seeking an abortion. On expedited appeal, the Supreme Court found that neither the Quebec civil code nor the Quebec Charter on Human Rights provided legal rights to a fetus.

In Supreme Court's last major abortion decision in 1992, Henry Morgentaler again was the respondent in the case. The Nova Scotia government passed the Medical Services Act in an attempt to prevent Dr. Morgentaler from establishing a free standing abortion clinic in Halifax. The Act prohibited abortion services to be provided outside of hospitals, and that provincial health insurance would not cover any abortions performed elsewhere (free standing clinics). The provincial law also stated that any persons providing such services outside of a hospital, upon conviction, could be fined between $10,000 and $20,000 dollars.

After establishing his clinic, Morgentaler was charged with 10 counts of violating the Act. Accepting the case on appeal from the Nova Scotia Appeals Court, the Canadian Supreme Court struck down the Act, concurring with lower courts, that the law was in 'ultra vires' of the federal criminal law. The Court asserted that the NS law was "...designed to serve a criminal purpose", and found that since criminal law was the authority of the federal government, Nova Scotia could not make legislation to this effect, although provinces are responsible for implementing health policy (3 SCR 436).

COURT ABORTION POLICY DIRECTIVES

State protection of fetal life and the rights of the woman

In contrast to the German Constitutional Court's strong claims regarding fetal rights or the weaker discussions found in the US Supreme Court decisions, none of Canadian Supreme Court's major abortion decisions (*Morgentaler* I (1975) or *Morgentaler* II (1988)) directly establish the legal status of the fetus. The Canadian Supreme Court avoided the issue for years. The Court either rejected cases addressing the status of the fetus (*Borowksi*) or addressed it obliquely in its 1989 decision of *Tremblay v Daigle*. As noted above, in *Borowski*, the plaintiff had argued the fetus had rights protected under section 7 of the Charter and that the S.251 federal abortion statute contravened such rights. The Court dismissed the case, stating that since it had struck down S.251 as in violation of the Charter in *Morgentaler* Borowski's case was moot.

Since the majority could not agree on the reasoning as to *why* S.251 of the Criminal Code was invalid In *Morgentaler II,* each majority opinion differed on the extent to which they addressed the rights of the woman. Only Justice Wilson addressed whether S.251 actually violated a woman's constitutional right to choose. She attempted to balance the rights of the woman with protections afforded to the fetus by referencing the 'early stages' and 'later stages' of fetal development. Her approach clearly echoed the US Supreme Court's majority reasoning in *Roe v Wade,* and cited the case in her decision (1 SCR 30, 183). Though Wilson asserted that the section 7 guarantee protected the rights of women to assert their personal dignity and autonomy, she acknowledged it was Parliament's responsibility to determine the factual question of when the state's interest in protecting fetal life should restrict the rights of the woman. "The precise point in the development of the foetus at which the state's interest in its protection becomes "compelling", I leave to the informed judgment of the legislature which is in a position to receive guidance on the subject from all the relevant disciplines" (1 SCR 30, 183).

In contrast, the other two majority opinions refrained from determining whether the Charter protected a woman's right to choose an abortion. Instead, both the Dickson and Lamer and Beetz and Estey opinions agreed Parliament had, in principle, the power to prohibit non-therapeutic abortions. Both opinions also limited their analysis to procedural rather than substantive issue of abortion rights. Dickson noted, "is neither necessary nor wise [to address the substantive issue] ..."[it] will be sufficient to investigate whether or not [section 251] meets the procedural standards of fundamental justice" (Morgentaler v Queen (1988) 1 SCR 30, 151). Both opinions focused on whether S.251 allowed legal exceptions to criminal sanction, and whether the procedural requirements (such as the requirement of prior approval by a TAC committee) were sufficiently available in order for a woman to obtain an abortion "in a timely and reasonable manner. Both opinions concluded that *"in practice it was not"* (Morton 1992: 243).

While addressing the same procedural issues, the two opinions differed in the degree to which they found the S.251 regulatory regime unconstitutional. Chief Justice Dickson found that Parliament's failure to define 'health' in the statute was an important procedural flaw of

S.251. Since health was not clearly defined, TAC's did not have a standard in which to determine when 'lawful' abortions could be permitted. Dickson relied on evidence from a 1977 Federal government report on the status of the abortion law in Canada (known as the Badgley Report) and a 1987 report on the availability of abortion in Ontario (the Powell report) (Morton 1992:243). Both reports showed that some TAC's defined health to include psychological as well as physical health, while others limited it to only physical health. Given this variation, areas in the country using the latter definition were found to restrict women's access to abortion, while the use of the prior definition provided broader access.

For Dickson and Lamer, this lack of a consistent standard used by TAC's made the application of the defense of a legal abortion uncertain (Ibid 244). "The combined effect of all of these problems with the procedure stipulated in s. 251 for access to therapeutic abortions is a failure to comply with the principles of fundamental justice.... [W]hen Parliament creates a defence to a criminal charge the defence should not be illusory or so difficult to attain as to be practically illusory" (1 SCR 30, 70). On this last point, all four judged agreed. The defense of legal abortion in s.251 *as applied* violated the Charter.

In addition, the four Justices disagreed on whether or not these procedural flaws could be remedied. Chief Justice Dickson, like Wilson, broadly interpreted section 7, stating that the 'security of person' guaranteed against "state interference with bodily integrity and serious state imposed psychological stress". The federal abortion law infringed upon this guarantee by "forcing a woman, by threat of criminal sanction to carry a fetus to term unless she meets criteria entirely unrelated to her own priorities and aspirations" (Morgentaler v Queen [1988] 1 SCR 30, 56). Therefore, Dickson's concern centered upon unconstitutional restrictions of access, or self-determination of the woman, and seemed to suggest that any third party (TAC) intervention in woman's decision would violate the Charter guarantee (Morton 1992: 245). Given Dickson's interpretation, Parliament's possible means and *ends* to amending s.251 could be constitutionally suspect.

On the other hand, Justices Beetz and Estey emphasized it was only the *potential* threat of criminal sanctions in application of S.251, which violated the procedural protections of section 7. The justices found no problems with the legislature requiring a third party provide "a reliable, independent and medically sound opinion in order to protect the state's interest in the fetus" (Morgentaler v Queen (1988) 1 SCR 30, 110). Beetz and Estey believed the S. 251 regulations, *as they were currently implemented, not written as a whole*, imposed delays in access to abortion leading to increased risks to the health of pregnant women (Morton 1992: 245). Therefore, a few revisions to the law could be enacted in order to limit health risks to the woman and to clarify the defense of a legal abortion (Ibid).

While the opinions in *Morgentaler* II did not discuss the 'rights' of the fetus, in *Tremblay v Daigle*, the Canadian Supreme Court rejected an injunction application by a Quebec man who attempted to prevent his girlfriend from obtaining an abortion by asserting he had a custodial interest in the fetal life, basing his arguments on relevant sections of Quebec's Charter of Human Rights and Freedoms and Quebec's Civil Code. In the case the Supreme Court unanimously determined the fetus did not possess legal rights or status under Quebec civil law. In addition, through its examination of the Quebec legislative record, the Court determined there was no legislative intent "to recognize the fetus as a legal person" (Jackman 1995: 2, citing the case).

In order to preclude similar injunctions filed in common law jurisdictions, the Court determined whether the fetus had legal status in common law or under federal criminal law. Under common law, the Canadian Supreme Court found that the fetus has no legal right of its own until it is born alive and separate from its mother (Jackman 1995: 3). Regarding the Civil Code and its legislative history, the Supreme Court found no evidence that legislature intended "the word 'person' to have a meaning different from that of 'human being', which was defined as a child which "has completely proceeded, in a living state, from the body of its mother"(Jackman 1995: 4). Finally, the Court stated it would not provide its own answer to the question of when the fetus obtained legal status: "The tasks of properly classifying the fetus in law and in science are different pursuits.... Decisions based upon broad social, political moral and economic choices are more appropriately left to the legislature" (*Tremblay v Daigle* 1989 2 SCR 530, 533). The Court once again asserted that it was the legislature's responsibility to legally determine when life begins and is afforded legal protections.

Role and Duty of the State in abortion policy

Compared to the US and German high courts, the Canadian Supreme Court cast a smaller net over abortion policy and was more deferential to legislative authority. However, by the time of *Morgentaler II*, the Charter' presence clearly shifted the Court's perception of its own authority and its willingness to exercise that authority since it decision in *Morgentaler I*. In *Morgentaler I*, the majority concluded,

> Parliament has made a judgment [about the criminal status of abortion] which does not admit any interference by the courts...Any unevenness of the relieving positions is for Parliament to correct and not for the courts to monitor as being in denial of equality before the law and the protection of the law (1 SCR 616, 613 636 1975).

This statement of deference to the legislature contrast with Chief Justice Dickson opinion in *Morgentaler II*,

> Although no doubt it is still fair to say that courts are not the appropriate forum for articulating complex and controversial programmes of public policy, Canadian courts are now charged with the crucial obligation of ensuring that the legislative initiatives pursued by our Parliament and legislatures conform to the democratic values expressed in the Canadian Charter of Rights and Freedoms (1 SCR 30, 46).

Not surprisingly, all of the majority opinions in *Morgentaler II* supported this view of the Charter and the authority of Court.

Yet, even with this new institutional authority supporting the constitutionality of s.251, the Court provided few directives leading to specific *policy requirements* that could shape future abortion policy. Even though the Justices noted there were aspects of s.251 that were constitutionally troubling, such as requirements that abortions take place in a hospital or that doctors performing abortions were prohibited from being on TAC's, none of Justices in the majority provided policy directives nearly as specific as those of the German Constitutional Court or to a lesser extent, the US Supreme Court. For example, regarding the appropriate constitutional balance between the rights of the fetus and that of the woman, Justices Estey and Beetz went only as far to say; "It is possible that a future enactment by Parliament...could achieve a proportionality which is acceptable under s. 1. As I have stated, however, I am of the view that the objective of protecting the foetus would not justify the complete removal of the exculpatory provisions from the Criminal Code." (1 SCR 30, 128). While this one statement indicates that complete abolition of abortion would likely be unconstitutional according to the Justices, it hardly provides any clear direction to Parliament as to how and where to draw the appropriate exceptions. Although the Supreme Court's majority decision in *Morgentaler II* may be relatively narrow, unspecific and provide few policy directives as compared to the decisions of the other courts in this study, nonetheless within the Canadian Supreme Court, the dissent believed the majority significantly overstepped its authority by striking down S.251. While concurring with Chief Justice Dickson that the Court had the authority to determine whether legislative acts were consistent with Charter guarantees, Justices McIntyre and LaForest believed the majority had made its decision based upon values not "clearly found and expressed in the Charter" (1 SCR 30, 138).[37] Justice McIntyre found that the Charter did not provide any new justification for striking down S.251 and disagreed with the majority opinion that the definitions and application of the abortion regulations in S. 251 infringed upon the section 7 rights of women.

Funding Regulations

In 1989, one year after *Morgentaler II*, the Nova Scotia government passed regulations prohibiting the performance of abortions of anywhere other than a hospital and refused to pay for such abortions. If an individual were found to be performing abortions outside a hospital, the province would levy a fine anywhere between $10,000 and $50,000

---

[37] The US Supreme Court, in its majority opinion in *Webster* (1989), makes a similar argument by stating that the viability and trimester principles of *Roe v Wade,* cannot be found in the text of the Constitution; thereby implying none too subtly, that it was wrong to assert such propositions in *Roe.* See the discussion of administrative regulations of abortion in the next chapter for further elaboration of this point.

dollars. Henry Morgentaler was charged with 10 counts of violating the Nova Scotia Medical Services Act soon after opening an abortion clinic in Halifax and subsequently sued the Nova Scotia government. At trial and on appeal, Nova Scotia courts found the Medical Services Act in ultra vires since it was in the 'pith and substance' of criminal law, mean that such regulation is the authority of the federal government. The Canadian Supreme Court affirmed these rulings in *Morgentaler III* (1993) stating that the Medical Services Act and the Medical Designation Act had "an effect on abortions in private clinics virtually indistinguishable from that of the now defunct abortion provision of the Criminal Code and this overlap of criminal effects is capable of supporting an inference that the legislation was designed to serve a criminal purpose" (3 SCR 463, headnotes).

The Court justified it decision on its examination of the provincial legislative debate records (Hansard). While the Nova Scotia government claimed it passed the legislation due to its concerns with the quality or costs of health care services, which are provincial policy matters, the Court found no evidence in the legislative record supporting those claims. Instead, the Court concluded that, "...the Medical Services Act and the Medical Services Designation Regulation were aimed primarily at suppressing the perceived public harm or evil of abortion clinics....The primary objective of the legislation was to prohibit abortion outside hospitals as socially undesirable conduct" (99 N.S.R 293, 12).

The Canadian Court left open the question of whether and to what extent the provinces by stating provincial regulation of abortion would be valid only if it was, "...solidly anchored in one of the provincial heads of power" (99 N.S.R 293, 493). As one Court commentator noted, by rendering the Nova Scotia legislation invalid solely due to the inclusion of a criminal sanction, the Canadian Supreme Court failed to address the broader and obvious question of whether provinces *are required* to cover payment for abortions performed outside hospitals (Farid 129*).* By providing such a narrow basis for its ruling the Court failed to settle such obvious policy issues raised by the case, which subsequently become a point of contention between the provinces and the federal parliament.

Summary of Canadian Court's directives on abortion policy

Overall the Supreme Court provided relatively narrow rulings regarding abortion. The court repeatedly refrained from both expanding its analysis of the abortion debate and subsequently providing meaningful direction to legislative actors. With the Charter's presence, the Supreme Court Justices did assert that the Court had the authority to determine whether legislative acts were consistent with the Charter. However, the presence of Charter guarantees did not move the policy needle significantly beyond the Court's deferential position to the parliamentary authority. As the next section illustrates, even though the Court was deferential to parliamentary authority, the federal government was neither particularly pro-active in exercising that authority, nor was it successful when it attempted to do so.

FEDERAL POLICY RESPONSE

The federal government evaluates the application of S.251 across Canada, while Joe Borowski argues that S.251 violates Charter guarantees. *1975-1982*

After the Supreme Court's ruling *Morgentaler v the Queen I*, the Quebec Attorney General indicted Henry Morgentaler with new charges, hoping he would plead guilty and serve concurrent terms (Campbell & Pal 1991:17). Declining the plea, Morgentaler was acquitted for a second time in 1975 using the defense of necessity. The Crown appealed, but this time the Quebec Court of Appeals set aside the jury acquittal and ordered a re-trial (Ibid. 18). For a third time, a jury acquitted Morgentaler. After the third attempt, the new justice minister of Quebec, of the recently elected Parti Quebecois government, did not appeal the case and Morgentaler was free.

Largely due to Morgentaler's efforts, abortion became more accessible in Quebec, yet in other areas of the country abortion access was severely limited. Therapeutic Abortion Committees were shutting down around the country due to public protests. In response, the federal government established the Committee on the Operation of the Abortion law in 1975 (known as the Badgley Committee). The federal government charged the Committee with determining the extent of public support of abortion across Canada and whether the Criminal

Code abortion procedure was 'operating equitably' across provinces but it was not expected to provide recommendations on abortion policy (Dunsmuir 1998: np).

In 1977, the Committee found that "the procedures set out for the operation of the Abortion Law [were] not working equitably across Canada" (Dunsumir 5 citing the Badgely Report). The Report found regional disparities due to inconsistent provincial and local applications of the law, particularly due to variance in the establishment and procedures of TAC's. The Committee said, "It is not the law that has led to inequities in its operation...It is the Canadian people, their health institutions, and the medical profession, who are responsible for this situation" (Committee on the Operation of the Abortion Law 1977: np).

The determination that the medical profession was responsible for these inequities as opposed to the federal government framed much of the subsequent policy debate on abortion. Consequently, this approach kept the debate at a provincial and local level, which also limited the ability of the Supreme Court (or courts generally) to shape the nature of abortion policy, since questions of 'individual rights' were not the locus of the debate. In addition, this construction of responsibility enabled the federal government to delay taking any immediate legislative action and foreshadowed the eventual struggle between the provinces and the federal government over health policy. However, two individuals, Joe Borowski and Henry Morgentaler took their respective cases to the courts and into the abortion debate.

While Henry Morgentaler pursued his acts of disobedience in Quebec, his actions had not yet made an impact public opinion on abortion, although they evoked responses from anti-abortion activists. One activist who was stirred to respond to Morgentaler's actions was Joseph Borowski. Borowski was a former trade unionist and NDP (New Democratic Party) cabinet minister in Saskatchewan, who became an active anti-abortionist campaigner (Campbell & Pal 1991:19).

Even though the Supreme Court refrained from determining that a 'right to an abortion' was protected under the Canadian Bill of Rights in *Morgentaler v the Queen I*, Borowski pursued the competing argument. He argued that the 'fetus' was a human life from the moment of conception, and therefore a 'person' protected under Canadian law. Employing one of Canada's most respected jurists, Morris Shumiatcher, to argue his case, Borowski sued the federal government, claiming that the federal criminal abortion regulations (Sect. 251) were unconstitutional. The case began in 1977, in Shumiacher's hometown in Saskatchewan. The Crown argued Borowski had no standing to bring the case in the first instance (Campbell & Pal 1991:19). Four years later, after first losing and then appealing his case in the lower courts, the Canadian Supreme Court accepted the case only to hear the issue of Borowski's standing. Examining its own precedents, the Court found that Borowski had standing to challenge the federal law on the behalf of the unborn. However, the Court also decided that his substantive challenge to the federal abortion law (Sect. 251) must originate in a provincial, not federal court. In August 1982, Borowski returned to Regina to argue his case on the merits (Ibid. 20).

Borowski and Morgentaler eventually find themselves at the Supreme Court 1982-1988

Hearing of Borowski's success, Morgentaler, who had been rebuilding his medical practice and life in Montreal, re-entered the abortion fray. In April 1982, he sent a letter to then Federal Justice Minister Jean Chretien, advocating for reform of the federal abortion law and stating that he would be opening a Winnipeg abortion clinic (which is in Manitoba and essentially Borowski's backyard). Soon after, Chretien received telegrams from League Life of Manitoba (an anti-abortion activist group) and Ronald Penner, the Attorney General of Manitoba, stating they would block Morgentaler's attempt to open a clinic there (Campbell & Pal 1991:20). While Penner's NDP government was on record as supporting greater access to abortion, Penner said he was bound to uphold the current law and would bring charges against Morgentaler if he attempted to carry out his plan (Ibid. 21). Morgentaler also announced plans to open a Toronto clinic, due to local support of a coalition of pro-abortion rights organizations. As in Manitoba, Ontario Attorney General Roy McMurtry said he would bring charges if Morgentaler attempted to perform illegal abortions in Toronto. Undaunted, by 1983 Morgentaler had opened clinics in both Winnipeg and Ontario.

Meanwhile, that same year, the Saskatchewan Court of the Queen's Bench (lower provincial court) heard Borowski's case that the federal law on abortion was unconstitutional. Due to the adoption of Canada's Charter of Rights and Freedoms in 1982, Borowksi's lawyer argued that the Charter's 'security of person' guarantee (section 7) protects the unborn's 'right to life'. The Federal government ignored this claim in its presentation. Instead it argued that the federal government had the authority to establish the criminal law and that the fetus was not a 'legal person' under the law (Ibid. 21). In October 1983, rejecting Borowksi's arguments, the Saskatchewan trial court upheld the federal law. Two years later, Borowski appealed his case to the Saskatchewan Court of Appeals and eventually to the Supreme Court of Canada (Ibid. 21).

In June 1983, less than one month after its opening, police raided Morgentaler's Winnipeg abortion clinic. Morgentaler was not there at the time, but was later charged with conspiracy to perform abortions. Two days after being charged, he went to Toronto to open his other clinic. As in Winnipeg, there were large anti-abortion protests in front of the clinic. On July 5, 1983, Toronto police raided the clinic and arrested another doctor, Dr. Smoling, who had been working in the clinic. Two days after the raid, Morgentaler surrendered to the Toronto police (Ibid. 22).

The Toronto case moved quickly to trial and began in the Supreme Court of Ontario (Judge W.D. Parker) on November 21st 1983. Morgentaler's attorney, Morris Manning asserted that the federal abortion law was unconstitutional under various Charter provisions, including section 7. Like Shumiatcher, Manning's strategy was to force the court to consider the constitutionality of the federal law itself before it could proceed with the charges against Morgentaler. Since the Toronto case moved so quickly, the Manitoba government postponed further action in the Winnipeg case against Morgentaler until the outcome of the Toronto trial (Ibid. 23). Manning made both constitutional and federalism arguments to support his case. He argued the federal abortion law violated the Charter guarantees of life, liberty and security of person, the right to freedom of thought, opinion, belief and expression and the right not to be subject to cruel and unusual treatment. In addition, he argued that the law infringed upon provincial authority over health matters since it regulated hospital procedures.

In contrast, the Crown lawyers argued that it was not for the judge to review whether the laws were consistent with the constitution (judicial review) but to determine only whether the regulation was procedurally legal. In their arguments, they warned against an "American" jurisprudence, by imposing the decisions of unelected judges on the people and that the political debates during the ratification of the Charter indicated that section 7 was not to apply to abortion. The Crown lawyers also asserted that it was unnecessary to determine whether or not the fetus is a person, but that the fetus does have value and the government's interest was to balance the rights of the mother against those of the fetus. They asserted that unequal access to abortion facilities across Canada did not invalidate the law, since there were other existing instances of unequal or inconsistent application of federal laws (Campbell & Pal 1991:24).

On July 20, 1984, four months after oral arguments had concluded, Justice Parker rejected Morgentaler's claims and ruled for the Crown. Parker stated that the Charter protected only those rights that had a long history and tradition in Canada; " 'No unfettered legal right to abortion can be found in our law, nor can it be said that a right to an abortion is deeply rooted in the traditions or conscience of this country' " (Campbell & Pal 1991: citing the decision 25). Morgentaler's appeal to the Ontario Court of Appeal was denied, and a trial on the original criminal charges began in October. Since a Charter justification was now inadmissible for the defense of his client, Manning used the defense of necessity as in Morgentaler's Quebec trials in the 1970's. During the trial Manning provided evidence which questioned the safety of clinical abortions in Ottawa and how limited access drove women to the US or Quebec to obtain abortions (Ibid. 25). The government failed to address this line of argument and asserted only that Morgentaler and his fellow doctors "conspired to perform abortions outside of section 251" (Ibid.). After six hours of deliberation, the jury acquitted Morgentaler on November 8, 1984. This outcome was even more surprising than the Quebec trials, since in Toronto Morgentaler openly had admitted to his intent to break the law, and therefore did not truly fulfill the defense of necessity. This acquittal, perhaps more so than the earlier ones, was a clear response of jury nullification of the federal law. In a limited way, through jury nullification, the court system and its legal rules provided an avenue even for the public to have a say on the direction of abortion policy, when more 'representative' political institutions remained silent.

The Attorney General of Ontario appealed the case and in spring 1985, Morgentaler was back in court. The Crown charged that the defense of necessity should not have been introduced and Manning should not have encouraged the jury to ignore the law (Ibid. 26). By October 1, 1985, the Ontario Court of Appeal agreed. Once again, the need to interpret the application of legal rules provided the opportunity for the Supreme Court to become involved in the abortion debate. With increasing political protests on both sides of the debate, it seemed clear that the case was going to the Supreme Court of Canada. The Supreme Court first heard the case in October 1986 but issued its ruling 15 months later.

After Morgentaler's case wound through the Ontario court system, Borowski arrived at the Saskatchewan Court of Appeals in 1987. The Appeals Court summarily rejected Borowski's claim that the Charter protected the rights of the fetus, and he immediately appealed to the Supreme Court of Canada. The Supreme Court accepted the case but did not hear it until after adjudicated Morgentaler's case in January 1988 where the Court ruled the federal abortion law (Sect. 251) was invalid. As discussed previously, the Court found the federal abortion law as unconstitutional due to the security of person Charter guarantee (section 7). Given that the federal law was no longer valid, the Court simply ruled that Borowski's claims and case against S.251 were moot. Having failed to provide any substantive direction as to what reforms could make the law consistent with constitutional guarantees, the Supreme Court of Canada provided a decisive victory for only one man, Henry Morgentaler, leaving abortion policy to other political actors.

Federal government fails to pass a new abortion law after Court's decision in Morgentaler II (1988)- 1988-1989

Both the federal and provincial governments were sucked into the political vacuum left by the Supreme Court's decision.The Conservative federal government immediately pledged to propose and pass a new abortion policy, but internal party divisions made this unlikely. Even with a majority government, Prime Minster Mulroney stated that any new policy would be put to a free vote in Parliament. By employing a 'free vote', the Conservatives tried to insulate themselves from being held accountable in the next election for passing such controversial legislation. This approach, however, was essentially self-sabotage. Parliamentary debate commenced the government in late spring and summer 1988, and the Mulroney government proposed a vote on three possible legislative draft proposals on abortion, with no amendments permitted. After the Liberal party voiced its criticisms, the government said it would allow 'amendments' to be proposed for any draft legislation but then it submitted only a resolution, not a draft law, prohibiting an abortion except under certain conditions. By submitting a resolution, the government could gauge the positions of parliament members and allow public discussion without specific legislation structuring the debate or revealing the government's policy direction (Brodie, Gavigan, & Jenson 1992: 69).

Subsequently, the government's proposal, along with two pro-choice and one pro-life amendment were defeated. With no party discipline, all female MP's in Parliament voted for both pro-choice amendments proposed. After this failure, Prime Minister Mulroney dissolved Parliament and called for new elections in November 1988. Effectively deferring to and deflecting responsibility on to the Supreme Court, Mulroney declared that his government would not take any further action until the Supreme Court of Canada's announced its decision on *Borowski* (Brodie, Gavigan, & Jenson 1992: 88, Morton 1992: 251).

The Supreme Court rejects Borowski's claims, the federal government fails again to revise federal abortion law -1989

The Canadian Supreme Court *Borowski* ruling came down on March 9, 1989. One could easily argue that since the Court had struck down the federal abortion law in *Morgentaler*, how could Borowski argue the unconstitutionality of a law that did not exist? In oral arguments, the Court asked Borowski's lawyer, Mr. Shumiatcher that very question. Justice Lamer said, "There is no law prohibiting abortions and there is no law prohibiting pregnancy and ordering abortions as in some countries. Where are we going to latch onto...a proper judicial function as distinct from a policy pronouncement?...I can only express an opinion as to what maybe the law should say" (Morton 1992: 263 citing pg. 17 Transcript of Appeal Proceedings on October 3, 1988, Supreme Court of Canada).

Mr. Shumiatcher tried convincing the Court that since it had entered the abortion fray, it should answer the question of whether the terms 'everyone' and 'person' of section 7 of the Charter included the fetus. The Court found neither Shumiatcher's assertions nor the Crown's arguments compelling. Justice Lamer chastised the Crown's lawyer Mr. Sojonky for asserting a mootness claim, while failing to ask the

Court to dismiss Borowski's appeal in the first instance, "'Mr. Sojonky, I realize that you follow instructions. I understand the position…In other words you would like us to quash it, but you do not want to ask for it'" (Morton 1992: 265 citing Transcript pg 65). Yet again, the federal government attempted to place any responsibility for directing abortion policy on the Court by failing to make a real effort to pass abortion legislation, asserting it would not pass a law till the Court ruled in *Borowski* and then asking the Court dismiss the case as moot.

Five months later, the Supreme Court ruled that Borowski's claims were indeed moot and refused to address whether the fetus had a right to life under the Charter. In the decision, the Court chastised the federal government for deflecting its responsibilities onto the Court. The Court justified its actions by stating it would have looked like a 'private reference' to the federal government had the Court rendered a decision on the merits. To elaborate, had the Court entertained Borowski's claim, the Court would have appeared as if it was "preempt[ing] a possible decision of Parliament by dictating the form of legislation it [Parliament] should enact" (1 SCR 342). The Court noted in its ruling that the federal government could have utilized the formal 'reference' procedure, providing a legitimate platform for the Court to evaluate the constitutionality of any 'new' abortion legislation. However, it was clear that the Mulroney government wanted the Court to make a decision without the government directly asking for such a ruling.

Both branches of government were passing the 'hot potato' of abortion back and forth and neither was willing to go out on a limb for the other. It is likely that the government did not pursue the reference option since it would have had to put forth a question for the Court to answer, and then publically respond to the Court's reference even though such a decision is not formally binding. Yet, the Mulroney government could have easily forced the Court to provide some direction regarding the constitutional parameters of abortion and the degree to which the Charter protects the rights of the woman and the fetus. Since the Court's hand was not forced, the Court strategically used the legal rules available to deny the case as moot and easily insulating itself from any negative fallout. The Court was not going to do the government's bidding unless it formally and publically requested the Court to do so. In summary, neither institution chose to extend a 'friendly' hand to the other, instead, each actor chose to exercise (or not) the rules and institutional supports available to protect their political power and institutional legitimacy.

This incident contrasts with the German case where the institutional presence of abstract review provides both the necessary incentives for the political actors to seek the court's review and the constitutional guarantees protecting the Court's legitimacy. In Germany, many different political actors, including Länder and minority party members in Parliament, may make an abstract review appeal, establishing review as part of the 'normal' legislative process whereas in Canada, only the ruling government has this authority. In addition, abstract review binds political actors to the court's decision, contrasting with the advisory nature of the reference procedure. Making a reference shines a spotlight on the ruling government's actions without being able to defer full responsibility to the Court. These limitations of the reference procedure relegate its application to 'extraordinary' events (like issues of secession) inhibiting its integration into the 'normal' political process and providing insufficient means for the Canadian Supreme Court to act as a 'third' legislative chamber as the German Constitutional Court can through abstract review.

The abortion issue returns to the Court in Daigle v Tremblay and the Court addresses the question of 'personhood' -1989

Due to the minimal parameters set out by the Supreme Court and the continued inaction of the federal government, abortion politics were being played out at the provincial level. This activity brought the abortion issue back to the Court in the form of an 'abortion injunction' case from Quebec-- *Daigle v Tremblay.* On July 7 1989 in Montreal, Quebec, Guy Tremblay sought a temporary injunction against his girlfriend Chantal Daigle, to stop her from having an abortion (Campbell & Pal 1991:38). Justice Jacques Viens of the Quebec Superior Court upheld the injunction. Basing his decision upon the Quebec Charter of Human Rights and Freedoms, articles 1 and 2, which protected rights of the 'etre human' (human being), he concluded that the fetus was a human being and thus guaranteed a right to life (Campbell & Pal 1991:39, Morton 1992: 277).

Chantal Daigle immediately appealed the decision to the Quebec Court of Appeal who upheld the injunction in a fractured 3-2 decision.

Each member of the majority provided a different justification for upholding the injunction. One found no basis in either the Quebec or Canadian Charters, but through Canadian common law and custom, while another found that only the civil code justified the injunction (Campbell & Pal 1991: 40). Only one member of the majority supported Superior Court Judge Viens argument that the Quebec Charter supported fetal rights (Ibid.). The dissenters all agreed, however, that injunctions should not be used in personal matters, and that the question of fetal rights was one that should be determined from precedents ruled under the Canadian Charter (Ibid.).

Now in an advanced stage of pregnancy, Daigle appealed to the Canadian Supreme Court and the Court interrupted its summer recess to hear the case on August 8, 1989. A number of pro-choice and pro-life groups sought intervener status in the case.[38] The federal government also sought such status asserting it was not supporting either side, but "defend[ing] [its] right to legislate at the federal level" (Campbell & Pal 1991: quoting Federal Minister of Justice Doug Lewis). This position obviously seemed disingenuous since the federal government had done little to assert its legislative authority up to that point.

The case was cut short. Halfway through the first day of hearing arguments from various interveners, Daigle's lawyer informed the Court that Chantal Daigle crossed the border into the United States and obtained an abortion. At that point, the case could have been determined moot, but the Court asked Tremblay and Daigle's lawyers if they wished to continue. Bedard, Daigle's lawyer said yes, noting that the issues supporting the injunction remained and other women could easily face such injunctions (Morton 1992: 281). In contrast to *Borowski,* the Supreme Court decided to continue to hear the case on the merits. A few hours after oral arguments concluded, the Court set aside the injunction.

Four months later, on November 16, 1989, the Court provided a unanimous ruling supporting its decision in *Daigle.* The Court failed to find any existing legal precedence of 'personhood' as applied to a fetus

---

[38] "Intervener status' allows third party groups to present oral and written arguments to the Supreme Court on either side of the case at hand. It is similar to interest groups in US who submit amicus briefs to the US Supreme Court.

in either common law, or under the Quebec Charter. The Court also asserted that if the Quebec Assembly had wanted 'human being' to include protection for a fetus, it would have done so. The court justified its examination of common law precedent in order to avoid similar cases from being brought forth on common law grounds (Dunsmuir 5). The Court refrained from settling the broader and lingering question of whether the section 7 'security of person' protections *in the Charter* included protections for a fetus. The Court cannily asserted that it could not answer that question because the Canadian Charter does not apply in civil cases between private parties; there must be some 'state action' involved for the Charter to apply, an oblique reference to the Quebec Appeals Court's dissenting opinion (*Tremblay v Daigle* (1989) 2 SCR 571). Lastly, the Court quickly dismissed the position that a father has 'veto' rights when it came for a woman to make a decision on whether or not to have an abortion (Brodie, Gavigan, & Jenson 1992:96, Dunsmuir 1998: np)

While one could argue that the *Daigle* decision was narrow and left the larger questions of abortion and fetal rights to the legislature, it could also be said that the Court showed less restraint that it had claimed necessary in previous decisions. First, once Daigle obtained her abortion, the case was moot; the Court did not have to continue with the case. Second, although the Court refrained from making a constitutional pronouncement, the Court extended its reach to include an examination of common law, which was not relevant for a case appealed from Quebec (Morton 285). What was the Court's justification for continuing with the case? The Court stated it was "in order to resolve the important legal issue raised so that the situation of women in the position in which Ms. Daigle found herself could be clarified" (*Tremblay v Daigle* (1989) 2 SCR 571). While this justification may be compelling administratively in order to preempt similar cases attempted in common law jurisdictions, there was not a clear legal basis for the Court's digression into this area.

In addition, while the Court didn't directly address the section 7 Charter questions, extrapolations could logically be made from the Court's interpretation of rights afforded to a 'human being' under the Quebec Charter, to that of 'rights' of 'person' under the Canadian Charter. If a 'human being' is a broader concept than 'person' yet the Court found no protection for a fetus under 'human being' this brings into doubt whether a fetus would have 'rights' under Canadian Charter section 7 guarantees of 'security of person' (Morton 1992: 286). As F.L Morton notes, "Intentionally or otherwise the Supreme Court seemed to have used the facts of *Daigle* to decide the issues of *Borowski*" (Morton 1992: 286). If this is true, as Morton claims, then why did the Court fail to make such a ruling in *Borowski* in the first instance?

Perhaps instead we can explain the Court's contrasting approaches in these two cases in light of institutional authority and the relative position of the Court to other political actors. In *Daigle*, the Court was reviewing a lower court's ruling and even resolving conflicting interpretations of law by lower judicial officials, actions appropriate for the 'highest court' in Canada and part of its institutional authority. In *Daigle*, the Court could justify making a 'policy' decision because it justified its intervention on purely 'judicial' grounds—reconciling legal interpretations even if such legal interpretations would easily have policy implications. The distinction between these two cases is a good example of what Jeb Barnes has noted as the crux of 'Interbranch research'; revealing "how legal rules and procedures shape ongoing policy [and reveal] the political significance of seemingly technical legal matters" (Barnes 2007: 25).

In *Borowski*, however, the Court was essentially being pressured by other political actors to make a policy decision in the absence of clear institutional authority to do so. As the Court itself noted in oral arguments and its decision, the federal government wanted the Court to make a decision on the 'fetus' rights question but did not want to grant it the institutional cover or 'legitimacy' to do so. As stated previously, the Court had no interest in risking its credibility and power in order to provide political cover to the federal government. The Canadian Supreme Court, understanding its predicament, strategically refrained from acting (in *Borowski*) when it did not have the institutional authority to do so, and chose to act (in *Daigle)* when it did. Yet, even though the Canadian Supreme Court in *Daigle* placed some parameters around the abortion debate by limiting the father's veto rights over a women's decision to have an abortion, and by asserting that common law precedent and civil law did not afford legal rights to a fetus, once again the Court still left major questions central to abortion policy unresolved.

Parliamentary response to Daigle; a second failure to pass a federal abortion law-1989-1991

After *Daigle,* the federal government again attempted to craft a new federal abortion policy. This time the Conservative government first convened a caucus committee of its members, representing all sides of the abortion debate, to come up with a new bill that could be introduced in Parliament. By November 3 1989, the committee presented Bill C-43. Instead of a free vote, the Cabinet (40 members) was instructed to support the bill, whereas backbenchers were not required to do so (Campbell & Pal 1991:41). After three months of committee hearings, the bill was submitted to the House of Commons for debate. The bill provided a general prohibition of abortion within the Criminal Code and provided sentences of up to two years in jail, "unless the abortion is induced by or under the direction of a medical practitioner who is of the opinion that, if the abortion were not induced, the health or life of the female person would likely to be threatened" (Campbell & Pal 1991: 43 citing text of Bill C-43). The Supreme Court's *Morgentaler* decision did influence the shape of the bill as the government addressed the procedural issues that the *Morgentaler* majority declared unconstitutional. The new bill provided a definition of 'health' which included physical, mental and emotional health, and eliminated TAC's and the hospital requirement, effectively making abortion a decision made between a woman and her doctor (no second opinions were required) (Campbell & Pal 1991: 42). In addition, a woman could not be culpable under the law unless she knowingly attempted to procure an abortion beyond the exemption provided (Ibid).

The debate in the House was fierce, and pro-choice advocates criticized the proposed bill for not addressing the issue of equitable access to abortion. Speaking in support of the measure, Minister of Justice Lewis stated that the bill defined a national standard regarding the entitlement of abortion while "issues of access and delivery of health services was a matter of provincial jurisdiction and responsibility" (Brodie, Gavigan, & Jenson 1992: 98 paraphrasing from Lewis's remarks in Parliament). By claiming that the burden of access and delivery was the responsibility of the provinces, this position reinforced what was already occurring, as provinces had been already been regulating abortions via their control of health delivery services. On May 29, 1990, with ardent pro-life and pro-choice supporters opposed, the bill passed in the House of Commons by a slim margin of 140-131 (Campbell & Pal 1991:45). The victory was short-lived as it was ultimately defeated by a free vote in the Senate.

Liberals dominated the Senate at the time the bill was presented. Debate on the bill was initially suspended due to the Senate's protracted consideration of the controversial GST (federal tax) (Brodie, Gavigan, & Jenson 1992:110). Finally, the Senate held a free vote almost eight months after the House had first passed C-43, on January 31, 1991. The vote ended in a 43-43 tie (Ibid. 115). A tie had never happened before in Canadian parliamentary history, and under Senate rules, a tie was recorded as a defeat. After this defeat, Prime Minister Mulroney announced that his government would not attempt to pass another abortion bill (Ibid.).

Why did C-43 fail in the Senate, while passing in the House? A number of factors could be considered. First, the federal government ordered cabinet support in the House, insuring 40 votes, which was about 1/3 of the votes the bill received in the House (Campbell & Pal 1991:45). Second, the ambiguity of the bill satisfied neither hard core abortion rights supporters nor the right to life contingent (Ibid.). The Senate delay only allowed more opportunity for criticism of the bill to be heard. In addition, doctors fearing criminal prosecution under the proposed law began refusing to perform abortions (Brodie, Gavigan, & Jenson 1992: 112). This created severe shortages of doctors willing to perform the procedures and in some areas women were unable to obtain the procedure at all (Ibid.). Lastly, while clearly under its jurisdiction to do so, the federal government chose to use the vehicle of criminal law to create and ground its abortion policy, which limited the federal government's ability to address essential questions of access that fell under provincial authority over health services (Campbell & Pal 1991:46; Brodie, Gavigan, & Jenson 1992:113). Some pro-choice groups and health experts encouraged the government to enforce abortion regulations through the Canadian Health Act by withholding federal medicare transfer funds to provinces denying access to abortion and reproductive health services (Brodie, Gavigan, & Jenson 1992: 107). The federal government rejected this approach. Federal Health Minister Lewis stated "The lack of or extent of medical facilities in any region of the country...[was] the responsibility of the province in question "(Brodie, Gavigan, & Jenson 1992: 107 citing the Minister). As with its ambivalent approach in the *Borowski* case, the Tory federal government tried to play both sides, by proposing a bill that provided a limited entitlement to abortion, while supporting some protections for the fetus (Campbell & Pal 1991:46). As will be discussed later in this chapter, the succeeding Liberal government headed by Prime Minister Chretien eventually employed the tactic of withholding funds to keep provinces from de-insuring and limiting access to abortion procedures. However, even if C-43 had passed as it was written,

> "...all the crucial decisions about access and entitlement would have been thrown back onto the provinces. Provinces would have to decide whether abortions could be performed in clinics or hospitals and whether public funds would pay for them, and provinces would have to deal with third-party prosecutions. Provinces, in short, would have to pay the political price for Bill C-43 "(Campbell & Pal 1991:46).

Except for the criminal prosecution of doctors, not a threat since the bill's failure, these crucial policy decisions *did shift* to the provinces, with limited success by either the courts or the federal government to insure equitable access across the provinces. The following sections examine the provincial attempts to regulate abortion and their responses to the limited Supreme Court dictates on abortion.

Summary and analysis of the federal abortion policy response

Abortion is part of the criminal law in Canada, which is under federal jurisdiction. There was one criminal abortion statue determined by the federal government for the entire country. This system contrasts with the United States, where the responsibility for the criminal law is largely left to the states and Congress has done relatively little to shape abortion policy. However, even in a 'first past the post' parliamentary system with one party holding majority control, the Conservative government was unable to pass abortion policy reforming S. 251 of the criminal code. The first attempt to pass a reform bill failed because it was set up to fail—allowing a free vote and amendments released members from the typical party discipline found in a parliamentary system. The government wanted to take the 'wait and see' approach, deferring to the Supreme Court and hoping it would provide some sort of political cover or justification on such a controversial issue.

However, it seemed the government wanted it both ways, because it could have easily pursued a 'reference' to the Supreme Court, but it chose not to do so.

With the pressure on, the second attempt to pass legislation was more straightforward and did in fact address some of the concerns the Supreme Court had presented in *Morgentaler v the Queen II* ; the vague definition of health, and eliminating the requirements of having TAC's and having abortions only performed in hospitals. However, this time, the 'veto point' of the second legislative chamber came into play; the Senate, with members who have lifetime appointments, produced a tie leading to the defeat of the bill.

Given the dodging and weaving behavior of the federal government, it was not surprising that the Supreme Court chose to protect its own interests and did not provide the decision that the government had hoped for in *Borowski*, by declaring his case moot. However, the Court did exercise it authority in *Daigle. Daigle* was a case where the Court could claim it was resolving lower court conflicts and providing clarifying interpretations of civil and common law. Remaining safely within its own institutional authority, the Court *was not* reviewing the acts of another branch of government as it would have had to do in *Borowski*.

Lastly, the presence of federalism played a role, since the government failed to pass a new criminal abortion statue and there was no regulatory policy at the federal level. Provinces, which had the legal responsibility for implementing health policy in Canada, were effectively responsible for regulating abortion. As the next sections will show, provinces responded to this situation by attempting to regulate abortion directly and indirectly. Also, the new Liberal federal government used its power over federal funds to ensure provinces provided adequate access to abortion.

In summary, the presence of the Charter emboldened the Supreme Court to overturn the federal criminal abortion law, but it was not sufficient support to enable the Court to provide extensive directives shaping the direction of abortion policy. The federal government attempted to defer to both the Supreme Court and the provinces on the issue of abortion. The Supreme Court did not take the bait, and with the failure of federal reforms, the regulation of abortion defaulted to the provinces.

NOVA SCOTIA

Provincial political orientation and brief summary of provincial activity on abortion

For most of Nova Scotia's history, its political culture has been 'traditionalist', conservative and cautious of change (Bickerton 49). The Progressive Conservative party has often been the ruling party in the province. Resistance to change was evident in Nova Scotia's approach to health and abortion policy. Compared to the other provinces in this study, there was much less debate over abortion in Nova Scotia and most of the provincial government's actions were attempts to limit the impacts of said controversy in Nova Scotia. The government attempted to dampen the controversy over abortion by passing legislation barring Henry Morgentaler from establishing an abortion clinic in the province. After this failure, the Nova Scotia government made few attempts to bar abortions, but also did not actively try to implement policies furthering access.

Henry Morgentaler threatens to open a clinic in Halifax, the PC government said it will enforce the 1969 Federal Abortion law, 1970's-1988

In the 1970's Canada's attention to abortion mostly centered on the federal policy and the acts of Henry Morgentaler in Quebec. Abortion had not been a particularly contentious political issue in Nova Scotia, until the 1980's, where as in most other provinces Henry Morgentaler became the catalyst for actions by the provincial government. Before Morgentaler took on Nova Scotia, the main hospital in Halifax had been providing most abortions in the province according to federal laws and without controversy.

Provincial consideration of abortion policy began to rise in the early 1980's. In 1982, Henry Morgentaler visited Halifax and publicly stated he was considering opening a free standing[39] abortion clinic

---

[39] Free-standing or private clinics are separate from the provincial hospital system.

(Canadian Press 1982: np). Asserting the government's position on abortion, Health Minister Sheehy (Progressive Conservative) stated that he supported stricter regulations on abortions and disapproved of abortion on demand, but that the Nova Scotia government could do little because of the 1969 federal criminal abortion law (Sheehy, House of the Assembly), and (MacDonald 1982: np). In an interview, Health Minister Sheehy responded that any abortion clinic would be "closed very quickly" and that he would not sign the license to approve the clinic (Ibid.). The Progressive Conservative (Tory) government repeatedly stated that it would oppose the opening of a free standing abortion clinic and would press criminal charges against Morgentaler if he went ahead with his plans ("May set up an Abortion Clinic in Halifax, Morgentaler says," 1985).

Nova Scotia said it would comply with the Supreme Court's decision in Morgentaler II, while prohibiting free-standing abortion clinics. CARAL attempts to challenge the prohibition in court, 1988-1989.

After the Supreme Court's *Morgentaler II* decision in 1988, the Nova Scotia Medical Board granted Henry Morgentaler a medical license to practice in the province. The Nova Scotia government, however, publicly continued to oppose the opening of the freestanding abortion clinic. Responding to the questions as to whether Nova Scotia would comply with the Supreme Court's decision in *Morgentaler,* Premier Buchanan stated his government's position in January 1989. "As far as Nova Scotia is concerned, with all the provinces of Canada, we're now adhering to the Supreme Court of Canada's decision and the accredited hospitals of Nova Scotia, where the boards have approved the procedure, are proceeding in that way according to the law. And we see no need of any additional clinics here" (L. Legge 1989e: 1, 16). In addition, Health Minister Nantes told reporters that the government would "use every method possible…including the courts if necessary, to try and stop an abortion clinic from being established in the province" (L. Legge 1989f: 1, 12). The Health Minister's comments about using the courts to defend its policy presages the actions the province eventually takes against Morgentaler.

Less than a week after the Supreme Court's *Borowski* decision, on March 16th, 1989, the Nova Scotia government announced it banned free standing abortion clinics from operating in the province by prohibiting abortions from being performed outside hospitals and imposed a $500 fine for violating this regulation under the provincial Health and Hospital Act (Cox 1989: 1). In addition, provincial health insurance would not cover any abortions performed outside a hospital. Premier Buchanan said the policy change was in response to the public's hostility to free standing clinics, as a recent poll showed that 63% of Nova Scotians opposed them (Fendick1989: 1). In addition, Health Minister Nantes stated, "We've simply established the policy as determined by government and we feel these policies...fit within the context of the current Canadian law" (L. Legge 1989b: 1, 20). Anticipating a response from Henry Morgentaler and pro-abortion forces, Attorney General Tom McGinnis said the government would vigorously defend these regulations in court (L. Legge, 1989a: 1). The Canadian Abortion Rights Action League (CARAL) immediately challenged the validity of the new Health and Hospital Regulations (CP 1989b: A10). Morgentaler delayed the opening his Halifax clinic, due to the court date set for June 22, 1989 (L. Legge & Proctor 1989: 1).

In anticipation of the case, on June 12, the Nova Scotia government introduced new legislation, Bill 107, "Act to Restrict Privatization of Medical Services" (referred to as the Medical Services Act), days before the closing of the legislature's spring session and ten days before the trial started. The debate over the bill was intense and members of the opposition (NDP and the Liberal parties) criticized the government's last minute tactics; resistance to the bill even came from those opposed to free standing clinics (Fendick & Lightstone 1989: 1). Health Minister Nantes openly admitted on the floor of the legislature that of all the medical procedures prohibited from being performed outside a hospital by Bill 107, abortion was the only one that could be safely performed outside a hospital setting. He further noted that the bill would help the government's case in court (Ibid.). Clearly stating the province's strategy of using the courts to validate the province's policy preferences, Nantes said, "Very seldom will you ever get an opinion from the lawyers that you're going to lose. But they discussed some options with us about ways we can strengthen our position and frankly that's what we're attempting to do" (L. Legge 1989d: np). The legislation also imposed a fine between 10,000 and 50,000 dollars on anyone found violating the law (Ibid). The bill passed the Assembly three days after it was introduced. While the government believed it had the jurisdictional authority to pass the legislation given its constitutional responsibility for administering health policy, the law's inclusion of a fine indicated a criminal sanction. Since provinces do not have control over criminal law in Canada, Nova Scotia was treading on authority of the federal government. The inclusion of the criminal sanction would be the eventual undoing of the law.

With this new law on the books, CARAL asked to postpone their court date in order to address the new legislation in its legal challenge. CARAL now asserted that the Nova Scotia government was attempting to circumvent the Supreme Court's *Morgentaler II* decision, which struck down the procedural requirements of the federal abortion law since those requirements delayed access to abortion procedures, and thereby implementation of the Nova Scotia law put women's health at risk. "No matter how this government tries to disguise it, that's exactly what they're attempting to do with their legislation" said CARAL spokesman Nancy Bowes (The Daily News 1989: np).   CARAL challenged the law on three grounds, that Nova Scotia: one, did not have the authority to establish the initial regulations, two, it could not exercise criminal law powers of the federal government and three, violated a woman's security rights under section 7 of the Charter of Rights and Freedoms by passing the law (L. Legge 1989c: 1).   In its brief to the court, the Nova Scotia government asserted that CARAL did not have standing to challenge the legislation on the grounds that only those who would be directly liable for prosecution under the law would have standing (Roberts 1989: 1).

The trial was postponed twice due to an inability of both sides to agree on the basic facts of the case. In early October 1989, Trial Judge Nunn denied standing to CARAL in a pre-trial hearing, agreeing with the Nova Scotia government's claim that since the organization does not own or operate an abortion clinic it did not have grounds to bring the case (Tibbetts 1989: np). In his ruling, Judge Nunn stated, "I am unable to accept that CARAL has any special interest greater than any other member of society in this matter which is presently the subject of strong emotional contest and national concern" (Ibid.).[40] CARAL quickly appealed to the Nova Scotia appellate court (Ibid.).

---

[40] Judge Nunn's construction of standing was narrower than Canadian Supreme Court precedent as seen in both *Borowski* and *Nova Scotia Board of Censors v*

Morgentaler steps in to challenge the province; the courts repeatedly strike down Nova Scotia's claims that their restrictions on abortion are legal, 1990-1991

With CARAL denied standing, Morgentaler immediately returned to Halifax to perform out-patient abortions in order to challenge the Nova Scotia law. Nova Scotia police charged him with 13 counts of violating the Nova Scotia Medical Services Act and his trial began in March 1990 (Canadian Press 1989a: np). While Morgentaler's case dragged on, CARAL continued with its appeal regarding standing to challenge the Nova Scotia legislation. On April 17, 1990, the Nova Scotia Supreme Court provided a 'split decision'. The Court stated that CARAL and other such interest groups may be granted standing "for the purpose of challenging the constitutional validity of legislation", yet since Morgentaler had been charged and in court, there was no need for CARAL to pursue the issue (Moulton-Barrett 1990: 43). In November 1990, the Canadian Supreme Court denied CARAL's appeal of the Nova Scotia Supreme Court decision, leaving the Nova Scotia Supreme Court ruling intact.

Finally, on October 19th, 1990, a year after the charges against Morgentaler were first filed, the Nova Scotia trial court cleared Morgentaler of all charges and found that Nova Scotia went beyond its constitutional jurisdiction by passing the Medical Services Act. The court found that the matter of abortion law was of *federal* and *not provincial* jurisdiction, and that the Act specifically targeted Morgentaler from opening his clinic. The Nova Scotia government immediately appealed. On July 6, 1991, the Nova Scotia Supreme Court upheld the lower court ruling, concurring that the Medical Services Act was unconstitutional because criminalization of abortion

---

McNeil. Borowski, in bringing his case on behalf of the fetus, had no more justification for 'standing' than CARAL. One could also argue in his case that a 'fetus' needs someone to speak for it, whereas in this case there is a class of persons or person (Morgentaler) that would have standing in this case. However, in light of , *Nova Scotia Board of Censors v McNeil*, a citizen was allowed to have standing to challenge a provincial law, when a class of persons who were directly harmed by the law; theater owners did not challenge the law.

is solely within the federal, not provincial, government's jurisdiction (Moulton-Barrett, 1991a: 43). Writing for the majority, Judge Gerald Freeman concluded, "There is little in the evidence of the purpose of the Medical Services Act to suggest that its primary thrust was privatization, and a great deal shows it was primarily intended to prohibit Morgentaler abortion clinics" (Ibid.).

Responding to the appellate court's decision, new Health Minister George Moody asserted that the provincial government should have the authority to decide where medical procedures are performed. Soon after the decision, NDP opposition leader Alexa McDounough questioned the Premier on the Assembly floor as to why the government continued to pursue matter through the courts, "given the fact that this is a public policy decision, a health decision, not a legal matter..." (*Assembly Debates*, 1991). The Premier asserted that the government's justification in pursuing the case was to contain provincial health costs, not an attempt to limit access to abortion:

> The courts...seem to think that it is simply an issue of wanting us to stop abortion when in fact we have abortion. It is available in this province, available now in this province, has been and will continue to be....We want to have the right in this province as a government on behalf of the people to control the cost of health care. We think it is wrong to allow anyone to come in here and set up a practice, for any medical procedure, and send the bill to the taxpayers. Mr. Speaker, if we can carry out that policy by appealing this and if that is the decision of the independent prosecutor that that is the right road to go, then that is the one we will follow..."(*Assembly Debates*, 1991)

This statement indicates that the Nova Scotia government was attempting to shift its justification of the law from its authority to regulate health policy, to asserting it passed the law because of the province's concern over rising health care costs. This rhetoric of controlling health care costs became the dominant theme/argument of the provincial government (and other provincial governments, particularly Alberta) when attempting to justify provincial acts limiting access to abortions. The 'health cost' discourse provided stronger 'jurisdictional ground' on which the province could justify abortion regulations, as opposed to making arguments based upon women's rights, the life of the fetus, or Charter concerns, all issues upon which the province can assert minimal authority.

Nova Scotia appeals to Canadian Supreme Court and loses; the Court asserts province improperly usurped the powers of the federal government, 1991-1998

Refusing to back down, the Nova Scotia government appealed to the Supreme Court, who accepted the case in December 1991. The Nova Scotia government, now led by Premier Donald Cameron, continued to argue that the case was not about abortion rights but about jurisdiction and that the provinces had the authority to regulate health matters and control the costs of health care. "I know the issue of abortion will never be resolved, but the issue of making sure that we protect the health care system, that we are allowed to manage it and are allowed to make sure we keep costs in an area we can afford, I think is a very important principle" (Moulton-Barrett, 1991b: 50). In addition to its concerns over health care costs, the Nova Scotia government, as stated by the director of public prosecutions, John Pearson, signaled to the Supreme Court it should take the case by saying that the case was "a matter of public importance in that it deals with the constitutional question of division between federal and provincial jurisdiction" (Moulton-Barrett, 1991b: 50). The phrase 'matter of public importance' is one that the Canadian Supreme Court has stated as justification for accepting an appeal from a lower court. While publicly opposing free-standing clinics in court, in July 1992, the Nova Scotia government quietly began complying with the Nova Scotia Supreme Court ruling in part, by paying doctor fees for abortions performed in Morgentaler's Halifax clinic.

As noted in the previous sections, in February 1993, the Canadian Supreme Court heard oral arguments on the case and by September, unanimously ruled in favor of Morgentaler, stating that the Nova Scotia government attempted to legislate in the area of criminal law by prohibiting abortions in free standing clinics. The Supreme Court determined that the provincial legislation had a 'moral' character because it "took a 'moral' stance, it seems, on free standing or profit oriented versus public institutions" (McConnell 1994: 420). The Court found the Nova Scotia government guilty of taking this 'moral stance', because the law included criminal sanctions for non-compliance.

The Court came to its conclusion though its 'pith and substance' (determining the matter and intent of the law) analysis, beginning with the fact that "regulation of abortion with penal consequences was suspect as a matter traditionally viewed as criminal" (McConnell 1994: 426). As did the lower courts, the Supreme Court of Canada based its decision on its examination of the Hansard (legislative) records that indicated the government's intent to prohibit the establishment of free standing abortion clinics. The Court rejected the province's argument that the law's primary intent was related to public health consistent with the provincial authority granted under section 92 of the Canadian constitution. The Court did not deny the authority of the provinces to regulate abortion as a *health matter*; "[T]here is no dispute that the heads of s.92 invoked by the appellant confer on the provinces jurisdiction over health care in the province generally, including matters of cost and efficiency, the nature of health care delivery system, and the privatization of the provision of medical services" ("R v. Morgentaler," 1993: 491). However, the intent to regulate abortion enforced by penal sanctions made Nova Scotia's actions suspect. The Court did not address any Charter concerns and "did not deal with funding of abortions as an access issue" (McConnell 1994: 328).

All three courts that heard the case had asserted that Nova Scotia had acted in 'ultra vires' because it attempted to legislate in an area of federal jurisdiction (criminal law). First, one could say that it was surprising that the Supreme Court of Canada chose to hear the case at all, since there was no lower court conflict to resolve and denying the appeal would have let the lower decision stand. The Supreme Court's decision, for the most part, reiterated the points made by the lower courts. However, the province did appeal on the basis that the case was 'a matter of public importance in that it deals with the constitutional question of division between federal and provincial jurisdiction'. Therefore, the Nova Scotia government was justifying its appeal, in part, based on Court's own rules for taking cases. By taking the case, the ruling would affect all provinces in terms of what actions they could legally take in fashioning provincial abortion policy. However, Nova Scotia's attempt to 'interpose the friendly hand' of the Canadian Supreme Court failed to lead to the outcome they wanted and enabled the Court to re-affirm its role (and political power in) refereeing the proper division of authorities between the federal government and the provinces.

Second, by hearing the case at all and ruling the way it did, the Court also could be seen as again 'inviting' the federal government to resolve the abortion debate by stating in its decision that "abortion is clearly a federal criminal law matter, an area of authority which is understood to include the exclusive jurisdiction to determine what is not criminal activity as well as not legislating that the activity is a crime" (McConnell 1994: 420). This statement echoes the position the Court took in *Morgentaler II*; that it was the federal government's responsibility to fashion a new criminal law on abortion.

Lastly, by sticking to the issue of federal-provincial authority, the Court refrained from making any significant statements directing abortion policy. The decision did not address any Charter principles or the question of how provincial regulations may limit access, an issue that may violate security of person guarantees (s.7) as the Court discussed in *Morgentaler v Queen II*. The Court considered the latter fleetingly by stating, "One of the effects of the legislation is consolidation of abortions in the hands of the provincial government, largely in one provincially controlled institution. This renders free access to abortion vulnerable to administrative erosion" ("R v. Morgentaler," 1993). However, the Court went no further in exploring this issue.

After the Court's ruling, Morgentaler pressured the Nova Scotia government to pay for the full cost of clinic abortions. While provincial health insurance was paying doctor fees, the province refused to pay the additional facility and clinic staff fees, which Nova Scotia insurance covered for hospital abortions (The Medical Post 1994: 13). Despite the threats from the federal government, Nova Scotia refused to fully fund clinic abortions by January 1995. Ottawa threatened the provinces that they must fully fund clinic abortions or force such clinics to be fully private and charge patients the full cost of the service (Lightstone 1995: 3). Provinces had to comply with this order by October 15th; otherwise the federal government would withhold federal health transfer payments (Ibid.). Nova Scotia Health Minister Ron Stewart stated that the province was willing to lose up to $130,000 dollars a year in federal transfer fees for not fully funding private clinics and continued using health care costs rhetoric as justification for the province's actions (Ward 1995: 1). Stewart said, "The best way to preserve a single-tier, publicly funded system, which is open and accessible to all, is to resist funding these facilities. The unregulated spread of private clinics could become financially unsustainable, inefficient in terms of public spending and could pose a significant risk to the health and health care of Nova Scotians" (MacLean 1995: np).

Stalwart on the facility fee issue, Nova Scotia lost $130,000 in federal health transfer fees from 1995-1997 (M. Kennedy 1997:A6). In response to the province's actions, Federal Health Canada spokesperson Guy Bujold said, " 'The federal government cannot force a province to change anything. We cannot regulate an area of provincial jurisdiction. At best, what we can do is, through the levying of a penalty, exert some kind of pressure' "(Ibid). Mr. Bujold also believed that the province would eventually agree to pay facility fees, and that Nova Scotia's actions violated an essential principle of the Federal Health Act that of "equal access on the basis of need and not ability to pay," was not being upheld by Nova Scotia (Ibid.).

Summary of the Nova Scotia Case

In conclusion, the Nova Scotia government attempted to limit access to abortion within the province through legislative acts. However, the province was unsuccessful in large part because its attempt exceeded its jurisdictional authority and imposed criminal sanctions on individuals opening free standing abortion clinics in the province. The courts consistently put Nova Scotia in check on this issue, even though it seemed to believe that it would receive a 'friendly' ruling from the courts. It was also clear that the Nova Scotia government's initial purpose in passing the Medical Services Act was to limit access to abortion, but when the government found that position to be problematic, it changed its rhetoric to financial considerations in order to justify the law. It seemed that the province was trying to find a more constitutional and (more publically palatable) basis for it actions by asserting its authority to regulate health services and insurance. However, since the Supreme Court ruling focused solely on issues of federalism, asserting that the provincial government improperly usurped a federal power, the Court ruling left the issue of abortion financing open for debate between the federal government and the provinces.

The financing issue became the central conflict between the federal government and the province regarding abortion, where the federal government attempted to wield its fiscal 'stick' of transfer payments to get Nova Scotia to follow its policy on abortion. As the next chapter will discuss, the United States federal government also used the fiscal 'stick' of withholding Medicaid funds from states in order to influence state policy on abortion. However, similar to the US, where Oregon refused federal funds and its corresponding restrictions, and chose to use state monies to fund Medicaid abortions, Nova Scotia refused federal funds and refused to fund abortions in free standing clinics. The withholding of funds was not always a sufficient harm inducing states or provinces to comply with federal wishes. With no other institutional authority or rules that could be used to enforce compliance, the federal government can only do so through indirect means. A significant difference between the US and Canadian cases though, is that the Canadian federal government *had* the authority to dictate abortion policy to the provinces, due to its control of the criminal law. Its failures to *successfully exercise that authority*, however, lead to conflicts with the provinces over abortion funding.

Lastly, the Canadian Supreme Court, in its decision, again stayed on 'firm' authoritative ground by basing its decision on issues of federalism and avoided making any substantive policy pronouncements on the direction of abortion policy.   It again deferred to the federal government as the institution responsible for fashioning a criminal abortion law and it provided minimal direction indicating to either the provinces or the federal government on where the policy should go next.

ALBERTA

Provincial political orientation and brief summary of provincial activity on abortion

While Alberta, like Nova Scotia, also has a conservative political culture, it is a conservatism resembling American western plain states than eastern Canadian traditionalism (Wiseman 1996: 54-55). Many settlers of early 20th century Alberta were American fundamentalists, and "the religious-political experiment in Alberta resembled very closely that which was tried much earlier in Utah" (Ibid.). In addition, over the last twenty years, rather than resisting change, Alberta has embraced market capitalism, more so than 'conservative' eastern provinces (Smith 2001: 297-298).

These two elements, religious fundamentalism and pro-market views were background forces present in Alberta's debate over provincial abortion policy. Alberta's government, consistently ruled by the Progressive Conservatives, attempted to shape the direction of abortion policy through its jurisdiction over health care and concern over health care costs, leading to significant friction between Alberta and the federal government. However, not only did Alberta fail to comply with the limited directives of the Supreme Court decisions, but enforced other policies contradicting the intent of the Court. The provincial government also chose to act 'passively' in other policy debates over health care, which hindered abortion access in the province. While Nova Scotia strategically sought the intervention of courts as support for its policies and failed, Alberta avoided the courts and instead relied upon its constitutional authority over health policy to limit abortion. This approach was somewhat more successful in insulating the province from legal challenges. This approach, however, set up a showdown with the federal government over health care costs, in which Alberta eventually had to back down due to public and financial pressures.

Debate over 'extra billing' allows Alberta to defer responsibility and shift blame to the federal government and doctors-1980-1988

As in the other provinces, except Quebec, there was little significant legislative activity on abortion in the 1970's. In the early 1980's, conservative-religious interest groups like the Voice of the Unborn pressured the Alberta government to investigate the operations of Therapeutic Abortion Committees, asking for a precise definition of the word 'health' as noted in the Federal Criminal Code on abortion (McGarry 1980: 8). In addition, these groups also pressured medical boards of local hospitals to not create TAC committees, effectively prohibiting abortions from being performed in those hospitals (Miller 1984: 1). The Alberta government took no action to limit the influence or actions of these groups. The issue heated up further when Henry Morgentaler, in the midst of his legal battles, visited Alberta in January 1983, in the hopes of opening an abortion clinic in Calgary or

Edmonton. Morgentaler found resistance to his plan and failed to obtain a lease on a building to house his clinic (Terry 1983: 19).

In 1984, after Morgentaler's first jury acquittal in Toronto, Morgentaler returned to the province to try opening an abortion clinic there again. The Alberta government opposed any opening of a Morgentaler free standing clinic, asserting it was against the law to perform abortions in private clinics (Dedyna & Creswell 1985: 1). Alberta Health Minister David Russell said, "We would respond as we have in the past that we only pay for and license therapeutic abortions when they're carried out under conditions laid out in the Criminal Code of Canada" (Canadian Press, 1985: np). Clearly the province wanted to assert that it would merely enforce the requirements of the federal law, thereby deflecting any interpretation of provincial action as construing a particular position on abortion.

While the controversy over Morgentaler's increasing presence in Alberta brewed, the 'competitive' dynamic played out among the provinces and the federal government. They were engaged over the other major controversy surrounding abortion at the time, the issue of extra-billing. Extra billing was a practice in which doctors charged additional fees for medical services beyond the fee listed by provincial insurance. By early 1986, the federal government had withheld over 20 million dollars in transfer payments to Alberta for not cracking down on this practice since federal Canadian Health Act had outlawed it in 1984 [41] (Harrington, 1986: np). Alberta set an October 1st 1986 date to end extra billing, in order to get the withheld money back from the federal government.

---

[41] The Canadian Health Act, passed in 1984, gave the federal government authority to "penalize any province denying its residents comprehensive, universal, portable, and accessible health care" (*Marleau ready to go after renegade provinces,*" *1994)* (34). The Act was passed in order to deter provinces from imposing user fees, and from doctors from charging more than the listed current medicare service fees (Ibid.). Yet, the federal government systematically decreased its financial contribution to provincial health care programs over time, leaving provinces to make adjustments. Provinces concerned with cuts in federal health transfers tried to find ways to cut health insurance costs.

Alberta doctors, upset with the province's low reimbursement rates for medical procedures and facing the loss in extra income from extra billing, used abortion as a political wedge after the government set the date to ban extra billing. Doctors began charging a $75 administrative fee for completing paperwork needed for the therapeutic abortion committees (TAC's) (Cunningham & Kondro 1986: np). Some doctors began refusing to perform abortions outright after the extra billing ban went into effect (Morningstar 1986: B2). During this same time, doctors in other provinces, like Ontario, began using similar tactics to oppose the extra billing prohibition.

In response, Alberta's Health Minister Marv Moore suggested either increasing the medical fee for abortion or removing (deinsuring) the service entirely from the Medicare plan. Removal would force patients to pay for the full cost of abortion. The province had previously 'deinsured' chiropractic and optical services in order to cut provincial Medicare costs (Cunningham & Kondro, 1986: np). Opposition leaders criticized the proposal to deinsure abortion as jeopardizing women's health (Ibid.). The Alberta Medical Association asserted that the TAC report fee was justified, since a third party required the report and it had nothing to do with the actual abortion procedure (R. Kennedy, 1986: np). During this standoff between the government and the doctors, women found it very difficult to obtain an abortion either because doctors refused to perform the procedure or the costs due to the extra fee for the TAC paperwork (R. Walker 1986: A1-2).

With doctors refusing to perform abortions, Minister Moore claimed the province could not compel doctors to perform the procedure, " 'I'm not responsible for whether or not doctors provide required medical services, that's entirely up to them. If they are refusing to do so, because of the fee schedule, it's something their patients should request the [Alberta] College of Physicians and Surgeons should look into' "(Locherty & Pratt, 1986: np). Opposition party critics and pro-abortion supporters questioned Moore's claims; since Alberta banning extra billing, Alberta Health had increased the fees it paid for other medical services but *not for abortion*. This action fueled criticisms that Tory government was trying to limit access to abortion without being held responsible for doing so (Schifrin, 1986: A17).

During this debate over doctor's fees, the Alberta government also proposed to drop birth control counseling services, tubal ligations and vasectomies, as well as pre-marital counseling from the Alberta medical insurance in order to cut health care costs. Opposition party leaders again met this news with criticism. On the floor of the legislature, NDP member Barrett asked Health Minister Moore, if he would "give his guarantee that his department will under no circumstances deinsure therapeutic abortion from provision of the Medicare plan in Alberta?" (*Legislative Debates*, 1987a). Moore responded to these critiques that Alberta had no choice but to fund abortions,

> [W]e are following a federal law with regard to therapeutic abortions…each hospital has a committee that judges whether or not an abortion is medically required and whether or not continuation of that pregnancy might affect the life or health of the mother. So theoretically at least --and all of us know that there are some doubts on occasion about whether or not abortions are really medically required--we have a situation where federal law requires to provide us assistance in that regard….I do have some concerns about the access, particularly in the city of Edmonton…But that's not something that our government has any direct control over (*Legislative Debates*, 1987b).

Moore's statement shows he was trying to deflect provincial responsibility for securing access to abortion, while government actions (by refusing to increase the fee for abortions) were, in part, responsible for limiting access. The province could claim it was adhering to the 'letter' of the federal law, but it was certainly not following its 'spirit'.

Alberta's rejects the Supreme Court's ruling in Morgentaler II and refuses to take actions that would provide more access to abortion-1988

Health Minister Moore reiterated his assertion that the Alberta government had little power over abortion even after the Supreme Court's *Morgentaler* decision in January 1988. The provincial government first responded to the Court's decision striking down the use of Therapeutic Abortion Committees by invoking an old Alberta Hospital Act regulation requiring a second doctor consultation before a woman can obtain an abortion (R. Walker 1988: np). When asked by the opposition whether such regulations were legal in light of the Court's ruling, Minister Moore replied, "It is our view, Mr. Speaker, that the hospital regulations in Alberta do not in any way contravene the Criminal Code of Canada (*Legislative Debates* 1988).   Moore pointedly ignored the fact that the Supreme Court had *struck down* the federal criminal law regulating abortion. The questioning continued, asking why the government failed to crack down on two provincial hospitals continuing to use TAC committees;

> Is the Minister of Health saying that he will let two hospitals break the law, as articulated by the Supreme Court decision in its interpretation of the Charter of Rights, in keeping in place therapeutic abortion committees or that he is going to allow them to break the spirit and intent of the Canadian Health Act by denying access to health care for women seeking abortions? (Ibid).

Clearly hostile, Moore responded,

> Well, the hon. Member, Mr. Speaker is wrong on both occasions. First of all, it's certainly not in any way clear that those two hospitals are breaking the law. The Supreme Court decision, as I understand it, didn't deal in any way, shape or form with the conditions under which hospitals operate in the province of Alberta. Secondly, the Supreme Court decision did not deal in any way, shape or form with a firm requirement that every hospital in this country provide abortion services." (Ibid.).

One could agree with Moore's interpretation that the Supreme Court decision did not require that hospitals *must provide* abortions services. However, to assert that the decision did not deal with the conditions of Alberta hospitals is false. *Morgentaler's* majority (1988) agreed that process of obtaining abortions via TAC's committees hindered the rights of women under s.7 (security of person) of the Charter.   Health Minister Moore's statements indicated, therefore, Alberta's intent to avoid compliance with the Canadian Supreme Court's decision. It took three years after the Court's decision, in 1991, for the new Alberta Health Minister Nancy Betkowski to quietly announce Alberta's two doctor consultation requirement was invalid. That little noticed change in policy came after the government "determined that they [the regulations were] not consistent with the Supreme Court decision that struck down Canada's abortion law" (R. Walker 1991: A1).

Given the provincial government's refusal to initially enforce both the Court's decision and the Federal Health Act, regional hospitals limited access to abortion services to women living only within the hospital's region, thus limiting the ability of women from other areas to obtain an abortion. When the Queen Elizabeth II hospital in Grand Prairie announced its plan to limit its services, it asked the Alberta Health Minister to consider allowing free standing abortion clinics in the area. The hospital board stated it had changed its policy due to the increasing numbers of women seeking abortions from Edmonton and Fort McMurray (Moysa, 1988: np). Premier Don Getty ignored the request, and stated that the Alberta government would not intervene regarding the decisions of any hospitals to limit or refuse to perform abortions until the federal government established a new federal abortion law (Ibid.). In addition, in 1989, the province deinsured a follow-up procedure often performed after late term abortions, one which Alberta Health had previously covered (Gilbert, 1989: np). After removing the reimbursement fee from Alberta Health, no doctors in the province performed abortions after 12 weeks (Ibid.).

By denying the expansion of abortion clinics and deinsuring procedures from provincial health insurance, the provincial government effectively wielded its authority over health insurance policy to limit abortions. In addition, by using these tactics, and by asserting it was the federal government's responsibility to pass a new federal abortion law, the province effectively insulated itself from possible legal challenges.

Federal-provincial conflict escalates with Liberal control of the federal government and its enforcement of the Federal Health Act - 1990-1995

With the failure of the Progressive Conservative's abortion bill C-43 at the federal level, and the party's subsequent defeat in parliamentary elections, October 1993 ushered in a Liberal government intent on getting provinces to comply with the terms of the Canadian Health Act and enforce national health standards. Alberta, with the highest number of private out-patient clinics of any province, was a target of the new federal health minister, Diane Marleau. Marleau asserted that provinces would have to shut down private clinics in order to stem the tide of the development of a two tiered health system (Ibid.). The threat induced a response by recently elected Alberta premier Ralph Klein (PC), who stated that federal health minister should call for Morgentaler to close his abortion clinics in addition to her critiques regarding MRI and eye surgery clinics (Bray & Fisher 1994: 21).

The feud between Alberta and the federal government grew, and in early January 1995, Federal Minister Marleau sent a letter to all provincial health ministers, stating that any province allowing private clinics to charge user/facility fees that exceed medicare fees for medically necessary procedures must shut down these clinics by October 15 or the federal government would withhold federal transfer payments to the province (Ferguson 1995: A6). At the time, about a third of Alberta's health care budget came from federal transfers; this would be a significant blow to the province's health budget (Ibid.). While Alberta was opposed to the federal government's aggressive stance, British Columbia, Quebec and Ontario (the three other largest provinces in Canada) quickly adopted legislation banning such fees. Ontario Health Minister Ruth Grier noted, " 'This issue crosses all political stripes,' she said, 'It will be interesting to see how Alberta complies in light of its approach that the marketplace ought to play a role in the provision of health care (Borsellino, et al 1995: 1, 51).

Much of this conflict between the federal government and Alberta surrounded the question of which medical procedures were 'medically necessary', and therefore must be covered by provincial health insurance. Federal Health Minister Marleau initially asserted that the provinces must decide that question, "In some cases, it's been defined by the courts, but certainly not by the federal government", alluding to the fact that health policy is within the provincial authority (Pole 1995: 33). Yet, Marleau also asserted that 'core' medically necessary services should be "provided on uniform terms and conditions" by all provinces (Ibid.). Not surprisingly, the federal government was trying to have it both ways, likely because it knew that the provinces had the right to decide and that Alberta was the outlier compared to the other major provinces. By March 1995, as the struggle between Alberta and the federal government escalated, Marleau softened her charge stating that while a "comprehensive range of services" should remain available, that "d[id] not mean that Canadians in one province should have their health needs met in exactly the same way as in another province" (Ha, 1995).

In response, Alberta's Health Minster stated at the first minister's conference of provincial health ministers that Alberta would consider de-insuring certain procedures deemed not 'medically necessary', therefore privatizing such services. Other provincial leaders felt this approach would open the door to privatization and the erosion of universal Medicare. At the end of the conference, the ministers called for a meeting with Federal Health Minister Marleau in order to clarify the meaning of the Canadian Health Act and the services that are to be insured by all provincial health plans (Cernetig 1995: np).

The conflict between Alberta and the federal government dragged on through the summer as Prime Minister Chrétien stated that the Canadian Health Act did not allow provinces to unilaterally deinsure medical services, which would effectively allow one set of services for the wealthy and those who only have Medicare. During a visit to Alberta, he said, "There cannot be a two tiered system in Canada. We will not give more flexibility to one province. Why more to Alberta than the others? If we have a law that applies to Canadians across the land, then it has to apply to Albertans like its applying to the people of Nova Scotia" (Feschuk, 1995b: A1, 9).

Alberta fails to 'de-insure' abortion, then says it will only fund 'medically necessary' abortions, deferring to the medical community to determine what is 'medically necessary'. 1995

As Chretien's remarks were made public, conservative backbenchers in Alberta seized the opportunity to eliminate public monies for all abortions unless the life of the woman is at risk (Feschuk, 1995a: A1, 2). Local pro-choice organizations believed the proposal contravened the Canadian Health Act (Ibid.). Susan Fox, executive director of the Morgentaler Clinic of Edmonton, said "What we have here is a small group of people trying to dictate moral issues by disguising them as financial issues'" (Ibid). Fox was referring to an interest group that sprung up to support the legislative proposal, The Committee to End Tax Funded Abortions.

Alberta Prime Minister Ralph Klein said that he would allow a free vote on the proposal if it came to the floor, though he personally wanted to keep the status quo on abortion, and was likely to vote against the proposal himself (Ibid.). Since his election campaign two years earlier, Klein had consistently stated he believed abortion was a decision between a woman, her doctor and God (Laghi 1995: A12). By September 1995, the Alberta legislature failed to pass the legislation deinsuring abortion. Immediately after the failed vote, the government announced a new tactic; it would insure only 'medically necessary' abortions. Klein asserted the province would no longer fund " 'abortions on demand for birth control reasons' " (Network 1995: A6). The government stated it would work with the medical community to draw up guidelines as to what would constitute a 'medically necessary' abortion (Mitchell 1995: A1, 2).   Pro-life groups applauded the decision, while pro-choice groups were upset and Canadian Abortion Rights Action League threatened to challenge the law in court if it resulted in limiting access to abortion (Ibid.).

The Alberta Medical Association was upset about the province's unilateral declaration that the medical community would be responsible for determining what constituted a 'medically necessary' abortion. Not surprisingly, it did not want to be involved in this debate and believed it was the province's responsibility to decide medical insurance guidelines (G. Legge 1995: A10). The deputy registrar of Alberta's College of Physician and Surgeon's said," 'The decision whether or not an abortion should be paid for is a social or political one, not a medical one" (Kaufmann 1995: 5). After discussing the issue, both the College and the Alberta Medical Association refused the government's request to define what constitutes a medically necessary abortion (Canadian Press 1995a: np). Alberta Health Minister McClellan responded to the news by stating, " 'If physician's don't feel that they can determine when the need to terminate a pregnancy is medically required, I don't think politicians can' " (Canadian Press 1995c: np). The government's plan never got off the ground. At this point, the province exhausted all its options for getting other actors to take responsibility for and make the policy decision it wanted but would not do itself. Alberta could have attempted to pass legislation that defined a 'medically necessary' abortion, but clearly it did not want to take that route.

MOUNTING FINANCIAL COSTS AND PUBLIC PRESSURES FINALLY FORCES ALBERTA TO AGREE TO COVER MEDICAL COSTS FROM PRIVATE CLINICS 1995-1997

On October 12, 1995, three days before the federal deadline to withhold transfer payments if provinces continued allowing private clinics to charge 'facility fees', the Alberta government asked to postpone the deadline while it sought a compromise with the federal government (Henton 1995: A3). In its letter to the federal government, Alberta proposed to incorporate private clinics into the public system. The federal government responded by not immediately deducting funds from the federal health transfer, but tracked the facility charges and planned to deduct an equal proportion from the transfer later (Greenspon 1995: A5). One month later, talks between Federal Health minister Diane Marleau and Alberta's Health Minister McClellan broke down over Alberta's insistence that doctors could receive payments from both private and public sources (Canadian Press, 1995b: np). The federal government said it would penalize Alberta $420,000 a month if the province failed to ban immediately ban the practice (Ibid.).

By February 1996, the federal government had docked 1.4 million dollars from Alberta's federal transfer money and polls showed Albertans were opposed to their government's position on the issue (R. Walker 1996: np). Finally on May 30, 1996, the Alberta government relented by announcing it would ban facility fees starting July 1, 1996. In a plan approved by the federal government and new Alberta Health Minister David Dingwald, Alberta Health agreed to pay the 'facility fee' charged by any existing or new clinic that provided an insured medical procedure (R. Walker 1996: np). Soon after, the province began paying clinics fees including payments to the two private abortion clinics in the province. After the clinic fee issue was resolved, there was little subsequent Albertan governmental activity on abortion.

Summary and analysis of the Alberta case

Alberta played the game of trying to dodge and evade implementation of abortion policy, similar to Nova Scotia, although Alberta was more aggressive in using some of its provincial authorities to limit abortions in the province. As with Nova Scotia, the federal government used the stick of transfer funds in order to restrain Alberta from completely de-insuring abortion. Alberta was somewhat more successful at limiting abortions using its authority over insurance, since it was more careful than Nova Scotia to ensure its actions did not encroach on federal authority. The provincial government repeatedly deferred to anyone it could, i.e., the federal government, the medical establishment, to take responsibility for abortion policy when it though it would be politically advantageous to do so. As the next chapter will show, the Alberta government behaved somewhat similarly to the Utah government, where the Utah government held on to its campaign to restrict abortion as long as possible, even when state public opinion began to turn against the state government. Similarly, Alberta chose to drag out the extra-billing conflict with the federal government as long as possible; however, it did finally back down after it could no longer avoid the looming financial costs and the public's disapproval.

Given the fact that there were no legal challenges to Alberta's actions, this can be explained by the fact that when Alberta acted, it repeatedly asserted that its actions were based upon financial considerations (a good basis for public support, till it wasn't) or that it *wasn't* acting because other actors (like the federal government or doctors) were responsible. Therefore, there was little that Alberta was *actually doing* that could have been the basis for a legal challenge. The one attempt to pass a bill which would have removed provincial funding for abortions 'unless necessary to protect the life of the woman', was given a free vote and failed. Once again using the 'free vote', (as the federal parliament had) and releasing members from party discipline was an effective method to insure the legislation failed. If the law had passed, Alberta would have been exposed to a potential legal challenge.

With the absence of any other institutional features that could have provided an avenue for court review, there was little likelihood the Supreme Court could sanction Alberta and insure adequate access to abortion in the province. In addition, given the unwillingness the Supreme Court to provide any directives determining whether or not the Charter provided any protections over abortion access, even if a legal challenge had be mounted in Alberta, the possibility of the Supreme Court intervening to provide answers when neither the provinces nor the federal government were willing to do so seemed highly improbable. Lastly, the role of federalism was again significant, in creating a competitive dynamic between the federal government and the provinces, particularly when the Liberals gained control of the federal government. The overlapping authorities of the federal government's authority to enforce the Canadian Health act and the province's responsibility to provide health insurance exacerbated this conflict. The federal government used the extra-constitutional institution of a first Minister's conference, to get other provinces to approve its policy and to put pressure on Alberta to comply.

ONTARIO

Provincial political orientation and brief summary of provincial activity on abortion

Ontario occupies a significant place in Canadian politics, since it is the home to forty percent of the country's entire population (Macdermid, 2001: 163). Yet, unlike Alberta, which has embraced much of American political culture, ideologically Ontario has often been referred to as the 'not-American' province, and has become more so in recent decades. It has most embodied [English] Canadian nationalism which is "largely defined by what it is not: American" (Weisman 1996: 47). For example, when Liberal and NDP governments ruled Ontario in the 1990's the province consistently opposed free trade policies with the United States. Much of the Canadian political activism over abortion was centered in Ontario, because it is the largest province and it is home to the capitol, Ottawa. Therefore, it is not surprising that the *Morgentaler II* (1988) arose out of Ontario. Though the 1980's and 1990's, depending on which party was in power, the provincial response and orientation to abortion policy shifted. When the Liberals were in control, they tried to appease both sides of the debate; the socialist NDP government actively enacted provincial policies supporting abortion access; and finally the Conservatives, who took no actions to limit abortion, yet refrained from ensuring access to abortion within the province.

Extra billing controversy focus of the abortion debate, Ontario eventually bans the practice -1980-1986

As in the Nova Scotia and Alberta, there was little significant provincial activity on abortion in the 1970's. Things picked up in the early 1980's when, as in Alberta, 'extra billing' was in the center of the debate between the provincial government and doctors. Ontario doctors had been charging more than double the listed rate for abortions under the Ontario Health Insurance Program (OHIP) and had required advance payment from women, something they did not require for other medical services (*Globe and Mail* 1980: np). A number of doctors had opted out of OHIP entirely; therefore, women could not get an abortion from these doctors using provincial health insurance. Due to these issues, hospitals were rationing appointments to women seeking abortions. In addition, given the centrality of Ontario to Canadian politics, it became a focal point for interest group protest activities. Anti-abortion forces called for the province to de-insure abortion. Feminist organizations and pro-choice organizations built support for out-patient clinic abortion services.

The debate intensified in June 1983, when on the invitation of women's and pro-abortion groups, Henry Morgentaler set up his Toronto clinic. Ontario Attorney General Roy McMurty responded to the clinic's opening by threatening to prosecute any doctors performing abortions at the clinic (Slotnick 1983: 9). The clinic drew large numbers of anti-abortion protesters and pro-choice supporters when it opened. Ontario police raided the clinic and arrested Morgentaler. By 1985, the recently elected Ontario Liberal government chose not to re-raid Morgentaler's clinic, though pressured to do so by anti-abortion forces. Eventually acquitted, as noted earlier, his subsequent appeals finally resulted in Supreme Court's decision in *Morgentaler II (1989),* which struck down the entire federal criminal law on abortion.

Meanwhile, the struggle over extra-billing continued, and doctors were requesting payment for letters written on behalf of patients that were necessary for TAC's approval for abortions, actions similar to those taken by doctors in Alberta. By this time, most gynecologists had opted out of OHIP and charged fees of $200-300 dollars for abortion, greatly above the standard insurance rate of $87 (Hossie 1985: 19). By February 1986, and under pressure from the federal government, the Ontario government announced its intent to outlaw extra billing. Some doctors resigned from TAC duties in protest of the announcement (McMonagle, Hossie, & Silversides 1986: np). By June 1986, the government threats failed to stop the protests, and the Ontario Medical Association supported a strike at all hospitals, keeping only emergency services open (Ubelacher 1986: np). The strike caused havoc throughout province. Pro-choice groups said that the strike exemplified the need for free standing abortion clinics (Delacourt 1986: np).

Due to the withdrawal of doctors from TAC committees, abortions were virtually unavailable at hospitals in metropolitan areas such as Toronto and Waterloo (Valorizi 1986: np). These hospitals referred the women to the Morgentaler clinic in Toronto, significantly increasing the number of abortions it performed (Ibid.). During this crisis, the Ontario Health Minister proposed a study of provincial abortion services to determine whether to provide more money to hospitals for such services (Ibid). Health Minister Elston hired Dr. Marian Powell to lead the study. Her report was eventually known as the "Powell Report".

Province bans extra billing and struggles to increase access to abortion-1986-1988

Due to the ongoing actions by the doctors and increasing outside political pressure, the provincial government banned extra billing in late June of 1986 through passage of the Health Care Accessibility Act in order to comply with the Federal Canadian Health Act of 1984 (Silversides 1986: np). Under the Canadian Health Act (CHA), the federal government authorized the withholding federal transfer payments to provinces allowing extra-billing (Ibid.). Ontario had lost about $4.4 million since the enactment of the CHA. In contrast, Nova Scotia had outlawed extra billing a month before the CHA went into effect, and thus paid no penalties (Ibid.). With the exception of British Columbia and Quebec, extra billing had flourished in the richer, more populated provinces, while 'poorer' provinces, such as PEI, Manitoba and Saskatchewan had not had to deal with the issue. As seen in the Alberta case, the issue of 'extra billing' revealed the cracks in Canada's universal health care program and the struggles the federal government faced in forcing provincial compliance with the act.

By September 1986, the Ontario government floated a proposal establishing a separate abortion center at Toronto's Women's College Hospital, and paying for travel costs for women unable to obtain abortions elsewhere. Deflecting possible critiques, Ontario Attorney General Scott noted that Ontario alone could not change the law regarding abortion, only the federal parliament or the Supreme Court of Canada could do so (Henton 1986: np). "Because of the shape of the federal law, it is not effectively possible to do much to encourage hospitals; except by moral persuasion, to establish [TAC] committees" (W. Walker 1986: np). Finally, in January 1987, about a year before the Supreme Court delivered its decision in *Morgentaler II*, the Powell Report was released. The report found that women largely sought abortions due to contraceptive failure and not carelessness. In addition, the report recommended that the province establish hospital affiliated abortion clinics. The report also found that the TAC requirement resulted in barring access to abortion and forced women to face delays, which increased the possibility of health complications due to having to obtain late term procedures.[42]

In March 1987, two months after the report was issued, Health Minister Elston said that the Ontario government would not support the creation of additional free standing clinics in the province (Maychack 1987: np).   She also stated that Ontario would not proceed with Powell's recommendation to establish abortion clinics affiliated with hospitals and instead proposed to upgrade hospital abortion services (M. Kennedy 1987, A1,2).   She also rejected Powell's proposal to establish grants for women who had travel long distances in order to obtain an abortion (Ibid.). While the Liberal government refused to put Powell's recommendations into action, the Supreme Court's decision in *Morgentaler II* eventually spurred provincial action, and the future NDP government implemented additional policies enabling abortion access in the early 1990's.

By November 1987, Elston was replaced, and the new Ontario Health Minister, Elinor Caplan again floated the proposal of women's health clinics affiliated with hospitals, as outlined in the Powell report, (Speirs 1987: D1). The provincial government would also provide funds to start a women's health clinic at a Catholic hospital in Toronto, though it would not provide abortion services. These funds were in addition to the 1.5 million proposed for the Women's College Hospital in Toronto that would run a women's health center and provide abortion

---

[42] This is precisely the justification the Supreme Court used in part to strike down the federal criminal law on abortion, by asserting the TAC procedure hindered access thereby threatening women's s.7 guarantees of security of person. It was widely known that the Supreme Court had access to the Powell report while making its decision on the *Morgentaler* case.

referrals. However, by trying to placate both sides, neither pro-choice nor anti-abortion activists supported the government's proposals. Pro-choice activists wanted more services and favored free standing abortion clinics, while anti-abortion supporters opposed the centers entirely (Canadian Press 1987: 16).

Ontario responds to Morgentaler II by providing monetary support to hospitals and allowing provincial health insurance to cover abortions in existing free standing clinics – 1989-1990

Days after the Supreme Court announced its decision in *Morgentaler II* striking down the federal abortion law; on February 2, 1988, the Ontario government declared provincial health insurance would cover abortions performed in free standing clinics. The province would cover the physician's fee, while the patient would still cover the administrative costs of staff and overhead (Canadian Press 1988: np). Once again, this payment plan violated the Canadian Health Act's ban on extra-billing. The Ottawa government also announced it would provide over 1 million dollars to three provincial hospitals offering abortion services, allowing them to hire more staff and to open on weekends (Heinrich 1988: C1)

During the summer, Ontario considered legislation governing the licensing and regulation of free standing clinics performing eye surgery, in vitro fertilization or abortions. Some commentators argued that Ontario's decision to regulate these clinics was in response to free-trade policies (NAFTA) being debated at that time. Many Canadians were also concerned with the threat of United States based for-profit abortion services looking to set up shop in Toronto (Speirs 1988: D5). New Ontario Health Minister Caplan, noted these concerns when she introduced the Independent Health Facilities Act in the legislature, stating, "Despite an international treaty or obligation to which Canada is a party and any legislation implementing such an obligation, preference will be given to not-for-profit and Canadian proposals."(Berube 1988: 2,46).

The Independent Health Facilities Act, which was quickly passed by the legislature, ensured government licensing, regulation and financing of independent health care clinics and payment for surgeries that could otherwise performed in hospitals. The act allowed the two freestanding abortion clinics in Toronto to operate for one year without a license, and thereafter had to apply for a provincial license if they wanted to receive government funds (McLaren 1988: A5). In addition, the law did not provide funds that would enable additional free standing abortion clinics, but did allow the licensing of regional women's health centers affiliated with hospitals, which could provide a variety of health services, including abortion (Ibid). On the request of the Health Minister and in conjunction with the Act, the Ontario College of Physicians and Surgeon's established guidelines and standards for the performance of abortion services. The guidelines allowed for abortions to be performed in clinics as well as hospitals (Rich 1988: np).

A new governing party provides more pro-abortion access policies and opposes the federal attempts to re-write the federal criminal law on abortion- 1990-1995

The 1990 elections ushered in a NDP government in Ontario that was considerably more favorable to abortion rights. At the time, Federal Parliament was debating Bill C-43, its attempt to re-write the criminal code on abortion, and the new Ontario NDP government publicly stated its opposition to the bill. The NDP government even started collecting evidence against the bill for a possible court challenge to the law (Allen, 1990). Speaking out against the bill Premier Bob Rae said, " We are right now gathering evidence with respect to the effect that the proposed law is having...and when we've gathered all that evidence, we will be announcing further measures" (Allen 1990: np.). Rae cited the Supreme Court as support for the NDP's position, "The Supreme Court of Canada in the (Henry) Morgentaler [*Morgentaler II*] case was very clear and that there had to be equality in terms of the way in which services were provided" (Ibid). In addition, the Ontario government submitted a brief to the Federal Senate regarding the bill, restating its opposition to the bill (Ontario, 1991). Pro-choice organizations lobbied the Ontario government to declare proposed federal law C-43 unenforceable should it become law, although the NDP government declined to go that far in its opposition of the federal law (Todd 1990: np).

Responding to leaked information to the press about the province's possible new abortion policies, and the pending vote in the Senate on Bill-C43, the Ontario government announced its intent to license and fully fund free-standing abortion clinics in November 1990. In the legislature, New Ontario Health Minister Gigantes stated, "I speak on the behalf of this government when I say that while we strongly respect the fundamental freedoms of the people of Ontario, illegal conduct which infringes or interferes with the decision to undergo an abortion is contrary to public policy" (Legislative Assembly of Ontario 1990). This was clearly the strongest public statement supporting abortion an Ontario government had taken up to this point.

After the failure of federal bill C-43 in March 1991, the Ontario government pledged to fund abortion clinics fully, to treat abortions as a health not criminal issue, and to encourage doctors to work in such clinics (Maychack & Millar 1991: np). By June 1991, OHIP was paying for all abortions-related services performed in the province, including clinic fees and administrative costs (Bagley 1992). In addition, Health Minister Gigantes also changed provincial policy on Northern Health Travel Grants to include women seeking abortions from general practitioners at free standing clinics, rather than just paying for travel costs to hospitals (Legislative Assembly of Ontario 1990).[43]

While the Ontario government was taking actions to provide greater access to abortion services, on May 18, 1992, an explosion destroyed Morgentaler's abortion clinic in downtown Toronto. Pro-choice leaders were angry and pro-life supporters were shocked that such an act of violence occurred. No one claimed responsibility and both sides condemned the act (Brent 1992: np). Many pro-choice leaders claimed that American anti-abortion activists were responsible for the violence (Ibid). New Ontario Health Minister Frances Lankin responded to the violence by saying, "...[I]ncreasing harassment activities is not going to prevent this government from ensuring that women have access to this service" (Ferguson & Brent 1992: A1, 7). Solicitor General Allan Pilkey announced Ontario would spend $420,000 to increase security at abortion facilities to insure safe access for women and staff (Ibid). In addition, the province considered providing monetary support for rebuilding and temporarily relocating the clinic (Ibid).

Under pressure from pro-choice groups, the provincial government sought an injunction banning protests and harassment of staff at

---

[43] A provincial program that provides travel expenses for individuals who must travel outside their local area to see specialists.

abortion clinics and began collecting depositions in March 1993 (W. Walker & Moloney 1993: A13). By April 20th 1993, the government applied for a court order banning anti-abortion activity outside abortion clinics, doctor's homes and hospitals (Mickleburgh 1993: A5). Anti-abortion groups were very upset with the action and said it infringed on their free speech rights and vowed to fight the injunction (Ibid).

In July 1993, the NDP government solicited proposals to establish a free standing abortion clinic in Ottawa (Ministry of Health, 1993). Morgentaler's proposal was accepted in February 1994 and his clinic opened in October of that year (Ibid). That same month, lawyers for the government and for anti-abortion protestors named in the injunction presented arguments to a General Division Court judge (Payne 1994: A4). Six months later in August, Judge George Adams ruled largely for the government, granting an injunction requiring anti-abortion protestors to stay 20 meters away from abortion clinics and 160 meters away from doctor's homes (Blackwell 1994: A5). The government had wanted protestors further from abortion clinics, 150 meters, but the judged refused (Ibid.). In his judgment, Adams stated that any limitation on protestors was an infringement upon their Charter rights of freedom of expression, but said the injunction was a justifiable limit on those rights as allowed by the Charter (Section 1 analysis). This analysis was consistent with the rights outlined in the Charter in which the Charter would allow limits on rights if such limits serve the general interests of the community. He also ruled that most of the protestors named in the proceedings should be tried in court. The injunction was to remain operative until such trial would determine whether permanent measures would be necessary (Ibid.).

Conservative government elected, little subsequent action on abortion policy- 1995-1997

The injunction controversy was featured prominently in the 1995 government elections and the NDP lost to the Progressive Conservatives. The new provincial government had the opportunity to drop the case and the injunction, but it did not. Beyond maintaining the injunction, however, the Tory government did little to expand abortion access, but also did not do anything to limit it. The government tried to ignore the issue, refusing to create more abortion clinics and focusing instead on measures to consolidate hospitals and health expenditures.

The only significant government action taken during this time was Omnibus Bill 26, which restructured health programs and rationed services to save the province money due to escalating health care costs and decreasing federal transfers. Since 1995, hospital consolidation has had the biggest impact on abortion access, as non-sectarian hospitals merged with Catholic hospitals that refuse to provide abortion services. The Tory government did little to insure that abortion services would continue to be available in regions that saw such consolidation.

Summary of the Ontario case

The Ontario case shows the impact different political parties had on the provincial government's approach to abortion policy. In addition, much of the contentious politics surrounding abortion in terms of pro-choice/pro-life forces had converged on the province, largely in part because *Morgentaler II* originated in Toronto. Immediately after the decision was released, the Ontario government had acted to cover abortions in free-standing clinics. Yet, just like in Nova Scotia and Alberta, much of the debate over abortion was still filtered through the prism of health insurance and fiscal considerations. It was only when the NDP came to power that the Ontario government took aggressive actions on to insure access to abortions and opposed the Conservative's proposed revision of the criminal law on abortion at the federal level. Perhaps due to fatigue over the highly contentious (and violent) battle between pro-life and pro-choice forces in the province, the Conservatives did not take much of a stance towards regulating abortion when they assumed control of the provincial government.

Comparisons among the Canadian provinces and overall summary of Canadian case

There were both similarities and differences in the responses and actions provinces took in regards to regulating abortions. These varied responses were in part due to the fact that neither the Supreme Court nor the Federal Parliament provided clear policy rules on regulating abortion. These provincial policies often reflected the policy interests of the controlling party in government, yet also reflected regional concerns. Although Alberta and Nova Scotia were both ruled by conservative governments that opposed expansion of abortion services, they took different steps in regards to that position. Nova Scotia focused on limiting the expansion of abortion clinics, but did not make any other significant attempts to limit abortion access. The province also unsuccessfully attempted to use the courts to validate its policy, where it was overruled by every level in the court system up to and including the Canadian Supreme Court. The Alberta government also wanted to eliminate private abortion clinics, but since there were other pre-existing private clinics providing other medical services in the province, Alberta turned to the tactic of 'deinsurance'; it attempted to remove the abortion procedure from being covered by Alberta Health Insurance.

Both Nova Scotia and Alberta used concerns over health insurance funding as justification to limit the expansion of abortion services in the province. Nova Scotia did this by attempting to prohibit the expansion of all out-patient medical clinics while Alberta did so by arguing with the federal government over whether abortion was 'medically necessary' and therefore was covered by provincial health insurance. Alberta's fight with the federal government illustrates the 'competitive dynamic' inherent in the Canadian federal logic. In contrast, the Ontario's NDP government supported the view that abortions were medically necessary and provided programs that expanded access to abortions, such as the Northern Travel Health Grants. Ontario at this time also fully funded abortion clinics in the province and was willing to provide greater services by enabling the opening of additional abortion clinics in the province.

Some provinces did refer to the Supreme Court's decisions on abortion and provincial government discourse often reflected whether they generally agreed or not with the Court's ruling in the *Morgentaler* II decision. In Ontario, government discourse often referred to abortion services in the context of access to 'medical services'. When the NDP was in charge, the Ontario government actively voiced its support for the Supreme Court decision, and often stated its actions were to 'ensure equitable access' to abortion within the province. Alberta was publically more hostile to the Supreme Court's decision. Both Nova Scotia and Alberta governments attempted to put up road blocks to abortion access. Alberta asserted that the Supreme Court made no mention of regulating hospitals and both provinces used financial arguments to limit access and support for abortions.

However, a more direct role for the Supreme Court in shaping provincial policy was limited by lack of opportunity and initiative. For example, there were no legal challenges to Alberta's actions that would have triggered Court review, and the Court itself was reticent to provide clear directives on what kind of abortion policy would pass constitutional muster. When presented with an opportunity to address substantive abortion policy in both *Morgentaler II* and *Morgentaler III*, the Court made limited policy pronouncements and repeatedly deferred to the authority of the federal government to direct the nature of abortion policy. In turn, the federal government, which arguably had the greatest institutional authority to direct abortion policy given its responsibility for defining the criminal law on abortion, failed to create a new law, leaving abortion regulation largely to the provinces. Provincial debates on abortion often focused on insurance and financial aspects of abortion, issues the provinces were largely responsible for. This debate over finances highlighted the 'competitive' dynamic between the federal government and the provinces, resulting in the federal government using the 'stick' of withholding of federal transfer funds to restrict provinces from 'de-insuring' abortion and to insure provincial payment of out-patient abortion services

Table 5.1: Government compliance and implementation of abortion policies

TIMELINE

	Alberta	Nova Scotia	Ontario
Summary of activity:	Conservative government actively tries to circumvent/avoid providing abortion services- -leave hard questions to other actors/doctors.	Conservative government Tries to avoid having clinics in province, doesn't necessarily want to get rid of abortion but want them done quietly and in hospitals.	Liberals flip-flop on supporting abortion policies. NDP government provides strong support. Tories provide little support, but also minimal 'direct' attempts at restriction of abortions.

Table 5.1 (Continued): Government compliance and implementation of abortion policies

TIMELINE	Alberta	Nova Scotia	Ontario
Federal Government/ Supreme Court decisions			
75 Supreme Court decides *Morgentaler v the Queen I* **77** Borowski files his case on behalf of the unborn			
	80's Morgentaler fanned flames through visit, possible site of clinic **80's** Doctors use abortion as wedge issue w/ provincial government re: extra billing (billing patients for services that are not listed on Alberta Health Insurance)	**1985** Morgentaler comes to open free standing clinic in Halifax	**80's** Issue of 'extra billing' (similar to Alberta), doctors threaten and do opt out of OHIP, due to issue. Lack of abortion services under OHIP. **80's** Morgentaler comes to Toronto, leads to Morgentaler Supreme case.

Table 5.1 (Continued): Government compliance and implementation of abortion policies

TIMELINE

	Alberta	Nova Scotia	Ontario
	86 Government response floats deinsurance' of Abortion proposal, to cut fees -cut health care costs rhetoric		**86** Government bans extra billing, rhetoric is strong, saying Doctors are holding abortion hostage, compared to Alberta, where govt. says it's up to doctors to decide whether they choose to perform certain services **86** Powell report issued by Ontario govt. re: abortion services, critical account re: access. **87** Government waits to charge Morgentaler, Smolling&Scott again before CSC case **87** Government decides to pay for physician fees in abortion clinics (Before M case comes down)

Table 5.1 (Continued): Government compliance and implementation of abortion policies

TIMELINE	Alberta	Nova Scotia	Ontario
January 88 Supreme Court decides *Morgentaler II* **February 88** Federal Government begins 1st attempt to reform s.251 **Mar. 88** Supreme Court rules in *Borowski*	**88** Government tries to keep TAC's alive, after CSC struck them down as unconstitutional, through old Alberta law still on books, -government rhetoric hostile to CSC		**June 88** Government increases funding for hospitals providing abortions and passes Individual facilities act. regulations of independent clinics (also to limit influx of American clinics into Ontario)

August 89 Supreme Court issues *Daigle* ruling
 	
November 89 Federal Government 2nd attempt to reform S.251
	89 Deinsure procedures associated with late term abortions	**89**-Government response w/ regulation and then law re: prohibiting clinics
		    -CARAL files case (issue of standing)
		    -Morgentaler files case	

			90's New Elections-NDP government publicly opposes Federal Bill C-43 (criminal law on abortion)

Table 5.1 (Continued): Government compliance and implementation of abortion policies

TIMELINE

	Alberta	Nova Scotia	Ontario
			90's Government allows Northern Health Grants for abortion services, pledges to fully fund abortion, and treat as a health issue
January 91 S.251 bill fails in Senate		**91**-Government uses rhetoric about medical costs/provincial authority- Government appeals case to CSC	
			92 Arsonist blows up Morgentaler clinic
93-Supreme Court issues *Morgentaler III* ruling	**93** Clinic issue-- Alberta in contrast w/Nova Scotia wants 'free market'/two tier system, has # of clinics, conflict w/ fed govt. to close clinics. Ironic since Fed is threatens Nova Scotia to pay for clinic abortions		

Table 5.1 (Continued): Government compliance and implementation of abortion policies

TIMELINE	Alberta	Nova Scotia	Ontario
		93 Nova Scotia government loses- ***Morgentaler III*** -SC rules on basis of federalism and division of powers btw provinces and national government	
	94 Controversy over defining 'health' and 'medically necessary'-- important issue to 'deinsuring' procedures, attempt to 'deinsure' abortions. Stalemate		**93/4** Government funds re-building of clinic, Court grants injunction against protestors
	95 Federal government withholds transfer payments to Alberta re: clinic issue didn't want to pay clinic fees		

Table 5.1 (Continued): Government compliance and implementation of abortion policies

TIMELINE

	Alberta	Nova Scotia	Ontario
	Alberta relents after being docked money, pays clinic fees..	**95** Nova Scotia government refuses to pay clinic fees (only doctor fees) --standoff w/ fed. govt. willing to lose federal transfer money over issue --rhetoric about 'preserving single tier system	
			96 Injunction remains, new Tory Government; refuses to fund more clinics, and allows hospital consolidation-- leaves fewer abortion providers.
		97 Nova Scotia still not supporting private clinics operating separately from publicly funded system.	

CHAPTER 6

United States

INTRODUCTION

This chapter examines the development of abortion policy in the United States and in particular the role of the US Supreme Court both 'in time' and 'through time' emphasizing how institutional and federal arrangements present in the American political system structure interactions between political actors and lead to particular outcomes.

The historical and legal analysis presented below leads to a number of conclusions regarding how the presence or lack of institutional features has significantly shaped outcomes regarding abortion policy in the United States. First, federal political elites were largely unwilling to address abortion policy at the federal level due to the controversial nature the policy and because there was no jurisdictional requirement or incentive to do so. Since criminal law is largely the province of states, federal elites could 'wave the flag of federalism' (Graber 1993: 41) and claim deference to state authority. Therefore, states could establish and implement their own abortion policies and the courts would be largely responsible for providing oversight regarding the constitutionality of such actions.

Second, without any direct institutional mechanisms enabling political elites to challenge state laws, private individuals or interest groups took on this responsibility. In addition, with the support of a favorable political environment, state legislatures could pass controversial abortion laws with little concern that legislation would face immediate legal scrutiny, since such challenges would have to originate in lower courts and could only reach the Supreme Court on appeal, a time consuming process. The Utah state legislature essentially 'invited' such challenge through passing controversial abortion regulations that it believed were consistent with US Supreme Court decisions.

Fourth, since all courts in the American judicial system have the authority of judicial review, state courts in particular, could shield their decisions from Supreme Court review by grounding decisions on state constitutional precedent or law. This 'shielding' occurred in Oregon, where the State Supreme Court chose not to base its decision on the US Constitution or US Supreme Court precedent, which precluded the ability of the US Supreme Court to review the state court's decision.

In addition, the US Constitution itself, with few clear, comprehensive individual rights guarantees, provided a limited basis on which the US Supreme Court could fashion clear and comprehensive directives on abortion policies. The Constitutional guarantees on which the Court based its abortion decisions are largely 'negative' rights; directives that limit government action rather than 'positive' guarantees regarding government obligations to protect individual rights. This rights orientation provided few opportunities for the Court to assert what the government *must* do in order to enable such rights.

Therefore, through its decisions, the Supreme Court largely directed abortion policy only through vetoing or upholding state laws, and its decisions did not largely reflect a clear, comprehensive position on what kind of 'baseline' abortion policy the Constitution *would* 'require'. The Court's trimester framework in *Roe,* its major attempt to create a comprehensive abortion directive, erodes over time and is eventually replaced with a more general 'undue burden' standard. As we see, the Court repeatedly had to review various state abortion laws resulting in patchwork of decisions directing abortion policy.

The following provides a brief historical background about abortion in the United States, including a brief discussion of the major Supreme Court decisions on abortion. The second section examines in detail the significant constitutional issues framing abortion policy as determined by the Supreme Court. The third section examines the federal policy response, with the subsequent sections focusing on the legislative responses in Oregon and Utah, cases that illustrate contrasting political orientations and activity on abortion. Generally, Oregon's political orientation has been a fairly 'libertarian', while Utah has been consistently conservative. During the time-period examined,

Oregon enacted few restrictions on abortion, in contrast to Utah's near constant legislative activity to restrict abortion. The conclusion compares and contrasts the development of abortion policy in the two states and summarizes the impact of the relevant institutional features shaping the direction of abortion policy in the United States.

Historical background

Up until the mid-1800's, abortion was an unregulated procedure in the US performed mostly by midwives and not part of medical practice (Craig and O'Brien 39). The first real debate over abortion in the late 1800's focused on doctors claiming abortion was murder, yet necessary in some cases (Devins 58). Doctors asserted they were the only 'professionals' (unlike midwives) who could determine when such abortions were necessary; therefore, they could be the only ones able to perform the procedure (Craig and O'Brien 40). By 1910, almost all states had outlawed abortion unless necessary to protect the woman's life. Doctors were solely responsible for determining when and how the procedure would be performed (Ibid). These regulations on abortion existed without much challenge until the late 1950's.

By the late 1950's, forces such as the women's movement and supporters of reproductive rights, such as Planned Parenthood began to declare abortion rights as an important medical and political issue (Feree, et al 25). In addition, doctors, who were afraid of being sued for performing abortions without adequate justification, wanted state laws to be re-written in order to protect their interests (Craig and O'Brien 41). In response to these forces, and the fact that many abortions were being 'secretly' performed in cases of incest, rape or fetal deformity, the American Law Institute created a model abortion law for states. The law provided legal justification for abortions performed under these circumstances and included a requirement that two doctors must support the reasons for performing the abortion procedure (McFarlane and Meier 37, Feree, et al 28; Craig and O'Brien 41).

In the 1960's, many states adopted the ALI model abortion law, some did not, and a few went beyond the ALI's recommendations. In 1970, New York State adopted legislation essentially allowing unrestricted abortions in the first trimester (Craig and O'Brien 42). Many women traveled to New York to obtain abortions unavailable to them in their home states (Sheeran 1987: 57). The New York law sparked significant public controversy. Due to this controversy and the pressures of the surging women's movement, which included groups such as NARAL, abortion became a significant political issue[44].

In addition, the effects of the drug thalidomide and the case of Sherry Finkbine attracted further public attention to the abortion debate. Thalidomide, a sedative often given to pregnant women, affected the limb development of the fetus and thousands of infants were born with missing or defective limbs. In 1962, Sherry Finkbine, a mother of four and television personality from Arizona, could not obtain an abortion after she learned early in her fifth pregnancy that the drug she had been prescribed was thalidomide (McFarlane and Meier 37; Craig and O'Brien 41). Numerous interest group challenges against state abortion laws and the high profile cases of women such as Sherry Finkbine led to the Supreme Court hearing of *Roe v Wade.*

Brief summary of the Supreme Court's major abortion decisions

In 1972, the United States Supreme Court heard both *Roe v Wade and Doe v Bolton,* cases addressing the constitutionality of state abortion laws. In January 1973, in a 7-2 decision, the US Supreme Court accepted the claims of Jane Roe, who challenged the constitutionality of Texas's abortion law. Finding for Roe, the Court asserted that a constitutional right to privacy, established in previous case law such as *Griswold v Connecticut,* ensured a woman's right to terminate a pregnancy. In *Roe,* the Court established the trimester framework, which divided a woman's pregnancy into stages; in the first trimester the woman's privacy interest outweighed the state's interest in regulating abortion and protecting the health of the woman or fetus.

In *Doe*, the Court struck down a Georgia statute requiring the approval of six doctors before a woman would be permitted to have an abortion. The Court held that only one doctor's approval was necessary. The Court did not base its decision on upon a constitutional right to privacy, but on a "physician's right" to practice. The Court emphasized in *Roe* and in *Doe* the interest *of both* the woman and her doctor to determine whether an abortion was to be performed in the

---

[44] It was first named the National Association to Repeal Abortion Laws, which was later changed to National Abortion Rights Action League.

first trimester. With these decisions, the Supreme Court invalidated all but four states' abortion regulations in existence at the time, including those with the ALI reforms. The *Roe* trimester framework remained relatively intact until *Planned Parenthood v Casey* (1993). In *Casey*, the Court replaced the trimester framework with a pre/post viability standard, and asserted that the constitutionality of state abortion regulations would be determined by whether or not such regulations were an 'undue burden' on a woman's right to an abortion.

COURT ABORTION POLICY DIRECTIVES

State protection of fetal life and the rights of the woman

The United States Supreme Court has neither explicitly determined whether the fetus *is* a 'person' under the constitution, nor directly addressed the prior question of when life begins, contrasting with the German Constitutional Court, which chose to answer these questions. In *Roe,* the Court examined the Constitution's use of the term person in order to determine 'who' would be included in that term. The majority concluded that, "...the use of the word is such that it has application only post-natally. None indicates, with any assurance, that it has any possible prenatal application" (Roe v *Wade,* 410 US 113). Given this analysis, the Court concluded that 14th amendment use of the word 'person' did not apply to the unborn.

While the Court determined that the Constitution does not protect the unborn, it did not settle the question of when life or personhood begins. Justice Blackmun stated in *Roe*, "We need not resolve the difficult question of when life begins" (410 US 113, 159 (1973)). The Court came close in *Doe v Bolton*, where it noted that the Georgia law was unconstitutional in part "because it equate[d] the value of embryonic life immediately after conception with the worth of life immediately before birth" (410 US 179, 209-21 (1973)). This statement only alludes to the proposition that 'potential life' does not have the same constitutional protections as 'actual life'.

Moving past the foundational and essential questions of when life begins and whether pre-natal life is a person with rights, the Supreme Court in *Roe* focused its attention on whether the fundamental right of privacy encompasses a 'woman's decision whether or not to terminate her pregnancy'. The Supreme Court essentially answered 'yes', with the caveat that the woman's right was to be balanced with the state's interests in protecting the health of the mother and the fetus.

The Supreme Court adopted a trimester regulatory framework in *Roe* in order balance the interests of the woman and the state. The Court agreed that the state had legitimate interests in protecting the fetus and the health and life of the mother, and in establishing and regulating medical procedures. Within the trimester framework, however, the Court found that early in the pregnancy, the women's privacy interests took priority over the state's interests and as pregnancy progresses (through each 'trimester'), the state's interests become more compelling and may be balanced appropriately with the woman's interests. The application of this framework meant states could not outright ban or harshly regulate abortion in the first three months of pregnancy (1st trimester). In the first trimester, the decision whether to have an abortion, "must be left to [her and] the medical judgment of the pregnant woman's attending physician" (*Roe v Wade,* 410 US, 164). Since first trimester abortions posed a lower risk than carrying the fetus to term, the procedure would not compromise the woman's health. The state's ability to pursue its interest in protecting the woman's health (and that of the fetus) would be limited.

In the second trimester, however, the Court found state abortion regulations permissible as long as they were 'reasonably related' to the health of the woman. Since the fetus was not viable at this point, states could not outright ban abortions at this stage. Lastly, in the third trimester, with the fetus now viable, the state's compelling interest in protecting life would be sufficient justification to limit or proscribe abortion. Essentially, the greater the likelihood that the fetus could survive independently, the greater the state interest in protecting that potential life. This independence allows the fetus to approach 'personhood' where rights then can be conferred upon it. As seen in the next chapter, this view of fetal life and the protection of its 'rights' is significantly different from the German Court's assertion that 'potential life' is established immediately after conception, that such life has its own rights separate from that of the woman and that the state is obligated by the Basic Law to protect such life.

This trimester framework remained until the *Planned Parenthood v Casey* decision in 1993. In *Casey,* the Court reaffirmed the three principles of *Roe:* (1) a woman's right to choose an abortion without undue state interference in the first trimester, (2) the state has legitimate interests in regulating abortions post-viability, while protecting the life and health of the pregnant woman, and (3) the state has legitimate interests in protecting both the life and health of the woman and the life of the fetus. However, the major distinction between *Roe and Casey,* was the replacement of the trimester framework with a <u>less precise</u> pre and post viability rule ('undue burden' standard) determining the constitutionality of state regulations. The Court asserted that *Roe* had undervalued the state's interest in regulating abortion pre-viability, rendering the trimester framework was unworkable (505 US 833, 872). In addition, medical procedures advancing viability to time-points earlier than known at the time *Roe* was decided, as well as enabling safe late stage abortions, likely also contributed to trimester framework's demise (505 US 833, 860). Te Court affirmed that viability, even from the time of *Roe,* has been the crucial point in balancing the rights of the woman with the interests of the state.

Elaborating upon the 'undue burden' standard, the Court asserted that state action would be found unconstitutional when

> "...a state regulation has the purpose or effect of placing a substantial obstacle in the path of a woman seeking an abortion of a nonviable fetus. A statute with this purpose is invalid. In addition, regulations, which do no more than create a structural mechanism by which the State, or the parent or guardian of a minor, may express profound respect for the life of the unborn are permitted, if they are not a substantial obstacle to the woman's exercise of the right to choose. Unless it has that effect on her right of choice, a state measure designed to persuade her to choose childbirth over abortion will be upheld if reasonably related to that goal." (505 U.S. 833, 877, 878).

In addition, as noted above, the Court affirmed that it was constitutionally permissible for states to express their views on abortion and could 'persuade' a woman to not choose an abortion as long as such actions did not present a 'substantial obstacle' to the woman exercising her rights.

Subsequently, by applying the new 'undue burden' standard, the US Court in *Casey* affirmed more stringent state abortion regulations that previously would not have been permissible under the trimester framework. In addition, the 'undue burden' standard provided an opportunity for states to change their abortion policies resulting in greater variation of such policies across states (McFarlane and Meier 78). Indeed, as will be seen, attempts were made in both Oregon (few and unsuccessful) and in Utah (numerous, both successful and unsuccessful) to change state abortion policies.

Informed consent rules

In 1976, three years after *Roe* in *Planned Parenthood v Danforth*, the US Supreme Court determined that states could require doctors to inform a pregnant woman about the dangers of abortion and alternative options. In addition, doctors were to obtain the written consent of the pregnant woman after this counseling. The Court asserted that such counseling regulations were to be narrowly constructed only to reflect the state's interest in protecting maternal health.

Seven years later in *Akron v Akron Center for Reproductive Health,* the Court addressed informed consent rules again, striking down a city ordinance requiring physicians to *articulate particular statements* to the woman, which would then qualify as 'informed' consent (Craig and O'Brien 99). The ordinance stated that the doctor had to inform the woman on the details of fetal development, and that a fetus was a human life from the moment of conception (Craig and O'Brien 85). The Court struck down the ordinance because the regulations essentially required the doctor to *"persuade the woman to withhold her consent rather than merely inform it"* (*Akron v Akron Center for Reproductive Health*, 462 US 416, 444-45, 1983; Daly 95).

In *Casey,* rather than rejecting informed consent regulations, the Court upheld state informed consent laws requiring that a woman must be informed of the nature of the procedure, the health risks due to abortion and childbirth, and of the "probable gestational age of the unborn child". The law also required that the woman must also be provided with information describing the development of the fetus and explaining non-abortive options (*Planned Parenthood v Casey 112 SCT 2791(1992)*. The Court qualified its affirmation of these regulations by noting, "If the information the State requires to be made available to the woman is truthful and not misleading, the requirement may be permissible" (Ibid.).

Finally, in *Rust v Sullivan (1991)* the Court found that the federal government could prohibit the discussion of abortion options by family planning clinics receiving federal funds (500 US 173). At issue were Federal Department of Health and Human Services regulations (the 'gag' rule) limiting Title X fund recipients in their engagement of abortion-related activities (42 C.F.R. §§ 59.8-59.10). As a condition of receiving Title X funding, the government insisted that the doctor or other health professionals did not recommend abortions and did not refer patients to abortion facilities. The Court affirmed the lower court holdings finding that the regulations were a permissible extension of underlying legislation and did not violate Constitution guarantees of free speech or procedural due process. The Court asserted that regulation did not encroach on a doctor's ability to provide or a woman's right to receive information concerning abortion-related services outside of Title X. The Court also found that Constitution did not require the government to enlarge the program's scope in order to provide abortion information to indigent women; therefore, there was no justifiable due process claim.

Parental and Spousal Consent issues

In numerous cases, the US Supreme Court addressed the issue of parental and spousal consent, as compared to the German and Canadian courts, neither of which significantly addressed these issues. In its initial review of consent laws, the US Supreme Court ruled that states could not require parental consent for a minor's abortion unless they provided a confidential alternative to consent (*Belotti v Baird (1979)* 443 US 622). In other words, the state had to provide some sort of a judicial bypass option. Two years later, the issue was in front of the court in *H.L v Matheson* (445 US 959, 1981). *Matheson* concerned the constitutionality of a Utah statute requiring an attending physician to notify a minor's parents before performing an abortion. In this case, the Court found that the state could require parental notification for minors who are immature and un-emancipated. The Court attempted to distinguish this ruling from *Bellotti*, by stating that question of obtaining consent for mature and emancipated minors was not addressed in *Matheson* (McFarlane and Meier 67). Two years later, in *City of Akron v Akron Center for Reproductive Health* (462 US 416, 1983), the Court reaffirmed its guidelines for parental consent rules, noting exemptions for minors who are sufficiently mature, or "have good reason for not seeking parental consent and can demonstrate that an abortion would be in her best interest" (McFarlane and Meier 67). Such bypass options were to be executed expediently and confidentially (Ibid).

The next time issues of consent appeared before the Court, the Court upheld state restrictions on minors seeking abortions. In *Hodgson v Minnesota (1990)* (497 US 417), the Court affirmed that states may require notification of both parents as long as a judicial bypass option was available. In addition, they upheld a 48-hour waiting period between parental notification and performance of the abortion procedure. In *Ohio v Akron Center for Reproductive Health* (497US 502), the Court upheld that minors must meet a high standard of proof in order to obtain a judicial bypass; they must show that they are *sufficiently mature* to consent on their own or that parental notification was not in their best interest. Lastly, in 1993, in *Casey,* the Court reaffirmed that states may require a minor to seek consent either from a parent or judge, and that states did not have to provide absolute anonymity to minors seeking a judicial bypass. Cumulatively, these decisions substantially limited the rights of minors to obtain an abortion and enabled states to establish greater regulations in this area. By 1998, 39 states had regulations requiring minors to obtain either parental or judicial consent prior to obtaining an abortion.

In regards to adults and state consent laws, in *Casey,* the Supreme Court did strike down a Pennsylvania provision requiring married women seeking abortions to sign statements indicating they notified their spouse about undergoing the procedure. Although this provision provided exceptions to the requirement in cases of sexual assault, threat of bodily injury and assault, the Court still found the regulation on its face, to be an undue burden on women. The Court asserted that requiring spousal notification was repugnant to women's autonomy and present day views of marriage.

Waiting periods

Similar to its approach to on consent regulations, the US Supreme Court initially struck down and later upheld waiting period restrictions on performing abortions. The Court initially struck down a 24-hour waiting period in *Akron*, stating there was no medical basis for the requirement, and that it increased medical risks by delaying the procedure and creating scheduling difficulties. The waiting period also imposed a financial burden on the woman because of extra travel expenses. Nine years later in *Casey,* the Court overturned this restriction. Applying the 'undue burden' standard, waiting periods and the subsequent costs incurred were determined not to impose a 'substantial obstacle' or 'burden' to a woman's right to choose an abortion prior to viability (Tribe 245). Although acknowledging that the requirement would be a greater practical imposition on women with fewer financial and familial resources, the Court did not find such concerns sufficiently compelling in restricting the woman's right to choose an abortion. "These findings are troubling in some respects, but they do not demonstrate that waiting period constitutes an undue burden" (*Planned Parenthood v Casey 112 SCT 2791(1992)).* Only Justice Stevens clearly thought that waiting period was not constitutional. "The State cannot further its interests by simply wearing down the ability of the woman to exercise her constitutional right" (505 U.S. 833 918). Nonetheless, before *Casey,* only two states had passed legislation requiring mandatory waiting periods prior to obtaining an abortion. After *Casey,* 19 states responded by establishing regulations prohibiting a woman from obtaining an abortion for a specified time after she has received state mandated information or instructions regarding abortion (McFarlane and Meier 91).

Administrative and performance regulations

Since *Casey,* the US Supreme Court has found a number of state health regulations and administrative requirements constitutional due to the state's interest in protecting both the health of the mother and the life of the fetus. Prior to Casey, the Court struck down a number of these regulations, while upholding others. For example, in *Doe,* the Court struck down a 'fetal protection statute' that required doctors to use the available means to protect the lives of fetuses pre-viability (Craig and O'Brien 97). However, the Court did find recording requirements constitutionally permissible, such as requiring doctors to provide information about abortions they performed as long as such information was not intrusive, confidential and related to maternal health (Ibid). In addition, the Court upheld the filing of pathology reports for each abortion performed (*Ashcroft (1983)* but struck down Pennsylvania's reporting requirements in *Thornburgh (1986)*, because such reports could be made public and therefore intrude on the privacy of the patient. Yet, three years later in *Webster (1989)*, the Court upheld the constitutionality of Missouri's abortion law requiring doctors to confirm whether fetuses were viable prior to performing abortions on women believed to be pregnant for 20 weeks or more.

In addressing the actual performance of abortions, the Court struck down a requirement of the presence of a second doctor for all abortions and a requirement that 2nd trimester abortions must be performed in hospitals (*Thornburgh (1986) and Akron (1983)* respectively). However, in *Webster (1989)*, the Court affirmed regulations prohibiting state employed physicians from performing abortions unless needed to save the life of the woman, and upheld state regulations prohibiting abortions from being performed in state facilities. As Justice Blackmun pointed out in his dissent, the Court in *Webster* essentially invited states to establish more restrictive abortion regulations. He said, "...a plurality of this Court invites every state legislature to enact more and more test cases [in order to overturn *Roe*] *(492 US 490 539)*. The Utah state legislature succeeded in enacting such restrictive laws, while these attempts failed in Oregon.

Funding Regulations

The US Supreme Court has never ruled that any federal or state monies should be used to enable abortions for low-income women, whereas the German Constitutional Court determined that state welfare funds should be used to support indigent women seeking abortions. In *Harris v McRae (1980)*, the US Supreme Court affirmed the Hyde amendment, prohibiting the use of federal monies to fund abortions, except when the life of the woman was in danger (446 US 907). This regulation essentially prohibited the use of federal Medicaid funds to support poor women seeking abortions (McFarlane and Meier 66). Prior to *Harris*, all 50 states had funded most abortions performed on Medicaid patients. One year after *Harris*, only 16 states funded abortions for Medicaid patients and this number has stayed relatively stable since (McFarlane and Meier 89). The Court has also ruled that states or local municipalities are not required to fund therapeutic abortions (*Beal v Doe* and *Maher v Doe*).

Summary of Court abortion policy directives

In concert, these Supreme Court cases support the proposition that the State (Federal, state or local government) has no *affirmative responsibility* in insuring a woman's ability to exercise her right to an abortion. The woman may be the holder of the right, but the State is not responsible for enabling the right, can assert its own views opposing that choice and take actions consistent with that view. In addition, the constitution may permit the State to act in particular instances to limit or delay exercise of the right because of the state's interest in protecting the health of the woman and the fetus.

In addition, the limited nature of United States Constitution itself provides few affirmative guarantees regarding the exercise of rights by individuals and only provides limited grounds on which to limit governmental action. In addressing the foundational questions of when life begins or whether the constitution protects fetal life, the Constitution provides little guidance. The Court largely bases its determination that a woman has a constitutional right to choose an abortion on court precedent. That precedent, establishing a general right to privacy, is in itself based on broad interpretations of constitutional guarantees related to, but not explicitly providing for, a right to privacy. This provides a weak foundation on which the Court could have ground a comprehensive and detailed approach to abortion policy. Therefore, it is not surprising that the Court's major abortion decision in *Roe* tried to provide a rule (the trimester framework) in which to evaluate the constitutionality of abortion policy. However, since this framework bore a tenuous connection to constitutional guarantees, it could be (and was) repeatedly challenged and eventually led the Court to reject the trimester framework and replace it with the broader 'undue burden' standard in *Casey*.

Lastly, it is significant that the criminal law is primarily within the state jurisdiction. This factor facilitated the Court's repeated entrance into the policy process but also limited its influence in shaping the direction of abortion policy. With the states largely in control of the criminal law, this meant that the Supreme Court could potentially review fifty different approaches to the criminalization of abortion. This variation increased the number of opportunities the Court could (and did) review the constitutionality of state actions. This likely explains why the US Supreme Court reviewed more cases on abortion than either the Canadian Supreme or German Constitutional Court, since for both of these courts criminal law is the responsibility of the federal, not state governments.

However, even though the US Supreme Court had multiple opportunities to review state abortion policies due to the diffusion of criminal law across the 50 states, this influence was diluted by the federal design allowing 'all courts' to address constitutional questions. In combination, this structure facilitated the policy variance among states over which Supreme Court could not immediately control. Constitutionally questionable state abortion legislation had to be enacted and subsequently challenged in lower courts before an appeal to the Supreme Court could provide 'authoritative' review, resulting in a relatively slow and time-consuming process and allowing multiple interpretations of what is constitutional remain in existence. .Having only one time-consuming, yet, multi-faceted pipeline to the Supreme Court review contrasts with the German Constitutional Court where lower courts are obliged to forward constitutional questions to the Constitutional Court for resolution. In summary, the US system provided multiple opportunities, for the Supreme Court to address abortion policy, but the lack of clear, specific and positive constitutional guarantees provided a weak basis on which the Court could act authoritatively and the federal design enabled a proliferation of state abortion policies, of which some would evade immediate Supreme Court review.

FEDERAL RESPONSES AND POLICY DEVELOPMENT

Federal government prohibits Medicare funds for most abortions, no other major policy action is taken at the federal level-1970's

When Roe *v* *Wade* was appealed to the Supreme Court, President Nixon did not want to involve his administration in the case, so no amicus briefs were filed on behalf of the federal government. Failing to intervene might have seemed surprising since Solicitor General Erwin Griswold represented the government in *US v Vuitch* (1971), an abortion case prior to *Roe* originating in the District of Columbia (O'Connor 46). *Vuitch* involved a D.C. doctor charged with inducing a medical abortion that violated the D.C code, which stipulated that abortions could be performed only to preserve the life or health of the woman. The administration had no choice but to be involved in the case since D.C. statues are acts of Congress; D.C. is under federal jurisdiction and therefore the executive branch was obligated to defend the law. However, when it came to issuing an *independent policy* position on abortion through filing an amicus brief, Nixon deferred to the Supreme Court rather than take a potentially politically damaging position *it did not have* to take. Not surprising, Congress had a few hearings on abortion matters but also took no significant legislative action during this time (Ibid).

Soon after the Court's ruling in *Roe,* the federal government responded, albeit slowly, beginning with Gerald Ford's administration. Ford issued vague statements endorsing abortions in a few, limited situations and supported a constitutional amendment authorizing states to decide abortion policies (Tribe 148-150). Congress found this approach politically palatable, since this removed any pressures for it to take a public position on the issue and was consistent with a 'states' rights' view of federalism that was gaining momentum at the time (Ibid.). However, there were two constitutional amendments proposed in Congress that attempted to provide legal protection to the unborn (Herring 111). First, the Hogan amendment was to apply the due process clause of the 14th amendment from the moment of conception (Herring 110-112). The second, the Buckley amendment would have defined a person as " 'human beings including their unborn offspring at every stage of their biological development, irrespective of age, health, function or condition of dependency.' "(Ibid). This amendment also provided an exception in which continuation of a pregnancy would result in the death of the woman and provided that states had the power to enforce the amendment (Ibid 110). At the time both amendments failed to reach a floor vote.

Although most legal observers believed that the states, under their police powers, had the main authority to regulate abortion, Congress did exert authority over federal funding of Medicaid to limit abortions through passage of the Hyde Amendment in 1977. It "banned spending of federal funds [for abortion] in all but three circumstances; (1) when the mother's life was in danger (2) when two physicians certified that a woman would suffer "severe and long lasting damage" if she carried to term; or (3) when the pregnancy was the result of rape or incest, as reported to the proper authorities." (O'Connor 69). As discussed in the previous section, three days after passage of the Hyde amendment, the

Supreme Court ruled in a series of cases (*Beal, Poelker, and Maher v Doe*) that states and cities were not required to fund elective or non-therapeutic abortions (Craig and O'Connor 120).

Congress fails to pass legislation protecting abortion rights-1980-1992

In the late 1970's with both a Democratic president (Jimmy Carter) and a Democratic majority in Congress, there was little significant federal activity on abortion policy. However, during the Reagan years and continuing through G.H. Bush's tenure, there were a few attempts at the federal level to alter abortion policies even though the issue became more politically visible and viable nationwide. After failed legislation sponsored by Senator Jesse Helms to outlaw abortions completely, Orin Hatch, in 1982, proposed a constitutional amendment severely limiting abortion access. Hatch's proposal made it out of sub-committee; but a filibuster killed it on the Senate floor (Craig and O'Brien 145). A year later, a second attempt was made on the Hatch amendment, but it failed to receive enough votes to break a filibuster (Ibid 146).

A number of congressional attempts to direct abortion policy marked George H.W. Bush's tenure in office. This shift was likely in response to the Supreme Court's rulings in *Webster (1989)* and *Casey (1992)* upholding a number of state restrictions on abortion. For example, the Democratic-led Congress first responded to *Webster* by proposing House and Senate bills attempting to enshrine the protections of the *Roe* trimester framework. Both bills failed to make it out of Congress. Bush vetoed additional legislation intended to relax federal funding restrictions limited by the Hyde amendment (Ibid). Contrasting with Congress's general support of abortion rights, the Republican administration filed an amicus brief in *Planned Parenthood v Casey* in support of the state's restrictive abortion policies (Craig and O'Brien 315). These contrasting and competing views on abortion by Congress and the President effectively sent mixed signals to the states regarding the federal government's position on abortion and thereby emboldened states to take action when the federal government could not.

While the administration filed its brief in *Casey* supporting state restrictions on abortion, Congress mounted its most concerted effort to protect abortion rights through the Freedom of Choice Act of 1991. The bill was to "prohibit the states from enacting any abortion restrictions before the time of fetal viability or at any time that an abortion was necessary to save the life of the mother". Supporters of the bill argued that it was incumbent upon the Congress to pass the legislation as the increasingly conservative Supreme Court (populated with a number of justices appointed by Republican presidents since *Roe*) moved further away from abortion protections outlined in *Roe* (O'Connor 139). President Bush publicly stated his opposition to the legislation, but the Act never made it to his desk while he remained in office (Ibid).

As noted previously, the Supreme Court in *Casey* upheld state restrictions on abortion while preserving a general right to abortion under the broader 'undue burden' standard. The day after the decision, the House Judiciary committee passed the Freedom of Choice Act II. During the debate over the Act in Congress, amendments were proposed and rejected, including one requiring women to be informed of the fetus' development during counseling and another mandating a 24 hour waiting period. A 'conscience' clause amendment did pass, which allowed health care workers to refrain from participating in abortion procedures for moral or religious reasons (Ibid). By July 1992, the Senate Labor and Human Resources committee approved the Freedom of Choice Act II, and the bill moved to the floor of the Senate. Both the Senate and House versions of the bill stalled at this point, never making it to full floor votes, largely due to the fact there were not enough votes in either house to pass them or to survive a presidential veto if they did pass.

Clinton rescinds 'gag rule', Congress fails to pass partial birth abortion act- 1992-1998

Bill Clinton's inauguration led some to hope that the abortion legislation that failed to be enacted under George H.W. Bush would finally be passed into law. While the Clinton administration did take some pro-abortion policy stances, the hope for significant change at the federal level was short-lived with the election of a Republican House majority two years into his presidency. Immediately after being sworn in, Clinton issued a number of executive orders overturning previous executive orders restricting abortions that were issued during the previous two Republican administrations. Most notably, he rescinded the infamous "gag' rule on clinics receiving federal funds found to be constitutional by the Supreme Court in *Rust v Sullivan*.

Perhaps emboldened by the Supreme Court decision in *Casey*, the Republican controlled House brought new attempts to restrict abortion, most notably the Partial Birth Abortion Act of 1996, which Clinton vetoed (O'Connor 170-171). This bill was comparable to partial birth abortion bills that had been passed by a number of state legislatures in the early 1990's (Herring 166). Two times Congress passed the bill but failed to override the president's veto (171). Meanwhile by 1998, 22 state legislatures had passed similar legislation (166).

Summary and analysis of the federal abortion policy response

Over this time, the federal government's limited jurisdictional authority over criminal law and the partisan division (diffusion of party control between institutions) between the executive and the legislative branches significantly contributed to the federal government's inability to make sweeping changes to the direction of abortion policy. While the public controversy over abortion policy raged nationally, particularly during the late 1980's and early 90's, federal institutions made minimal changes to abortion policy and succeeded only when they pursued policies that fell most squarely under their constitutional authority. These included such policies as limiting the application of federal funds via Medicare, or when the executive acted unilaterally through either issuing executive orders or filing amicus briefs.

As discussed in chapter two, a number of scholars (Ginsburg, Graber and Whittington, et al), note that 'conflict' between political institutions/elites provides opportunities for political actors, like courts, to expand and exercise their power. However, with the presence of a federal structure, this 'conflict' did not just facilitate the Supreme Court's power to alter abortion policy but also the states' powers to do so. The Supreme Court had heard a number cases on abortion prior to *Webster* and *Casey*, however, in these latter cases the Court was largely upholding rather than striking down state restrictions on abortion. With no constitutional impetus to force federal action, deference to states was an easy route for federal elites to take. The federal government's deference to the Supreme Court was an indirect and effective one, since states would responsible for enacting any abortion policy changes, and oversight of such policy would lie with the Supreme Court and not the federal legislature. In addition, such challenges to state laws would take years before they reached the Supreme Court, and thereby could be 'off' the national agenda.

Therefore, in addition to the party diffusion among federal institutions, and the lack of incentive or legal obligation to craft abortion policy at the federal level, the diffuse logic of American federalism itself also facilitated the decentralization and fragmentation of legislative policy responses to Supreme Court decisions. As Barbara Craig and David O'Brien observed in their study of US abortion policy,

> The decentralized structure of American federalism--with fifty state jurisdictions, diverse populations, and distinctive regional political cultures--openly invites competition among political forces. In that structure, federalism affords multiple opportunities for thwarting compliance with, or implementation of, Supreme Court rulings" (Craig and O'Brien 77).

As the following sections will outline, the Supreme Court's piecemeal, rather than comprehensive and detailed directives on abortion policy combined with the diffuse federal structure established a context in which states could devise their own abortion policies with minimal federal direction or oversight.

In addition, having a judicial system in which any court can evaluate the constitutionality of state legislation and is dependent upon the willingness and resources of petitioners to appeal cases results in a slow review process with no guarantee that the Supreme Court will hear the case. The lack of institutional features enabling direct intervention by the Court diminishes the Court's *opportunity to* and therefore *ability to* shape policy. Combined, these factors facilitated state control and development of abortion policy and fostered the subsequent diversity of abortion policies found across states. The next two sections examine how two states, Oregon and Utah, compare and contrast in their responses to US Supreme Court rulings on abortion.

UTAH

State political orientation and brief summary of state activity on abortion

Within the United States, Utah is arguably the only state dominated politically by a single religious group. About 60% of Utah citizens are members of The Church of Latter Day Saints (Mormons). The Church has a long history in the state and strongly influences state politics. An overwhelming majority of state legislators are Church members and given the Church's conservative orientation, they are also Republican Party members. Utah has not supported a Democratic candidate for president since 1964. Since the Church has had a longstanding influence on Utah politics and the state's political orientation, it is not surprising that the Utah legislature continually and enthusiastically responded to Supreme Court decisions by passing a series of increasingly restrictive laws on abortion. Beyond just responding to Supreme Court decisions, the legislature attempted to anticipate and predict whether proposed bills would be upheld by the US Supreme Court (should they be challenged in court) and actively and knowingly passed bills that were constitutionally deficient under existing US Supreme Court rulings. The state government pursued seven years of litigation over an unconstitutional bill even in the face of public dissatisfaction over the legal costs. After exhausting every possible legal venue, including an appeal to the US Supreme Court, the state's legislation was ultimately ruled unconstitutional by the 10th Federal Circuit Court.

Legislative action to restrict funding succeeds, other abortion restrictions do not-1970's

In the 1970's, the Utah state legislature made a few attempts to pass restrictive abortion policies into law. The first major bill that was passed was in 1977, HB447, prohibited the use of state funds to pay for abortions unless the mother's life was in danger. The law did not go into effect immediately because the constitutionality of the law was challenged in Federal District court. The District court enjoined the law because of pending Supreme Court cases regarding the use of state Medicaid funds to pay for abortions (*Maher v Doe, Beal v Doe, Poelker v Doe*). After the US Supreme Court had ruled in favor of state funding restrictions on abortion, the restraining order against the law was lifted (Tinker 1977). Two years later in 1979, two bills severely restricting abortion rights, one making the killing of an unborn child while in a woman's womb a homicide, and the other requiring parental, as well as, spousal consent were introduced but failed in the House. Although these bills received little consideration and debate, in the 1980's the legislature stepped up its attempts to enact restrictive abortion policies.

The legislature passes constitutionally suspect abortion legislation- the 1980's.

While a second attempt to make abortion a criminal homicide failed in the Utah Senate, another bill requiring informed consent, Bill HB83, quickly passed and was signed into law in March 1981. The bill required informed counseling about abortion procedures, adoption services, and support agencies. The information included a description of the abortion procedure and the physical characteristics of the unborn child at two-week intervals up to the 24th week of gestation. The doctor was also required to provide written notification that the material was presented to the woman at least 24 hours prior to the procedure. This meant that the woman could not receive this information immediately prior to obtaining an abortion, effectively creating a 24 hour waiting period requirement without specifically legislating as such (HB 83 1981).

Prior to final approval of the bill, Governor Matheson (R) requested the Attorney General's office to provide a legal analysis of the bill. In his report to the governor, Chief Deputy Attorney General Paul Tinker stated that federal courts previously had struck down similar legislation in other states. He specifically questioned the constitutionality of the 24-hour waiting period and the written notification requirement. The Deputy stated that while the existing case law was not entirely consistent, he believed that the bill was most likely unconstitutional (Tinker 1981). In a letter responding to this report and to constituent concerns about the constitutionality of the bill, the Governor voiced his skepticism, "As a practical matter, House Bill 83 is essentially a window dressing bill, as it contains no methods of enforcement or penalties. I consider it to be political grandstanding. However, this does not make it [abortion] any less offensive"

(Matheson 1981). Even though he acknowledged the bill did not have any practical effect, Matheson said he would not veto the measure and did eventually sign the bill into law. Passage and signing of the bill signaled the legislature's determination to limit abortion regardless of contrary evidence and that the Governor was not going to stand up to the legislature. In addition, no interest group or private party sought to challenge the law. The passage of this likely 'unconstitutional' law indicates the extent of the freedom state legislators had to enact such legislation without threat of an oversight mechanism that would immediately sanction the legislature for passing such a law.

By 1985, the legislature passed a second informed consent measure (HB 82), requiring even more detail about the abortion procedure and the nature of the fetus to be communicated to the pregnant woman. Again the Attorney General's office provided a legal analysis, although this time Assistant Attorney General Clark Graves stated that the bill "[did] not present any patent constitutional problem or obvious legal deficiency" (Graves 1985).

While the US Supreme Court was considering how it would rule in *Webster v Reproductive Health Services* in 1989, the legislature anticipated the Court's decision by preparing a strongly worded abortion bill to be passed immediately after the Court issued its decision in *Webster*. Conservative Utah legislator R. Mount Evans asked the Office of Legislative Research and General Counsel to write up a bill prohibiting virtually all abortions (Evans 1989). The request was labeled confidential at the time it was sent on April 12, 1989. His request stated, "I want a bill to be drafted that prohibits abortions except in the cases of rape, incest or threats to the life of the mother, oh, I want the bill to be very similar to the bill currently before the US Supreme Court. I want the bill written and ready for the pre-file within two or three days after the announcement of the Supreme Court decision on abortion [sic]" (Evans 1989). Although he clearly put in his request for this bill before *Webster* was decided, no other record of the bill or evidence of movement on the bill was evident in the legislative records until *after* the *Webster* decision was announced that summer.

In the fall of 1989, Janetha Hancock, from the Legislative Research office, edited a draft of Evan's bill, which imposed the strictest restrictions on abortions possible, using as her guide the Supreme Court's ruling in *Webster*. The bill limited abortions after 20 weeks, and the state would only fund abortions necessary to save the life of the woman or to prevent 'serious and permanent damage to her health' (Hancock 1989). In addition, the bill included a provision stating that it was the legislature's position that life begins at conception, childbirth is favored over abortion, and abortion would be regulated "to the full extent permitted by the Constitution of the United States" (Ibid).

Ms. Hancock's notes indicate she analyzed the Webster decision in detail in order to determine what would be the greatest restrictions on abortion permissible under the law. For example, on the issue of viability she noted, "In *Webster*, the USSC upheld a presumption of viability at 20 weeks, which the physician must rebut with tests indicating that the fetus is _not_ viable [sic]"(Hancock 1989). Her notes also instructed to "Add regulations identical to those upheld in *Webster*", and proposed a strategy to get the bill approved; "first-conduct public hearings to ensure first rate medical testimony; 2nd-Elicit (probably futile effort) governor's support for the bill; 3rd-Present bill as _moderate_, _reasonable_, pro-life/anti-abortion bill that makes room for hard cases [sic]" (Hancock 1989).

Possibly anticipating a constitutional challenge to the new law, her notes also reveal that she attempted to predict which Supreme Court justices would vote to overturn Roe. She noted that "4 would overrule Roe; 4 would uphold Roe; O'Connor-Swing vote" and counseled the [legislature] "Don't go further than Webster, but less than all out prohibition--too many restrictions....Focus on O'Connor. Don't do everything all at once- one step at a time [sic]" (Hancock 1989). Her notes show that there was clear intent in the legislature to comply with the Supreme Court's decision in *Webster* through passing legislation that would be consistent with the ruling, yet go as far as constitutionally possible to place restrictions on abortion. These notes indicate the extent to which Utah legislators were strategically crafting legislation that would not *only test the limits of USSC's* previous decisions, but also provide a foundation *for future legislation by anticipating* which justices would favor possible further restrictions on abortion and therefore support state legislation should it be challenged in the future.

Constitutionally suspect bills again are signed into law, leading to a protracted legal battle-1990-1992

About a year after *Webster,* in October 1990, the Utah legislature held hearings on Evan's bill, HB 171-Abortion Limitations. While the bill was going through revisions regarding what constituted serious and permanent damage to the woman's health, it also began receiving attention from outside the legislature. The Utah chapter of the ACLU threatened to sue the state if the law was enacted (Crosby 1990). The Governor initially responded by stating, "I don't think I've developed a reputation for letting lawyers and lawsuits dictate good sound policy" (Ibid). However, he then quickly asserted that the legislation should have "a reasonable chance to be upheld by the [US] Supreme Court", foreshadowing the future litigation battle that would erupt over the law (Ibid). In addition, the public was divided over whether the bill should be passed. A poll by Salt Lake Tribune revealed that 35% surveyed found existing state laws acceptable, an equal amount favored more restrictions on abortion, 19% wanted to liberalize the state laws, and the last 11% were unsure (1991). These survey numbers showed that the mass public was not driving the legislature to pass the law, yet these poll numbers also indicated that the legislature was probably correct in assuming there would be no political ramifications from attempting to pass this bill.

A few weeks prior to the bill's passage (now known publicly as SB 23), the Office of Legislative Research reviewed the House and Senate versions of the bill for any conflicts with the US Constitution. Janetha Hancock's report for the Office stated that "Under current US Supreme Court rulings, a court would most likely find this legislation to be unconstitutional as violating a woman's rights to privacy" (Hancock 1991). Soon after she issued her report, the legislature conducted another round of public hearings on the bills and in a January 24, 1991, in a letter to the bill's sponsors, the state Attorney General supported Hancock's concerns that the bill was unconstitutional. He wrote, "You and your fellow legislators should be aware, as you consider this bill, that in the event it must be defended in the courts, as it appears it surely will there are provisions in the bill which will be of concern to the litigators who handle such defense" (Van Dam 1991). The legislature was clearly made aware that the bill was stepping over constitutional limits, which could expose the state to the possibility of a court challenge.

At this point, the latest version of the bill imposed greater restrictions on abortion than what was initially outlined. It now outlawed all abortions after 20 weeks unless it was necessary to save the woman's life; it prevented life threatening damage to her physical health; it allowed abortion only when it prevented a child being born with "grave and irremediable physical or mental defects incompatible with sustained survival", or if the pregnancy was the result of rape or incest. The bill also included a 'second tier' set of abortion restrictions that would go into effect in the event that the above regulations were enjoined or challenged in the courts. The second tier simply broadened the language to allow abortions only if preventing 'grave' damage either to the life or health of the woman or the child, while keeping the same overall restrictions on abortion as the first tier. By including this 'second tier' the legislature acknowledged it was passing a highly controversial law and was anticipating a legal challenge. In his monthly news conference, Governor Bangerter said, "My preference would clearly be to just go with the second tier. There's no question about that. We think that has the best chance of constitutionality"(Bangerter 1991). Again, regardless of his preferences, the Governor made no attempt to veto the legislation and signed SB 23 into law the following day on January 25 1991.

Immediately after the bill was passed, the Utah ACLU stated that it would challenge the law in court (Sisco 1991). Responding to the legal challenge, the Utah legislature hastily proposed and passed a bill titled "Abortion Litigation Trust Fund Account and Clarification Amendments". This bill revived the state's abortion law pre-existing to the enactment of SB 23, should the courts overturn the new law. The amendments also provided for a monetary account in which the state would collect private funds for litigation expenses necessary to defend the new abortion law (1991). It became law on March 19, 1991.

Litigation over SB 23 began in a federal district court where the state initially tried to postpone the lawsuit. Federal district court Judge Greene rejected the stay and scheduled the first hearings for the case for October 1991 (House 1991). While the costs of the case, initially estimated at 1 million, climbed rapidly, the public provided minimal monetary support for the litigation. The state received about $9,000 dollars in donations to the state's litigation fund when the case began (Ibid).

The suit dragged into 1992, when the legislature sought to respond immediately to the Supreme Court's *Casey* decision by proposing another new law further restricting abortion. On July 1, 1992, Senator McAllister, a sponsor of the previous bill now tied up in litigation, sent drafting instructions to the Office Legislative Research:

> Draft legislation to do whatever <u>Casey</u> allows, that we're <u>not</u> doing - include a parental consent w/ judicial bypass, add 24 waiting requirement, materials (stick to what seems reasonable) ?? Don't use the 20 week standard ??? Use <u>Casey</u>- -> whatever the USSCT says we can use "viability", or not less than 20 weeks or viability. A constitutional bill...only what we <u>know</u> the SupCt w/uphold. Check: If we amend the statue that's in litigation --will there be no basis for appeal? Moot? [sic] (Hancock 1993)

Again these instructions reveal the strategic intent to pass a bill that goes right up to the constitutional 'line' and to accept the Court's invitation in *Casey* to establish additional restrictions on abortion. The legislature was also clearly aware of the legal rules (mootness) that could stop an appeal of the current case. Lastly, McAllister's notes also indicated that he less willing to pass a law likely to be inconsistent with Supreme Court doctrine, perhaps a view that reflected the state's difficulties with its litigation over SB 23. This approach affirms the view of scholars who have argued that legislatures provide the political supports for judicial review by writing legislation in such a way that 'invites' (or *not* in this case) court review (e.g. Whittington, Frymer).

By the fall of 1992, the public began to voice its displeasure at the state government for continuing to pursue its litigation over SB 23, when the Supreme Court's decision in *Casey* signaled that the contested Utah law had little chance of being upheld. Even Governor Bangerter, who had been previously unwilling to challenge the legislature, publicly asked the legislature to give up the fight stating that it was "foolish, now that the Supreme Court, with numerous conservative Republican appointees, ha[d] still refused to go further [to restrict abortions]" (Press 1992).

Utah continues its appeals and the legislature responds to Planned Parenthood v Casey with new legislation -1992-1998

In December 1992, Federal District Judge Green issued his decision, striking down the law's ban restricting most elective abortions prior to 21 weeks, the ban on fetal experimentation, and the spousal notification. His ruling severed only these parts as unconstitutional from the rest of the legislation. The decision was consistent with previous US Supreme Court's abortion rulings, including *Casey*. In response to the District Judge's decision, Governor elect Mike Leavitt initially stated he was unsure whether the state would appeal the ruling, as the state had already spent more than $750,000 defending the law (Harrie 1992). Yet, after he took office in January 1993, he declared that the state would continue its battle over the law, and he would support McAllister's second abortion reform proposal based on the perceived opportunity *Casey* provided to the states to enact further abortion restrictions (Harrie 1993).

Soon after Levitt's public statements, McAllister's bill was on the fast track and Janetha Hancock reviewed a draft of the bill (SB 124). She noted possible constitutional conflicts, yet ultimately gave her approval, stating that, "Since Casey (USSCT) was an opinion based on a challenge to PA law 'on its face' any challenge to a similar statute such as this under a different constitutional theory could bring about a different ruling. However, under the Casey opinion there is a very strong argument that this statute is constitutional. [sic]". Governor Leavitt signed the bill into law on March 12, 1993, which amended the 1991 law (enjoined due to the litigation) and included a 24 hour waiting period, and informed consent provisions identical to those upheld in *Casey* (Fahys 1993). A few months later, the legislature again attempted to restrict abortions by requiring physicians to show a woman a ultrasound picture of her fetus as part of the required pre-abortion counseling procedure (Harrie 1993). This bill died in the House in the summer of 1993, likely due to fatigue over the continuing litigation battle over SB 23.

In early March of 1994, the Legislature strengthened waiting period stipulations requiring women to have face to face consultations with a doctor, although phone consultations had been deemed sufficient by existing case law (Semerad 1994). Meanwhile the Governor's office filed an appeal in the 10th Circuit Court in the fall of 1994 in the litigation battle over SB 23. The Circuit Court first heard the appeal in May of 1995, addressing the constitutionality of the 20 week time limit on abortions and issues of fetal experimentation in SB 23; the state had dropped the appeal concerning the spousal notification requirement (Massey 1995).

By August, the 10th Circuit court struck down SB 23 in its entirety, instead of just ruling on the constitutionality of prohibiting most abortions after 20 weeks and the prohibition on fetal experimentation, as District Court Judge Green had done. The Court asserted that these issues could not be severed from the entirety of the legislation. The Governor immediately asked for a re-hearing by the full Circuit Court, which was denied. Having been rejected at both the District and Circuit court levels, the Governor petitioned the US Supreme Court to hear the case in December 1995 (Harrie 1995). At this point, public opinion had soured on Utah's appeal of the 1991 abortion law (Harrie 1995). A poll taken by the Salt Lake Tribune indicated that 50% of Utahns opposed further state spending on the case, a third of residents were supportive and 16% were unsure (Ibid). After four years, the state had spent 1.1 million dollars in legal fees defending the law (Ibid).

Undaunted by public opinion, in 1996, the next winter legislative session, the legislature passed a bill requiring women to watch a video about abortion procedures prior to undergoing the procedure and mandating the state provide and pay for an ultrasound if a pregnant woman requests one. The legislature also passed another bill during the same session, which outlawed the use of the D&E abortion procedure (Dilation and Evacuation). The legislative counsel clearly communicated to Representative Kilpack, the sponsor of the bills, that these bills had dubious constitutional merit; "This bill goes further than what was specifically tested in *Casey*, because it directs the information be given, not just made available, and includes the viewing of a video as part of the informed consent requirements'" (Collins 1996). In response, Representative Kilpack said, "'It's important to realize it's true that this bill will be challenged. No question. But if it's going to be challenged anyway, let's take the strongest possible stance we can. If it's going to be challenged, let's have something worthy of challenge' "(Ibid). In conjunction with passage of these bills, this time legislators set aside $200,000 to be used for future costs of legal challenges to the laws (Ibid). Even with the federal courts rejection of the 1991 abortion legislation, the state legislature continued to pass likely unconstitutional laws with little concern that they would face sanction by either the public or the US Supreme Court.

Meanwhile, in June 1996, five years after the law was initially passed, the US Supreme Court ruled on the contested 1991 law (SB-23). In a narrow, technical decision failing to address the substantive merits of the law, the Court ruled that the 10th Circuit Court erred in its disposition of the case regarding the issue of severability. According to the Supreme Court, the 10th Circuit was wrong in ruling that unconstitutional sections of the law, such as the 20-week rule, could not be severed from the rest of the law, thereby upholding the District Court's ruling. The Supreme Court justified its position by noting that the legislature intentionally wrote the law so that some sections could still be enforced if other sections were struck down. By failing to rule on the substantive merits of the legislation, the Court 'punted' to the lower court and chose not to take the opportunity to expand its reach over abortion policy. The case was remanded to 10th Circuit with instructions to review its decision regarding the severability question (Bauman 1996).

Now back in the 10th Circuit in December 1996, the Circuit Court ruled that the 1991 law's ban on most abortions prior to 20 weeks and all abortions after 20 weeks (with its few exceptions) was unconstitutional. In a harshly worded opinion, the Circuit Court chastised the state for disregarding US Supreme Court precedent and intentionally passing an unconstitutional law (Costanzo 1996). The Circuit Court asserted that Utah attempted to definitively determine viability, which contradicted Supreme Court precedent in *Planned Parenthood v Danforth*. The state, " 'made a deliberate decision to disregard controlling Supreme Court precedent set out in *Roe* (and in other cases) and to ignore the Supreme Court's repeated directive that viability is a matter for an attending physician to determine' "(Ibid, citing the decision). The Circuit Court opinion also stated that establishment of the abortion litigation trust fund account indicated the state knowingly passed an unconstitutional law in order to have it challenged.

Even with the strongly worded 10th Circuit ruling, the governor immediately appealed to the US Supreme Court, regarding the 20 week viability issue and general ban on abortions after 20 weeks. On June 16, 1997, the US Supreme Court rejected the appeal without comment, effectively ending the case since the state ran out of appeals. Over the 6 years since the law was passed, the state paid 1.2 million dollars in legal costs (Hunt 1997). Responding to public criticism regarding the expensive legal battle that the state waged over the law, the Governor's spokesperson, Viki Varela said, "'this was a discussion of principles. Sometimes those are expensive discussions, but they are important discussions. So I don't think the governor or the attorney general regret spending that money on the behalf of taxpayers.'" (Hunt 1997). While it may be true that the Governor did not regret spending the money, it is unclear whether the taxpayers regretted it.

Summary of the Utah case

In conclusion, the Utah legislature passed numerous restrictions on abortion, strategically responding to the Court by anticipating and attempting to predict the direction the Supreme Court would take in its abortion decisions. After the decisions of *Webster* and *Casey*, both of which provided the opportunity for states to pass additional restrictions on abortion, the Utah legislature did not respond by merely following the new Supreme Court directives but by challenging the Court through enacting legislation that went beyond these new and previous Court rulings. With the legislature and the governor's office firmly in the hands of conservative Republicans, there was no political elite resistance to the legislation even if the attorney general and the legislative office of legal counsel warned that there could be legal challenges to state abortion legislation.

In addition, due to the Mormon Church's heavy influence in the state, which likely shaped the generally conservative nature of the public, it is not surprising that the public dissent was mild and inconsequential with no impact on electoral politics. Therefore even if the citizens of Utah had the opportunity to 'restrain' the legislature through a recall election or a ballot initiative, which was tried in Oregon (as the following section will show), it is unlikely that the public would have done so. Perhaps they would have rejected adopting a clearly unconstitutional law like SB-23, but it is likely they still would have supported abortion legislation consistent with US Supreme Court decisions, such as parental consent laws or a 24-hour waiting period.

OREGON

State political orientation and brief summary of state activity on abortion

As a western state, Oregon is known to have a strong independent/libertarian streak and retains some of the progressive era ethos in terms of its political orientation. Oregon has a biennial legislature; legislators still maintain careers outside the legislature and are not considered professional lawmakers. During the progressive era, the state adopted a number of direct democracy reforms including the ballot initiative, referendum and the recall. Both the ballot initiative and the referendum have been used to pass significant public policy measures including the death with dignity law, and anti-city sprawl measures. The state also has a relatively high voter participation rate compared to other states, which is due, at least in part, to the fact that the state has long used the 'vote by mail' approach to elections. The state has voted for the Democratic candidate in every presidential election since 1988. The state legislature was dominated by Democrats in the 1970's and early 1980's, but the Democrats slowly lost control to the Republicans, who gained a majority in the legislature in the 1990's, however, at that same time the governor's office was dominated by Democrats.

These features of Oregon politics are reflected in its approach to abortion policy. While abortion policy received increasing attention in the 1980's and early 1990's across the US, and the US Supreme Court rendered a series of decisions upholding restrictive state abortion policies, the Oregon legislature largely resisted taking advantage of these opportunities to pass new abortion laws. In addition, other state government actors, such as the Governor, acted to maintain access to abortion services. In addition, when faced with a series of ballot initiatives sponsored by anti-abortion organizations, the public rejected these restrictive abortion proposals.

The state asserts it will comply with Roe v Wade; voters reject attempt to ban the use of state funds for abortions- 1970's

In 1969, Oregon replaced its restrictive abortion law with a more liberal statute modeled on the American Bar Association recommendations. The 1969 law allowed abortions if the pregnancy posed a substantial risk to the woman's mental or physical health, if the pregnancy resulted from 'felonious intercourse' i.e., rape or if the child was to be born with serious mental or physical defect" (Laatz 1986). Four years later, *Roe v Wade* invalidated the Oregon law and the Oregon legislature did not immediately respond by amending the state statutes. Assistant Attorney General Lawrence R Young issued a statement that the state simply would abide by the guidelines set out in *Roe v Wade* (Ibid.). During the 1970's, conservative Oregon state legislators proposed a few bills that would have further regulated abortion, yet none of them made it out of committee for a vote.   In 1978, in response to the Supreme Court decisions about state funding of abortions, Oregon voters rejected an initiative that would have banned the use of state funds for abortions by 52 to 48 percent (Hortsch 1986).

Administrative rule restricting abortions struck down by Oregon Supreme Court, voters rejected attempts proposals to limit abortion- 1980-1989

In the 1980's there was virtually no state legislative action on abortion. The few attempts to limit abortion came from outside the state legislative area. Attempts occurred through ballot initiatives attempting to restrict abortions and an administrative rule created by the Department of Family Services in the early 1980's limiting how many abortions the state would pay for via state Medicaid funds.

The controversy over this administrative rule culminated in the Oregon Supreme Court case of *Planned Parenthood v Hegstrom (1984)*. The rule limited payment by Oregon Medicaid for elective abortions, stating that Oregon Medicaid would only pay for one elective abortion for women 18 years or older and only two abortions if the woman was under the age of 17 for her duration on Medicare. The only exception to the rule was if a physician certified in writing that the abortion was necessary to save the life of the mother. Planned Parenthood of Oregon asserted that the administrative rule violated a women's right to privacy under the Oregon Constitution, while the Department of Family Services argued that the US Supreme Court's prior ruling in *Harris v McRae,* upholding the validity of the Hyde Amendment, permitted the establishment of the rule (1984).

On appeal, the Oregon Supreme Court upheld the lower court's ruling, while providing a different justification for invalidating the law. Rejecting arguments provided by both the petitioners and respondents, the Court asserted that the agency actions violated the separation of powers between the executive and the legislative branch; stating that Department exceeded its authority by arbitrarily limiting the number of abortions women could obtain through Medicaid funding (*Planned Parenthood v Hegstrom* 1984 574). The only factors the Department could consider when providing services were the needs and financial status of the individual (Ibid.). By attempting to change the conditions under which someone could obtain services, the Court ruled that the Department usurped the legislative authority of the Oregon legislature when it enacted the rule (Ibid.).

The Oregon Supreme Court also effectively eliminated a potential opportunity for any federal court (including the US Supreme Court) to review the case by justifying its ruling on an improper division of power among state institutions, rather than basing its decision on rights guarantees under the US Constitution and US Supreme Court precedent. This case illustrates how the diffuse nature of the American judicial system (the "all courts" model) can both facilitate the diversity of existing abortion policies while also *limiting oversight opportunities* that would allow the US Supreme Court to shape comprehensive and uniform outcomes regarding abortion policy.

A few years after *Hegstrom,* local conservative interest groups turned their efforts towards the ballot initiatives, having failed in their attempts to get the Oregon legislature to enact restrictions on abortion. Since the US Supreme Court's ruling in *Harris v McRae* (1980), Oregon was one of only thirteen states still providing Medicaid-funded abortions. In 1986, Taxpayers for Responsible Government proposed an amendment to the Oregon constitution that would prohibit state payments for abortions (1986). In response, a pro-choice organization, Oregon Taxpayers for Choice campaigned against what was known as Ballot Measure 6 (Ibid.).

There was some controversy over the wording of the ballot measure and its estimated fiscal impact. Pro-choice activists were concerned that the broadly worded initiative would prohibit the teaching of abortion procedures in state medical schools. The Oregon Supreme Court eventually stepped in to evaluate the fiscal impact of the proposed measure (Hortsch 1986). The Court upheld the Secretary of State's estimation that the measure would save the state $243,000 dollars a year in abortion costs but would increase state expenditure by 2.6 million to support pregnancies to term (Ibid.). Although polls before the special election indicated a close split in the electorate over Measure 6, it failed decisively, 55% to 46% (Hortsch 1986). This is the second time a ballot initiative to restrict abortion failed.

Due to the failure of the ballot initiative, some pro-life organizations started to change their tactics, and Oregon Right to Life began raising large amounts of PAC money in order to support anti-abortion legislative candidates (Roche 2001). However, no significant abortion legislation was proposed or passed, largely because Democrats controlled the Oregon House and Senate.

The legislature fails to respond to Webster (1989), voters reject two more anti-abortion ballot measures

When the US Supreme Court handed down its *Webster* decision in July 1989, upholding state restrictions on abortion, there was speculation that the decision would provide the opportunity for states to pass more restrictive abortion laws. While the Oregon legislature did not respond to the decision by passing any legislation, legislators pledged to support abortion rights (Ames 1989).

Even though the USSC's *Webster* decision did not sanction state prohibition of abortion, Oregon's two major anti-abortion groups put forth anti-abortion ballot measures for the next election. The Oregon Citizen's Alliance initiative, Measure 8, outlawed all abortions except in cases of rape or incest, or if the life of the woman was threatened by the pregnancy. Oregon Right to Life's Measure 10 required parents of minors seeking abortion, to be notified 48 hours prior to the abortion procedure. The notification requirement would be waived in cases where the pregnancy had resulted from sexual or physical abuse confirmed by a doctor (Leeson 1990). Les Mabon, chair of the Oregon's Citizen's Alliance said, "There are those of us who are willing to try even if it is a risk or a reach. The *Webster* case opened up the door. And we want to get a test case before the court that will challenge *Roe v Wade* right at the heart [sic]" (1990). As was seen in the preceding section, Utah legislators made similar statements referencing *Webster* when introducing legislation to enact further restrictions on abortions in their state. As Justice Blackmun predicted in his dissent in *Webster,* these comments indicate that the *Webster* decision did signal that the states had both the opportunity and authority to establish further restrictions on abortion. However, the state chapters of Planned Parenthood and NARAL organized comprehensive voter education efforts that succeeded in getting their base to turn out and vote against the measures (Roche 2001). As Maura Roche, a longtime lobbyist for Oregon Planned Parenthood noted, Oregon NARAL, one of the 10 largest state NARAL's in the country, was well organized and had database of over 110,000 pro-choice registered voters, which in a state of about 1.7 million people, was "enough to move an election" (Ibid). Come Election Day, voters rejected Measures 8 and 10 ballot measures by decisive majorities (Wright 1990). The test case envisioned by Les Mabon and others never came to fruition.

Political shifts in the legislature do not lead to substantial changes in state abortion policy; Governor pledges financial support for family planning 1990-1998.

After conservative groups were defeated three times in their attempts to use the ballot initiative to change abortion policy in Oregon, these groups re-focused their efforts towards supporting and electing conservative legislators to the Oregon House. While this approach bore fruit in the 1990's, as political power in the House shifted from Democrat to Republican control, it still did not lead to any significant change in abortion policy, in spite of the new doors left open to the states by US Supreme Court decisions in *Rust* and *Casey* which upheld additional state and federal acts restricting abortion.

As stated above, after 25 years of Democratic control, Republicans gained control of the Oregon House while Democrats remained in control of the Senate (Roche 2001). The political shift in the House, however, did not spur a legislative response to *Rust v Sullivan*, which affirmed that federal monies could not fund discussions of abortion by family planning clinics receiving federal support. Roche, the Planned Parenthood lobbyist, believed that the legislative inaction was because Larry Campbell was elected as Speaker of the House. She characterized him as a pragmatist, who, as she put it, was "pro-life but not if it [was] going to cost the Republicans in the election cycle" (Roche 2001). He made it clear that there would be no pro-choice or anti-choice legislation coming out of the House (Roche 2001). While the legislature remained silent, the state's Democratic Governor, John Kitshaber requested a transfer of state family planning funds to county health clinics to compensate for these federal funds that were now made unavailable for abortion counseling (Hortsch 1991). Even after the USSC ruling in *Planned Parenthood v Casey* in 1992, which upheld a 24 hour waiting period and a parental consent law, the state legislature still took no significant action on abortion policy until 1995, when Republicans also gained control of the Senate. Even with both houses of the legislature in the hands of the Republicans, the only abortion legislation that had a floor vote in both houses was a parental notification bill that was almost identical to the ballot initiative that failed 5 years earlier. With intense lobbying by Planned Parenthood and a lack of such intensity by Oregon Right to Life, the bill failed in the House by six votes and the legislature took no further action on abortion (Roche 2001). No other significant legislative action was taken on abortion policy in the next three years (Athon 1995).

Summary of the Oregon case

In conclusion, the Oregon legislature made few attempts to increase restrictions on abortion, even though the US Supreme Court, began providing numerous opportunities for the state to do so through its decisions in the 1980's and 1990's and even after political control in the state legislature had shifted from Democrats to Republicans. With the exception of a failed parental notification bill, the only significant attempts to change abortion policy in the state came from outside the legislative process; an administrative rule, eventually struck down by the state Supreme Court, and three failed ballot initiatives supported by conservative anti-abortion groups.

Moreover, it was anti-abortion groups, primarily using ballot initiatives, which made direct attempts to take advantage of the USSC decisions in *Webster* and *Casey*. In addition, the institutional presence of the initiative process alleviated pressure on the Oregon legislature to respond. As one Democratic Oregon House Member speculated prior to the Supreme Court's 1989 *Webster* decision, "[if *Roe v Wade* is reversed]...the legislature will probably handle it like all other controversial issues--duck it and put it on the ballot" (Thalman 1989).

If the state legislature was reluctant to respond, other state government actors, such as the State Supreme Court and the Governor, responded *by rejecting* restrictive abortion policies sanctioned by the US Supreme Court. Even with the opportunity to bypass the legislature and legislate through use of the ballot initiative, the public repeatedly rejected attempts to impose greater restrictions on abortion. The strong voter education and turnout efforts by pro-choice groups and the lack of such coordinated organizational efforts by anti-abortion groups likely shaped the outcome of these measures.

With no strong federal-state party connections, no institutions that require federal-state cooperation (like the Bundesrat in Germany), and without overarching federal legislation pre-empting state action, the Oregon case, similar to Utah, illustrates how the US federal system is more diffuse as compared to Canada and Germany. This diffusion provided opportunities for states to diverge in the approaches to abortion policy. In the Oregon case, state actors largely chose to *ignore* Supreme Court invitations to enact restrictive abortion policies and *rejected* coercive attempts by the federal government to change state abortion policies (through redistribution of state funds to cover the loss of federal funds regarding abortion counseling).

COMPARISON AND ANALYSIS OF UTAH AND OREGON CASES AND OVERALL SUMMARY OF THE US CASE

From these two cases, we see how two states may take different approaches in responding to US Supreme Court decisions on abortion and how the various political and institutional features created the conditions enabling these varied approaches. First, the political orientation of the state may be a necessary but not sufficient condition to spur legislative activity on abortion. Republicans dominated the Utah state government and conservative legislators were intent on passing as many restrictive abortion policies as possible, regardless of their constitutionality. Conversely, when the Democrats controlled the Oregon legislature, there was only one, failed attempt to pass restrictive abortion policies, regardless of the opportunities provided by Supreme Court decisions. Political orientation was not a sufficient condition in order to motivate the legislature to act in Oregon; even when the Republicans gained control of the legislature, almost all attempts to pass restrictive abortion policies came from the outside via the ballot initiative. Sensitive to their electorate, who consistently expressed their opposition to abortion restrictions through ballot measures and faced with a well-organized pro-choice lobby, Oregon Republicans had little incentive to take up abortion and risk electoral fallout. In Utah, the Republicans had long dominated the legislature and faced few political challenges from the Democrats. This unchallenged political dominance coupled with muted public concerns over abortion restrictions, created conditions where there would be little political risk in taking a consistently aggressive stance on abortion policy.

Second, while the US Supreme Court provided opportunities for states to implement restrictive abortion policies, these decisions did not necessarily provide clear directives mandating states to change their laws. In addition, when the opportunity to provide judicial oversight arose, such oversight depended upon the willingness of actors to bring cases and pursue appeals; this meant that it took some time before the Supreme Court had the *opportunity* to exercise its influence over abortion policy (i.e. Utah) and there were no institutional rules *requiring* the court to do so. After passing a clearly unconstitutional law, it took seven years to bring Utah back in line with the Supreme Court's directives on abortion. The 'all-courts' model of the US legal system significantly increased the likelihood that judicial enforcement of Supreme Court rulings would take time since cases must pass through each level of the judicial system (and often back again). As in the case of Utah, the state exploited this extended time horizon by consolidating its political support and passing additional constitutionally suspect legislation during the litigation process. As the next chapter will detail, this long response time contrasts with the relatively shorter period in which the Constitutional Court in Germany exercised review of Bavaria's abortion legislation.

In addition, the Oregon case also shows how the all-courts system of judicial review can facilitate the ability of state courts to shield their decisions from Supreme Court review thereby limiting the opportunities for Supreme Court oversight and constraining its ability to provide comprehensive and uniform policy. The Oregon Supreme Court eliminated the potential for federal court review, by basing its decision on separation of powers concerns, rather than on Supreme Court precedent or its own interpretation of the constitutional guarantees. State supreme courts can 'inoculate' their decisions by removing any basis for Supreme Court review. The developments in

Oregon and Utah illustrate how the diffuse nature of the American judicial system, in which virtually all courts can review the constitutionality of laws, can both facilitate the diversity of existing abortion policies while also *limiting oversight opportunities* of the Supreme Court, restricting the *ability*, and therefore power, of the Court to shape comprehensive and uniform policy directives. In other words, while there may be fifty separate jurisdictions in which laws may arise and provide the potential for review, the participation of lower courts (particularly, state supreme courts) may limit the number of cases that can be appealed to the Supreme Court.

Lastly, in addition to the complexities of the US court system, the unwillingness of the US federal actors to determine a national policy on abortion and the absence of centralized federal criminal abortion regulations (in contrast to federal criminal abortion laws present in both Canada and Germany) also contributed to the conditions enabling the creation of state abortion polices free from significant outside political interference. Compared to the Canadian case, there was very little of the competitive dynamic played out between the US states and the federal government over abortion. Perhaps this can be explained by the fact that the federal logic as determined by US Constitution does not outline clear policy jurisdictions of the state and federal authorities. Historically the US Supreme Court itself has often negotiated the dividing line between federal and state power. It is unclear what constitutional authority the US federal government has regarding criminal sanction of abortion. Even when the US federal government attempted to direct state abortion policy by withholding federal funds from the states (an uncontested area of federal authority), as it did with Title X funds, a state could, as Oregon did, evade such sanction by providing its own funds to support abortion counseling thereby negating the attempted intrusion on state authority.

In conclusion, these features of the US case--the federal design, the judicial structure, the patchwork nature of the Supreme Court abortion decisions and the relatively limited powers of the US Supreme Court provided the conditions enabling both Oregon and Utah to produce significantly different state abortion policies.

CHAPTER 7
Germany

INTRODUCTION

This chapter examines how the presence and nature of particular institutional features of the German system have political consequences both for shaping court policy outcomes and for the compliance with those outcomes by other political elites.

Through the historical-institutional and legal analysis presented below, this chapter draws a number of conclusions regarding how particular institutional features significantly shaped political outcomes regarding abortion policy. First, direct and timely access to judicial review through abstract review and the constitutional complaint procedure repeatedly enabled the Constitutional Court to insert its policy recommendations into the political process. In regards to abstract review, this procedure has effectively institutionalized the ability of legislative actors to 'defer' to the Court, thereby enabling the Court to exercise significant influence in the political process. Second, the Basic Law's establishment of the Court's judicial review authority and that such review is definitive and binding on other political actors further enhances the Court's power. These features provide the context in which legislative actors demonstrated compliance by revising federal abortion laws to be consistent with the comprehensive and detailed policy recommendations outlined in the Court's Abortion II decision. Third, the comprehensive and detailed nature of the Basic Law itself, providing both positive and negative rights guarantees, in combination with the Court's authority to definitively interpret the Basic Law and

233

the availability of the constitutional complaint procedure, enabled doctors to file a constitutional complaint and allowed the Court to review and strike down restrictive Bavarian abortion legislation.

Lastly, the 'interlocking' design of federalism in Germany which explicitly grants most policy making authority to the Parliament (including criminal law) and implementation authority to the Länder (sub-national government) and the Court's constitutional authority to rule on disputes between the federal and land governments provides additional justification for the Court's decision to strike down the Bavaria law.

The organization of this chapter is as follows. The first section provides a brief historical background about abortion in Germany, including a brief discussion of the major Constitutional Court decisions on abortion. The second section examines in detail the significant constitutional issues framing abortion policy and directives on abortion policy as determined by the Constitutional Court. The third section examines the federal policy response, while the fourth and fifth sections focus on the Land legislative responses in Bavaria and North Rhine-Westphalia respectively. Each section summarizes the impact of the relevant institutional features and makes comparisons with the other cases in this study. The following chapter engages in a more complete comparison and evaluation of the three cases in this study.

During the period covered in this project, the socialist-left SPD (Social Democratic party) dominated North Rhine-Westphalia politics and the Land largely implemented the federal laws on abortion without attempting to limit access to abortion or enact onerous regulatory policies of abortion providers. The Land did make some attempts to insure access to abortion counseling and services by passing regulations to subsidize counseling centers. In addition, the language in their supporting legislation was more 'supportive' of the rights of the pregnant woman than in Bavaria.

In contrast, the conservative-right, CSU (CDU at the federal level) consistently dominated Bavaria politics and its party elites repeatedly supported increasingly onerous and restrictive abortion policies at both the federal and Land level. North Rhine-Wesphalia' implementation legislation closely followed the directives of federal law, adopting language that echoed both the federal criminal law and the Constitutional Court's directives. Bavaria, however, passed implementation regulations that exceeded the directives outlined in the federal legislation. The Constitutional Court eventually determined that Bavaria's regulations violated individual rights guarantees and that the Land exceeded its competences by legislating in an area in which the federal parliament had explicitly *chosen not* to legislate, thereby effectively preempting Länder from passing legislation on these issues.

Historical background

In Germany, a federal law, outlawing abortion, Sect. 218, had been on the books since the country's establishment in 1871 (Ferree, et al 26). Yet, by the end of the 19th century, interest groups, such as the Bund für Mütterschutz und Sexualreform (League for the Protection of Mothers and for Sexual Reform), were advocating for the legalization of abortion (Ibid). While there were attempts in the Bundestag under the Weimar Republic to repeal Sect. 218, these efforts failed (Ibid). During the Nazi regime, the government established a 'eugenic' justification for abortion and inserted a clause into the law that required the death penalty for abortion where the life of the German people was threatened (Ibid). After World War II, when the Federal Republic of Germany was established, the Basic Law explicitly declared the state's obligation to protect human life in order to protect against atrocities that occurred during war and the Nazi regime.

As in the US and Canada, abortion began to be recognized as a political issue in Germany in the 1960's. The existing West German law on abortion prior to 1969 was a blanket ban outlawing all abortions (Quaas 42). The law punished both the woman and the doctor or anyone else who performed an abortion and made no exceptions to save the life of the woman or for any other reason (Ibid.). In the FRG (West Germany) in 1969, the newly elected left leaning SPD w/ its governing partner (libertarian-free market) FDP announced they would appoint a commission of law professors to reform Sect. 218 (Feree, et al 32). Protests led by women's organizations called for the repeal of Sect. 218, and opposition organizations such as the Catholic Church mobilized against the attempt to reform/repeal the law (Ibid 60).

In the early 1970's, a number of different bills were presented in the Bundestag, and in 1974, approved by a narrow majority, abortion was decriminalized in the first trimester, with counseling required prior to the procedure (Ibid). Abortions due to medical necessity could be performed at any point during pregnancy. Immediately after the law was passed, five conservative CDU/CSU Land governments and 193 conservative members of the Bundestag made an abstract review appeal to the Constitutional Court regarding the law.

Meanwhile in East Germany, the GDR, with relatively little controversy, legalized abortion in the first trimester in 1972 (Ibid). The preamble of the East German law stated women's equality in education, occupation and in the family; the law guaranteed women the right to make their own decisions about whether or not to terminate a pregnancy (Van Zyl Smit 308). In the GDR, abortion was treated similarly to other medical care, and the state covered a woman's abortion expenses. Abortions were allowed only on an in-patient basis and required contraceptive counseling (Feree, et al 60). The GDR also provided extensive support services, such as child care, to families and pregnant women (Van Zyl Smit 308).

Brief summary of the Constitutional Court's major abortion decisions

In February 1975, responding to the abstract review appeal, the German Constitutional Court addressed the legality and constitutionality of federal abortion policy in its *Abortion I* decision. The Court invalidated Section 218a of the Abortion Reform Act. In its decision, the Court proclaimed general guidelines outlining the future conditions that would shape German abortion policy. The major provisions of the decision were that abortion would be permitted during the first twenty-three weeks of pregnancy only for medical (protecting the life or health of the mother) or eugenic (severe fetal deformity) indications. In addition, pregnancies resulting from criminal assault and subsequently terminated within the first twelve weeks of pregnancy would also be unpunishable. Lastly, "courts would have discretionary authority to withhold criminal sanctions with regard to the termination of pregnancy by physicians during the first twelve weeks in those situations where abortion is the only remaining measure so reasonably expected to relieve pregnant women of a 'grave hardship' " (Kommers 1977: 94 citing 39 BVerfGE 2-3). This exception was widely understood as a 'social indication' allowing a woman to obtain an abortion.

Political pressure by conservatives and Germany's reunification in 1989 eventually brought the abortion issue back to Parliament and eventually the Court, because of the significant differences between

East and West Germany abortion policy. The Reunification Treaty charged Parliament with creating a new law that would reconcile the West and East abortion laws (Van Zyl Smit 308). In June 1992, after months of parliamentary debate over numerous proposals, a compromise bill was passed by an absolute majority. While supporters believed the law met the obligation to protect fetal life dictated by the first *Abortion I* decision, nevertheless, the law never went into effect as conservative members of parliament made an abstract review appeal to the Constitutional Court resulting in the Court *Abortion II* decision in 1993.

In *Abortion II*, the Constitutional Court largely struck down the compromise law. The legislation had required mandatory counseling and waiting period, yet allowed women free choice during the first 12 weeks of pregnancy. The Court found that the decriminalization of abortion during these first 12 weeks was unconstitutional and violated the guarantee of life in the Basic Law. In addition, the Court found the counseling provision was insubstantial in protecting the rights of the fetus, offered its own directives on what the counseling provision should look like and prohibited state medical insurance from covering abortions, although welfare provisions could pay for abortions sought by indigent women. Lastly, the Court found that the social support measures to help women raise children, such as childcare funding, were encouraging, and suggested additional policies in this area to be adopted by Parliament.

COURT ABORTION POLICY DIRECTIVES

State protection of fetal life and the rights of the woman

The German Constitutional Court's major constitutional justification for its policy pronouncements in the *Abortion I* decision focused on the determination of fetal life and the extent to which the state is obliged to protect it. In the case, the Court examined Articles 1 and 2 of Basic Law to determine the status and rights of the fetus. Article 1, Sect. 1 obliges the state to 'respect and protect' the dignity of man and article 2, sect. 2, of the Basic Law, states, "Everyone shall have the right to life and the inviolability of person." The Court read these two guarantees in concert, and through its referral to 'objective values', the Court asserted that the State is affirmatively required to protect and secure human life

(Kommers 1977: 94). The Constitutional Court interpreted 'everyone' in Art. 2 to include all living human entities. By providing such a broad interpretation, the Court could afford constitutional protection to unborn as well as born life (Ibid). The Court therefore held that the Basic Law Article 1 safeguards of human dignity and life require legal protection of the 'developing life', or the fetus. In addition, those objective values, which also emanate from the Basic Law, oblige the state to act or protect the 'rights' of the fetus from encroachment of others, particularly the mother (Klein-Schonnenfeld115, citing BverfGE 39; 1,42).

Contrasting with the vague or absent positions of US and the Canadian Supreme Courts respectively, the German Constitutional Court took a clear position on when human life begins. "Life in the sense of the historical existence of a human individual exists according to definite biological, physiological knowledge in any case from the 14th day after conception" (Kommers 1977: 94, citing BvefGE 39, 37). In addition, the Court understood the fetus to be a part of a continual developing process that did not allow differentiated states of protection by the Basic Law (BverfGE 39, 1, 37). "The process of development which has begun at that point in time is a continuous process," said the Court, "which cannot be sharply demarcated and does not allow a precise division of the various stages in the development of human life" (Kommers 1977: 94, citing BverfGE 39: 37).[45]

Having deduced these starting principles, the German Constitutional Court found the federal legislation (Sect. 218) unconstitutional because it did not adequately balance the rights of the fetus with those of the mother. The Constitutional Court acknowledged that pregnancy clearly would fall within the arena of private relations constitutionally protected by Art.2, Sect. 2 of the Basic Law which says, "Everyone shall have the right to the free development of his personality in so far as he does not violate the rights of others or offend against the constitutional order or the moral code."

---

[45] This understanding of fetal development and the state's role in protecting the fetus is quite different from the United Supreme Court's discussion in *Roe* and it seems quite possible that above statement is an overt critique of the US trimester framework.

However, given the Basic Law's hierarchy of values and rights of which human dignity and life is preeminent, the Court ruled that the state is obliged to provide more legal protection and status to the fetus than the woman (Klein-Schönfeld115-6, BverfGE 39; 34,38,51). " 'Es [das sich im Mutterleib entwickelnde Leben] genießt grundsätzlich für die gesamte Dauer der Schwangerschaft Vorrang vor dem Selbstbestimmungsrecht der Schwangeren. It [the life developing in the mother's body] fundamentally takes priority over the pregnant woman's right to self-determination throughout the entire period of pregnancy.' " (BverGE 39; 1, 44, translation Feree, et al. 3).

Since Article 2 does not provide an absolute right to a 'free development' of a woman's personality, the Constitutional Court "rejected any theory which would treat the decisions of a woman not to become pregnant in the first instance on the same level of constitutional protection as her decision to destroy a fetus once pregnancy has occurred" (Kommers 1977:95). The Constitutional Court again insisted that rights of the woman and the fetus had to be considered in light of 'human dignity', the underlying guiding principle of the Basic Law (Ibid). As noted above, the Court ruled that the under Article 1, the state is not only obliged not to infringe upon 'developing life' but required to protect such life from harm by third parties, which includes the pregnant woman herself (Kommers 1977:95-96). Therefore the rights of the woman were to be protected *as long as* they do not violate the rights of the fetus.

In its 1993 *Abortion II* decision, the court's language is even more forceful in its insistence that the pregnant woman has an obligation to carry out the pregnancy, "The fundamental rights of a woman do not mandate the general suspension of a duty to carry out a pregnancy, even within a limited time frame. However, a woman's constitutional rights permit--and in certain cases require--recognition of exceptional circumstances which such a duty shall not be imposed upon her..."(BverfGE 88, Lëitsatze (headnote) 7). Regardless of the rights a woman has regarding the free development of her personality and any privacy rights inherent in that right, the Court remained steadfast in the priority of protecting the developing life of the fetus over the rights of the pregnant woman. In both the Abortion I and II decisions, the Constitutional Court found the essential constitutional issue regarding abortion regards the constitutional protection of life, which includes fetal life, and the duty of the state (and the woman, with few exceptions) to protect that life.

Role and duty of the State in abortion policy

Given the duty of the State to uphold the objective value to protect life in the Basic Law, in *Abortion II,* the Germany Constitutional Court said the State must "fulfill its duty of protection by adopting adequate measures setting legal and factual standards whose objective -- in consideration of conflicting legal interests --is to provide for appropriate and effective protection (minimum protection)" (Lëitzsatze (headnote) 7). The Court re-asserted its position from *Abortion I* that the State has an affirmative duty not only to protect the fetus from state action but from other actors, including the pregnant woman. Therefore, the State was obliged to establish a regulatory scheme including both preventive and 'repressive' protection (Ibid.). These constitutional requirements frame the Court's instructions on abortion counseling for 'unindicated' or 'counseled' abortions. The Court declared Parliament's 1992 legislation decriminalizing 'counseled only' abortions unconstitutional because it conflicted with the State's constitutional duty in Article 1, to 'respect the dignity of man.' (Kommers1994: 19).

Consistent with its 1974 decision, in *Abortion II,* the Court held that legal exceptions to the general criminal prohibition of abortion could be permitted only when the duty of carrying the fetus to term would create an 'unreasonable burden' upon the woman. These exceptions could be for medical, embryo-pathological or criminological indications or in other situations (a counseling time-based model) where circumstances create a burden so difficult that carrying the pregnancy to term would go beyond 'reasonable sacrifice'. While the 1992 federal legislation stated that an operating physician was not required to determine the presence of an indication if a woman completed a counseling session within the first twelve weeks, the Court struck this provision down, stating that the State may not leave to the pregnant woman the judgment of whether said circumstance merits an exception (Walther 393) The Court observed that "...[i]f 'merely counseled' abortions could be justified solely upon the woman's own assessment of her reasons with no requirement of external review, the protection of unborn life would be dispensed with. Declaring a 'merely counseled' abortion is *nicht rechtswirdig* [not unlawful/illegal] despite the lack of ascertainable [independent] grounds would be understood as a general 'allowance' of abortion" (Walther 393 citing BverfGE 88 D III 2b aa). It would be easy to interpret the Court's determination as a paternalistic and giving little consideration of the rights of the woman to determine the severity of her own experience. Yet, the Court justified its assertion by noting that the abortion law could not contravene traditional concepts of criminal law by allowing the woman to be the 'judge' in her own case.[46]

The Constitutional Court argued therefore that decriminalizing the act of abortion by allowing a time-based counseling model would be incompatible with the state's duty to protect unborn life. The basis of legal justification in criminal law must be made on factual grounds. However, the legislature had altered its policy from the earlier social indication to the counseling model in the 1992 legislation in part due to the difficulty in determining factual, justifiable reasons for permitting abortion, hence the time-based exception (BverfGE 88 D II 2). The Court stated that under Parliament's legislation, only 'unreasonable burdens' could render the act of abortion 'justified'. Due the Basic Law obligations set out in Article 1 and 2, the Court found that 'merely counseled' abortions would have to remain unjustified and unlawful. The Basic Law prohibited the state from condoning abortion under any circumstances, though abortions obtained for criminological or medical indications could be characterized as 'not illegal'. Counseled abortions would have to remain <u>unlawful</u>, but could go <u>*unpunished*</u> if the proper procedures were followed. The majority of the Court held that "...even though the woman's decision will not be criminalized, it may not be viewed as legal; and the 'remaining legal order' must bring this fact to

---

[46] To allow decriminalization--'nicht rechtswirdig', within the first twelve weeks of pregnancy of abortion would also be contrary to the 'justification' doctrine in German criminal law. Any act that satisfies the elements of a crime may be not illegal, if justifiable reasons are demonstrated for committing the crime. This is analogous to the concept of justification in Anglo criminal common law. For example, if a defendant has killed someone, yet can prove he has met the elements necessary to prove self-defense, the killing is justified, and therefore a 'legal' or 'justified' killing. The defendant, therefore, will not be guilty of committing a criminal act.

the general public's consciousness" (Walther 392; BverfGE 88 D III 2,3). The Court stated that the moral and legal wrongfulness of abortion must be reflected not only through application of the law, but through the actions of any actors involved in the process of obtaining an abortion, including other public institutions, such as schools, and even private broadcasting (BverfGE 88 D I 3d; Walther 393).

In addition to keeping 'counseled' abortions 'illegal', the Constitutional Court also asserted in *Abortion II* that the State must provide additional policies indicating the state's duty to protect and support life. The Court supported Parliament's Pregnancy and Family Support Act, which was passed in conjunction with the abortion legislation, yet it also believed that additional legislation need to be established to support women in carrying their pregnancies to term (Kommers 1994: 21). The Court justified its position by invoking Article 6 of the Basic Law: "1. Marriage and family enjoy the special protection of the state; 2. The Care and upbringing of children are a nature right of, and a duty primarily incumbent upon the parents, 3. The national community shall watch over their endeavors in this respect...4. Every mother shall be entitled to protection and care of the community".   The Court detailed a variety of possible policies Parliament could provide in order to support pregnant women, such as; prohibiting landlords from terminating leases due to family size; easing credit repayment requirements for families after the birth of a child; and rewriting social security laws to excuse absences from the workforce due to pregnancy and child rearing (Neuman 281).

In addition, due to Basic Law provisions that obligate the state to further the equal participation of women in working life and enable the woman's right to the development of her personality, the Court asserted the State had to insure a women's job security or protect her from financial hardships during or after pregnancy: "The legislature [must] provide the basis for a balance between family activities and gainful employment and guarantee that the task of raising children in a family will not lead to any disadvantage in the workplace" (Kommers 1994: 21, translation 88 BverfGE 260). According to the Court, the state must adopt "legal and actual measures designed to enable both parents simultaneously to raise their children and pursue gainful employment and to return to their jobs without losing the opportunity for professional advancement following periods of child care" (Kommers 1994: 21-2, translation).

Provider-related abortion policies

While the Court, in its *Abortion II* decision, agreed with the legislature that the mandatory counseling procedure should indicate the state's intention to protect the unborn, the Court's ruling exceeded the legislature's intent by stating that the entire regulatory scheme must wholly attempt to protect unborn life. The Court, however, recognized that given the social reality women would continue to seek abortions regardless of whether or not the procedure was criminalized. The Court asserted that the state must not make an enemy of the pregnant woman and to provide assistance to her -- 'hilfe statt straffe' ('help not punishment'). In order to keep the woman open to the possibility of carrying the pregnancy to term, counseling procedures should be 'result open' (ergebnisoffen), thereby increasing the State's chances to convince her and 'win her over' (BverfGE, D II, D III 4).

The Court directed that counseling functions had to remain separate from the performance of the abortion procedure and that Land governments would authorize and regulate advice/counseling centers. These counseling centers would provide certification that the women had completed counseling, and maintain proper records proving that they fulfilled the requirements. This certificate would be a required prerequisite to contacting a doctor for performing the abortion procedure. The counselor would have the right to withhold the certificate if he/she felt that the woman did not fully engage in the counseling session, and the counselor could require continuation of the counseling over a number of days and even ask other individuals close to the woman (the husband or other family members) to attend the session(s) (Klein-Schonnenfeld131).

The Court specified in detail what a constitutional permissible abortion counseling session should look like. The counselor was required to explain to a pregnant woman that only 'unreasonable' demands would enable her to obtain an abortion. In addition, the counselor was to assist the woman in obtaining any assistance she might need.

> "... [T]he counselor must enter a dialogue with the woman, employing scientifically developed methods of 'conflict counseling'; an uninvolved, 'it's up to you' demeanor is unacceptable.... [C]onflict counseling' requires that the

woman reveal her motives; and while she cannot be compelled to do so, counseling must work towards this goal. Furthermore, the woman must be informed of the social and other support measures offered by the state, or by institutions like churches and foundations" (Walther, translation of decision section D IV, 1-3; 397-398).

In this scenario, there is little indication that the Court interprets 'counseling' in the therapeutic/psychological context of listening to the concerns of a person non-judgmentally. Yet, even though the counselors were to articulate the significance of life, the "ultimate responsibility" in deciding to have the abortion was to rest with the woman without threat of punishment. "In other words, the illegality' verdict on the woman (and her doctor) seeking a 'merely counseled' abortion must not be carried to the bitter end" (Walther, 1993). Although the Court's directions were specific that counseling should be 'result open', this requirement still left the potential opportunity of coercion or shaming by counselors. Even though the decision to terminate a pregnancy was ultimately that of the woman, the counselor, under the Court's terms, clearly would have significant influence in determining whether an abortion will be procured, since he/she could withhold the certificate and subjectively determine whether or not the woman 'actively' participated in the counseling. As seen in the subsequent section on sub-national implementation of the revised law, Bavaria passed onerous supporting counseling legislation outlining the process.

In regards to 'counseled' abortions, the German Constitutional Court also found that doctors also played a significant role in protecting the life of the fetus. The doctor had to insure that woman received counseling and could provide a certificate, to observe a three-day waiting period after the counseling before performing the procedure, and to conclude that the woman had not been pressured into having the abortion (Neuman 284). The doctor's role and determinations were still open to state scrutiny and threat of prosecution, since 'counseled' abortions were still 'illegal' (Klein-Schonnenfeld131-2). These counseling provisions are somewhat comparable to the informed consent policies reviewed by the US Supreme Court in its decisions, although the US Court was far less specific and proscriptive in its policy-making than its German counterpart.

Funding Regulations

Lastly, in *Abortion II*, the German Constitutional Court asserted that state medical insurance should not cover the cost of 'counseled' abortions, if the woman was financially able to pay for the procedure. The Court reasoned that if the abortion was 'unjustified', then the state would be participating in 'illegal' acts though its financial support (Neuman 287). Therefore, no insurance benefits could cover the procedure itself, any follow-up services, or allow sick pay to cover job absences. Yet, in order to prevent poor women from seeking illegal abortions the German Constitutional Court permitted the use of welfare payments for women unable to pay for the costs of abortion (Walther 399).

Summary of German Court's directives on abortion policy

The German Constitutional Court's abortion decisions relied on the specificity of various Basic Law guarantees in order to assert which abortion policies would be constitutionally appropriate. The detail and comprehensiveness of the Basic Law provided a strong basis for the Court's decision-making, which is in stark contrast to the limited rights afforded and detailed in either the US constitution or Canadian Charter of Freedoms. In addition, neither the US or Canadian constitutions clearly provide 'positive rights' or obligations on the state to effectuate individual protections as the Basic Law does. In addition to the Constitutional Court's uncontested authority of judicial review, the detail and scope of the Basic Law provides compelling support for the Court to issue comprehensive and detailed review of abortion policy. The Court's decisions specifying *how* abortion should be criminally defined and *what* supplemental policies the state is obliged to adopt due to constitutional guarantees effectively limited Parliament's options in its revision of the federal abortion laws. The following section reveals that the Parliament largely accepted the Court directives in its reform of the law after the *Abortion II* decision.

FEDERAL POLICY RESPONSE

Development of abortion policy at the Federal Level-1970's

In February of 1972, the federal government introduced its draft to reform the criminal abortion law (Section 218). The draft allowed abortions under certain 'indications' (conditions) and required a doctor to perform the procedure. These indications included a medical indication, preserving health and life of mother; a eugenic indication, preventing birth of a seriously defective child; an ethical-criminological indication, preventing birth caused by sexual assault; and a social indication, in which pregnancy and birth would seriously burden the life and well-being of the mother. The last two indications *could only* justify an abortion be performed in the first trimester of the pregnancy, as long as the pregnant woman submitted to professional counseling and a licensed physician performed the operation (Ibid.). In addition, under the other indications no criminal penalties would be imposed if the abortion took place during the first three months of pregnancy as long as the women sought counseling from a doctor before obtaining the procedure. Due to subsequent federal elections, this draft was never voted upon, and after the elections, the Federal government withdrew this proposal. In the absence of federal legislation, four competing proposals were debated in parliament.

The proposals ranged from highly restrictive 'indication' models (similar to what was outlined above) allowing abortions only under limited circumstances, to a more liberal ''fristenlosung' (time period regulation) model. The Bundestag debated for a long time and held numerous hearings on these proposals. While the conservative CDU/CSU minority faction may have supported a limited version of the indication model, the socialist-liberal SPD-FDP coalition, holding a majority in the Bundestag but not in the Bundesrat, was able to pass its 'time period' draft through Parliament by a slim majority over the objections of most CDU/CSU members (Quaas 44).

This time period regulation criminalized abortion the 13th day after conception, if the procedure was not performed by a doctor. In addition, the pregnant woman must have also received counseling before the procedure; otherwise, the doctor could be punished. Counseled abortions could only be performed during the first trimester, after which only medically indicated or necessary abortions would be allowed for up to 22 weeks. A separate expert authority had to confirm the presence of such indications (Van Zyl Smit, 305). Two weeks after the vote in the Parliament, on July 11, 1974, the CDU/CSU minority in Parliament made an abstract review appeal to the Constitutional Court over the constitutionality of the new abortion legislation. Five CDU/CSU Länder governments subsequently joined the appeal. (Klein-Schonnenfeld115) (Quaas 46).

With the presence of the abstract review procedure, there was little incentive for compromise to take place within Parliament if the opposition believed it would receive a favorable opinion from the Court. Why compromise if you can get your preferred policy approved by the Court? Employing an 'abstract' review appeal is essentially a constitutional means to 'defer' to the Court thereby enabling political elites in the minority an opportunity to have the Court strike down majority approved legislation. It gives the political minority a 'second chance' at getting their preferred policy approved.

Six months later on February 25, 1975, about two months after the law was to take effect, the Constitutional Court struck the legislation down as unconstitutional for violating Article 1 and 2 of the Basic Law (guarantees of human dignity and the right to life). As outlined in the previous section, the Court determined that life begins 12 days after conception and the developmental process of life cannot be subject to such time differentiation that would allow abortions to be constitutional. The Court interpreted Article 2's guarantee of a right to life to 'everybody', to include every living entity, which included the born and the unborn, and therefore the time indication law violated these constitutional principles.

Reform of Federal abortion policy as response to Abortion I decision

Parliament quickly responded by enacting new legislation closely adhering to the limitations outlined by the Court's decision. Parliament passed the newly revised criminal legislation, Revised Abortion Act, on May 18th, 1976 (Quaas 50). Since the court clearly found the periodic model of abortion unconstitutional, Parliament was left with fashioning a law based on the indication model which included protections for the fetus, while allowing for exceptions to consider the health or situations of the woman (Esser 374). The Court's determination that life began 12 days after conception and that the constitution protects life at all stages required parliament to keep abortion criminalized in all cases, and therefore the revised law did not include decriminalization of abortion within the first three months of pregnancy (Van Zyl Smit 305). Both the pregnant woman and anyone who attempted an abortion upon her would be held culpable and punished under the law. While the act of abortion remained 'criminal' it was not 'punishable' if the pregnant woman consented to an abortion performed by a doctor and if certain indications were present (Ibid.).

These indications were to be consistent and 'universal' justifications to exempt a woman and her doctor from punishment (Esser 375). Medically indicated abortions were not punishable if "the abortion of the pregnancy is according to medical knowledge advisable, considering the current and future living conditions of the pregnant woman, in order to avert danger to her life or the danger of a grave interference with the physical or mental condition of her health, and which danger cannot be averted by other means reasonable to her" (Quaas 50, translation of BGBL (BundesGesetzBlatt) 1976 I, at 1213 Section 218a, Part 1, subsection 2 of the Criminal Law). This indication included not only physical conditions but also psychological conditions due to pregnancy and the possible hardships following birth (Esser 376).

The following 'indications' also had to meet the above requirements: embryo-pathological/eugenic (birth defects), criminological, and sociological-general emergency. The embryo-pathological/eugenic indication would be present if "strong reasons argue for the presumption that the child, owing to a hereditary disposition or harmful influences before the birth, would suffer from an irremediable injury to its state of health which would be so severe that the continuation of pregnancy could not be demanded of the pregnant woman" (Quaas 51, translation of Sect.218a (2) 1). The criminal indication was present if rape crimes were committed against the woman or child (rape, including statutory rape) (Ibid.). The last indication, the 'medical-social' indication, allowed abortion "in order to avert the danger of a predicament which (a) would be so severe that the continuation of the pregnancy could not be demanded of the pregnant woman, and (b) cannot be averted by other means reasonable to the pregnant woman" (Quaas 51, translation Sect. 218 (2) 3,a,b). This emergency indication included other unforeseen problems which could overwhelm a pregnant woman, and reflected the position of the Constitutional Court that, "the overall situation of the pregnant woman and her family can generate conflicts of such magnitude that, beyond a certain limit, the measures of the criminal law cannot force further sacrifice in favor of unborn life" (Eser 376, translation of 39 BverfGE 49 (1975). Overall, these revisions to the federal law reveal that Parliament hewed closely to the Court's policy directives set out in its Abortion I decision.

Lastly, the law did not punish a woman if she received counseling from a doctor and obtained an abortion within the first 22 weeks of pregnancy, although this section did not allow the same doctor to perform the abortion (Esser 377). This 'personal exception' essentially allowed a woman not to be prosecuted for having sought an abortion abroad and some critics of the law said that it actually encouraged women to seek abortions abroad (Ibid.)

In addition to Sect. 218a, Parliament enacted Sect. 218b, which provided additional rules and guidelines to regulate the abortion counseling process (social and medical) consistent with the Constitutional Court's decision. Social counseling would occur three days prior to the procedure and was intended to provide early intervention and to decrease the rates of abortion over time (Esser 378). The woman would be "instructed as to the public and private aid available to pregnant women, mothers and children, especially with regard to such aid as eases the continuation of pregnancy and the circumstances of mother and child, and (2) being advised by a doctor as to the medically significant aspects" (Quaas 51, translation Sect. 218b (1)1,2). An officially recognized agency or a qualified physician was to perform the counseling session (Ibid.). Any doctor could provide medical counseling, since doctors usually conducted pre-operative counseling for other surgical procedures (Esser 378). Doctors were required to ensure that the performance of the abortion was consistent with a particular indication and they could be held liable if they performed an abortion in the absence of the required counseling, regardless of whether or not the abortion was indicated (Ibid. 379). The pregnant woman, however, would not be held liable under this section.

Finally, the legislation also outlined where abortions could be legally performed, in order to limit the rise of for-profit 'abortion clinics' and to insure the woman would be legally and medically protected should complications arise (Esser 379*)*. Länder varied in their implementation of this part of the legislation. "Many [Länder] authorized other establishments, especially private practitioners, to perform abortions soon after the reform. The more conservative states of the South [Bavaria], however, persisted in limiting abortions to hospitals. If an abortion justified by an indication [was] not performed in an authorized facility, the doctor, but not the pregnant woman, [could] be fined for an administrative violation (Ordnungswirdrigkeit)" (Esser 379).

As the following sections indicate, Bavaria was one of those southern Länder that created detailed administrative rules limiting the number of facilities allowed to perform abortions, whereas North Rhine-Westphalia essentially implemented the federal law as it was and did not enact strict regulations limiting abortion facilities. Given these disparities among the Länder, in the late 1970's and early 1980's women began traveling from more restrictive to less restrictive Länder and even out of the country (referred to abortion tourism) in order to obtain abortions, particularly socially indicated abortions (Van Zyl Smit 307). In addition, given that doctors were largely held responsible for determining under what conditions abortions could be performed, some doctors, "found that the burden that was being placed upon them was severe and that they did not always know what in practice would be expected of them; the majority of them did not expect to be prosecuted even if they did not follow the new law to the letter" (Ibid.). Given this complexity, some doctors were unwilling to perform abortions.

Doctors held criminally responsible for abortions; pressure to reform Federal Law S218 increases in the 1980's.

In 1982, a new federal election resulted in a new conservative-libertarian CDU/FDP coalition government, a shift from the previous 'left' leaning SPD/FDP government. The new government wanted to enact a law clarifying the counseling requirement for abortions; one that stated that the directive of counseling should be the protection of unborn life (Birkenfeld-Pfeiffer 123) However, the FDP, the CDU's coalition partner, would not agree to such directives (Ibid.). While drafts regarding the proposed legislation circulated over the years, the partners in the federal government could not agree upon any significant policy. This conflict presages the second debate and reform of the federal abortion laws, which ended up significantly focusing on the 'counseling' component and shows how cross-party pressures/coalition governments limits the ability of governing elites to enact their preferred policy objectives.

The pressure to reform the law did not abate, as conservatives argued whether the government should fund 'socially indicated' abortions and if such abortions are 'illegal', but 'permissible' (as had been determined by the Constitutional Court). In response to political pressure, particularly from southern Land governments like Bavaria (ruled by the CDU's sister party, the CSU), the federal government created a federal fund to provide monetary support to women who would have aborted their fetus due to a social emergency situation, thus trying to motivate them to not abort the fetus (Quaas 56).

Prosecution of doctors became a reality in the 1980's, when in 1988 in Memmigen, Bavaria, Dr. Horst Theissen was tried and convicted of performing abortions without the proper indications present (Klein-Schonnenfeld124). The case began as one of suspected tax evasion by Dr. Horst Theissen. When tax officers took his files as evidence, prosecutors sought out and interviewed women who had obtained abortions from him (Ibid). In order to avoid further legal proceedings, most women received an order of summary punishment and paid a fine (Ibid.). The initial case against Dr. Theissen began in September 8th, 1988, in which he cooperated and admitted that he performed out-patient abortions when no such procedures were allowed in Bavaria (Ibid.). He had also performed abortions on women without following the regulations of having proof of counseling and/or obtaining a second medical opinion. During his trial, the women who had been interviewed were compelled to be witnesses against Dr. Theissen. They could not refuse to answer since they already received summary punishment and could not be punished twice for their crime (Ibid.). After six months of a very public and drawn out trial, where the 'state of need' or socially indicated abortions became the focal point of the case, Thiessen was found guilty (Ibid.). Eventually after an appeal and a retrial, the Federal Supreme Court (Bundesgerichtsthof) found Dr. Theissen guilty on 36 counts of criminal abortion (from an original 79) and sentenced him to 18 months' probation (reduced from an original sentence of 2 years and six months) and a 3 year suspension of practice as a doctor by (Walther 388). The notoriety and attention that this trial received across Germany put significant pressure upon the federal government to amend Section 218.

Reunification of East and West Germany leads to revision of federal abortion law.

The notoriety of the Memmigen trial, and the failure of the coalition Federal government to revise Section 218, led the Bavarian government to file an abstract review appeal in 1990 asserting that the 1976 amendments to Section 218 were unconstitutional (Prützel-Thomas 473). Once again, failure to get their preferred policy enacted at the federal level spurred political elites to appeal to the Constitutional Court via the abstract review procedure. After years of asserting that abortion tourism and the social indication model allowed women to procure abortions too easily, the CSU-led Bavarian government claimed that the 1976 law essentially allowed abortion on demand, and if abortion was illegal then it should not be paid for by state health insurance (Prützel-Thomas 473). However, a larger political issue in Germany had to be resolved at the time, which was the reunification of East and West Germany. The historical event of German reunification altered the course of amending the federal abortion law when the federal government took on the responsibility to reconcile West and East Germany's abortion laws (Ibid). Therefore, the Constitutional Court put the Bavarian appeal on hold (Van Zyl Smit 307).

The Unification Treaty had allowed the more liberal former East German laws on abortion to continue operating until Parliament passed a new federal abortion law. Article 31(4) of the Unification Treaty required Parliament to pass a new law "which would protect the unborn life and would allow pregnant women, by means of legally guaranteed entitlements to counseling and social assistance, to cope with conflict situations in a way which would be in conformity with the constitution" (Van Zyl Smit 308). Parliament faced substantial hurdles as the former GDR law was much more liberal than its West German counterpart, yet the German Constitutional Court *Abortion I* ruling of 1975 essentially asserted that the state had a constitutional duty to do its utmost in protecting unborn life (Prützel-Thomas 468). This constitutional requirement was in direct opposition to the former GDR law that allowed abortion on demand within the first 12 weeks of pregnancy

(Ibid.). Parliament was charged with passing the new reconciliation abortion law by December 31, 1992 (Klein-Schonnenfeld125).

Over the next two years, Parliament debated and discussed a number of reform proposals. Every major party submitted a proposal, and they ranged from greater liberalization to greater restrictions on abortion. The 'liberal' proposals, not surprisingly, came from the FDP, SDP, the Greens and the PDS (former communist party). The most 'liberal' proposals came from the Greens and PDS who wanted to remove abortion from the criminal code entirely, and the PDS went even further by proposing an explicit right to abortion (Prützel-Thomas 476). Neither of these proposals received serious consideration. The more moderate SDP legislation allowed abortion on demand within the first 12 weeks, without requiring counseling services. In addition, the SDP legislation proposed removing abortion from the penal code, therefore removing any threat of criminal sanction. The legislation would replace Section 218 with social legislation providing resources for families and pregnant women (Ibid.). More conservative than the SPD legislation, the FDP proposal allowed abortion on demand during the first 12 weeks of pregnancy and only after women completed a required counseling session (475). It also upheld criminalization of abortion under Sect. 218 of the criminal code, in order to comply with the Constitutional Court's *Abortion I* decision of 1976, which required criminalization in order to indicate the state's moral disapproval of abortion as dictated by the Basic Law Article 1 guarantee (Ibid.).

The majority party in parliament, the CDU/CSU, had difficulty presenting a united position and policy; therefore, two main CDU/CSU proposals were presented (Ibid. 475). The first, a backbencher's[47] proposal, strengthened existing abortion regulations. Specifically, it kept abortion criminalized, removed all indications except for medically necessary abortions, and required the fetus to be treated as a living person (Ibid.). The 'Majority proposal' of the CDU/CSU (called that because the majority of party members supported it) allowed only medical indications and psycho-social hardship as justifications for legal abortion (Ibid.). The doctor was to be responsible for ultimately deciding whether an abortion should be performed and for providing

---

[47] A backbencher is a member of the ruling party in a parliamentary system that does not hold a ministerial/executive office position in government.

documentation proving such justification (Ibid.). The CDU/CSU proposed bills were not reflective of popular sentiment on abortion policy, as a national *Der Spiegel*[48] poll in the summer of 1992 indicated that 76 percent of Germans "supported a woman's right to an abortion in the first 12 weeks of a pregnancy." (475).

Even though there were two competing CDU/CSU proposals to choose from, some CDU members did not support either proposal. Most of these party members were female members who did not believe that the responsibility and final decision for abortion should be with the doctor. Instead they argued that the pregnant woman herself should have the final decision. These female legislators faced severe criticism and pressure from their party to support the 'Majority proposal' (Klein-Schonnenfeld125). These defectors, however, supported the FDP draft during the first reading of the bills in the fall of 1991.

The CDU party leadership threatened that the 'defecting' legislators should not be re-elected and that there should be strict party line voting on the proposals. One of the 'defectors' was Rita Süssmuth, a deputy party chair, was called 'un-Christian' by CDU cabinet member (Prützel-Thomas 476). However, the party leadership eventually backed down from its threats and announced a free 'matter of conscience' vote. This action was consistent with past practice regarding legislation with strong moral/ethical content (Prützel-Thomas 475). Similarly, the Conservative party in Canada made the same 'free vote' concession to their members when attempting to reform Section 251 of the Canadian criminal code in 1988. It seems that when faced with highly controversial legislation, even parliamentary governments will seek institutional mechanisms such as having 'free votes', which enable them to defer accountability on to individual members.

With the announcement of the free vote and the 'defectors' unwilling to support the existing CDU/CSU proposals, a 'Group Proposal' was created and ultimately passed. The 'Group Proposal' arose out of the fact that since there were so many varying proposals, none would garner a majority of votes in Parliament. Therefore, all were sent to a special parliamentary committee for re-consideration, the

---

[48] This is major national news magazine in Germany, roughly equivalent to Time in the US or McClean's in Canada.

"Protection for Unborn Life" committee (Ibid. 476). The SPD and the FDP female members of the committee worked together to create the 'Group Proposal', which was similar to the original FDP proposal. This group agreed to start with the principle, dictated by the Constitutional Court, that abortion legislation must uphold the Basic Law's instruction that the state's duty was to protect unborn life. However, the proposed legislation veered away from the Court's instructions as to *how* the legislature should carry out that duty (Klein-Schonnenfeld125-6). The proposal and eventual legislation allowed a woman to obtain an abortion within the first twelve weeks of pregnancy after required counseling (Ibid. 126 and Prützel-Thomas 477). The ultimate decision whether to proceed would lie with the woman and not the doctor, and a doctor would perform the procedure within a private practice or a hospital (Ibid.). The existing medical or eugenic/embryopathic indications would remain the same. The bill reworded Section 218, to make abortions meeting these requirements 'not punishable' as opposed to 'not illegal'. This change in wording was significant since it removed criminal (moral) sanction from the law and was to be one of the major objections the Constitutional Court eventually made about the legislation. In striking down this provision in *Abortion II*, the Court re-asserted its view that the Basic Law required the law to state a moral objection to abortion, thereby dictating the criminalization of abortion but allowing it to be 'not punishable' if it met the allowed indications (Prützel-Thomas 477).

In addition to the revised indications, the counseling provisions included in the legislation stated that the objective of counseling should be to protect life and offer medical, legal and social advice and to help the pregnant woman. The counseling could be anonymous and the details of a counseling session did not have to be recorded (Ibid.). After the required counseling took place, the counseling certificate was to be awarded (Ibid.). Lastly, in addition to these changes in the criminal code, additional supporting legislation ('Pregnancy and Family Support Act') was also passed and has remained in effect since August 1992. This supporting legislation guaranteed state-financed family, sex, and contraceptive counseling to both women and men. The legislation provided for free contraception for adolescents up to age 21, and provided child care or nursery school for all children ages 3 and up (Ibid. 477 and Klein-Schonnenfeld126).

Parliament passed both the 'Pregnancy and Family Support Act' and the 'Abortion Reform Act' (revision of Section 218) on June 26, 1992 and the Bundesrat did so on July 10, 1992. In the Bundesrat, 14 Länder voted for the bills, including three CDU-led Länder from the east: Berlin, Saxony, and Saxony-Anhalt (Prützel-Thomas 478). Not surprisingly, Bavaria, the CDU/CSU stronghold, was the only Länder that voted against the bills. Three other Länder, with coalition governments, whose partners supported the legislation in the Bundestag, abstained from the vote since they could not provide a unanimous vote as required in the Bundesrat: Baden-Württemberg (CDU/SPD), Mecklenburg-West Pomerania (CDU/FDP) and Thuringia (CDU/FDP) (Ibid.).

CSU members of the Bundestag and the Bavarian government ask the Constitutional Court to review the new federal legislation- 1992

Immediately after Federal President Karl Fromme signed the bill on July 27, 1992, the Bavarian Land government and 248 of the 318 members (all male) of the CDU/CSU in parliament made an abstract review appeal to the Constitutional Court. On August 4, 1992, the Court issued a temporary injunction against parts of the legislation amending Sections 218 and 219 of the criminal code. Four months later in early December 1992, the Constitutional Court held hearings on the 1992 Abortion Reform Act and the revived 1990 appeal by Bavaria in regards to the use of health insurance and sickness benefits to pay for socially indicated abortions under the 'old' law (Prützel-Thomas 479). At the hearings, opposition party members from the SPD, such as the minister president of Schleswig-Holstein and the deputy chair of the SPD party, asserted that the legislation had the overwhelming support of the public, citing as evidence a public opinion poll which indicated support for the liberalization of abortion laws (Prützel-Thomas 479).

Five months after the hearings, on May 28th 1993, the Court ruled in *Abortion II*, rejecting the main provisions of the law. It outlawed abortions performed on hardship (socially indicated grounds) and upheld Bavaria's argument against public health financing of such abortions. This time the Court took yet another policy option off the legislative table by rejecting 'socially indicated abortions' and by prohibiting public health financing of abortion. Strongly re-affirming its 1975 decision, the Court stated that the Basic Law demands the protection of life, including the unborn. As discussed previously in first section of this chapter, the Court found that only under a few conditions could abortions be considered 'not illegal', such as those done for medical or eugenic grounds or after the crime of rape; therefore, in all other instances abortions performed within the first 12 weeks of pregnancy were to remain illegal but 'not punishable' if they adhered to proper regulations. Since such abortions were illegal, government health insurance could not cover these abortions, but for women in dire need social services would be allowed to cover the costs.

The Court rejected most of the counseling provisions in the law, stating that the provisions neither sufficiently protected life nor provided an adequate pro-life stance in counseling. As noted in first section of this chapter, the Court extensively detailed what an acceptable counseling model should look like and determined that this model would remain in effect as a temporary measure until Parliament passed new regulations. The Court's counseling model insured every attempt was to be made to persuade the woman to have the child; however, the final decision would still be left to the woman. Rejecting Parliament's attempt to leave out required documentation of such counseling, the Court ordered that a woman's specific reasons for having an abortion were to be documented, though she could remain anonymous.

The Federal Government responds by largely implementing the Court's directives from Abortion II-1995

The Federal Parliament responded quickly to the Court's decision by passing new reforms in July 1995 that went into full effect in January 1996. The legislation hewed closely to the policy recommendations and requirements laid out in the Court's decision. The new section 218a (subsection 1) allowed abortions that were performed in the first 12 weeks to not be considered punishable offenses if certain conditions were met (Schlegel 45). The main conditions were that the woman was to have a mandatory counseling session at least three days before the procedure and the woman was required to provide the operating physician with a counseling certificate (Ibid.). In addition, the woman could also receive a medically indicated abortion at any time during the pregnancy or criminally indicated (pregnancy due to rape) one within the first 12 weeks of pregnancy (the description of these indications are identical to the 1976 version of the law) (Ibid.). Unlike counseled abortions performed under Section 218a (1), abortions performed due to medical or criminal indications would be lawful if a medical practitioner determined that such indications were present, and completed an indications certificate. The operating doctor (separate from the practitioner finding the indication present) would also inform the woman of the risks of abortion and this doctor would be held liable for punishment for performing such abortions without the indication certificate. Finally, the 1995 legislation completely abolished embryopathic indications and the 'socially' indicated abortions allowed in the 1976 law which was consistent with the Court's instructions (Ibid).

Responding to the Court's directive that the Basic Law required the state to indicate its preferences in the counseling procedure, the new legislation included these requirements. It required that counselors expressly encourage the woman to bring her pregnancy to term and "' to show her perspectives for a life with the child' " (Ibid. 46 quoting the law). A counselor must also tell the pregnant woman that the unborn has a right to life at all stages of pregnancy and abortion is legally accepted only if continuing her pregnancy would lead to an "extraordinary burden exceeding the extent of the sacrifice that can reasonably be expected" (Ibid.).

Parliament also passed the "Pregnancy Conflict Act", at the same time as the revision of S218, which was an additional supporting legislation providing further detail on the counseling procedure and largely followed the model outlined by the Court in *Abortion II.* This statute provided detailed regulation requirements for authorizing counselors, counseling procedures and counseling centers that were to be implemented by all Länder. Section one of the Act stated that counseling should result in neutral or open-ended 'ergebnisoffen' position on the procedure. This requirement reflected the Court's recommendations on how counseling should proceed. The counseling discussion had to "include a confidential talk about the woman's motivation to have the pregnancy terminated, but the woman must not be forced to reveal her reasons"(Ibid. 47). The counselor had to provide medical, legal and social information regarding the rights of women and children and about all available financial assistance. The pregnant women must be offered help with any housing, education or child rearing needs. Section 8 of the Act stated that all Länder must provide a minimum number of counseling centers within reach of any woman in that state. In order for Land certification of counseling centers, the law required such centers to have competent and qualified staff and to cooperate with all public and private institutions providing assistance to mothers and children. A counseling center's authorization was to be reviewed every three years to insure compliance with the regulations. The law only allowed abortion to be performed in facilities where post-abortion or follow-up treatment was available. The Länder were responsible for providing a sufficient number facilities for both clinic and hospital abortions.

Lastly, the financial obligations of the state were also included in the new legislation to reflect the Court's position on state health insurance payments for abortion. The mandatory state health insurance was obligated to pay for abortion-related services where the abortion is 'not illegal' or 'not unlawful' (i.e., performed under the medical or criminal indications) (Ibid. 48). If an abortion is performed within the 12 week provisions of Section 218a, which would be considered 'illegal' yet 'not punishable', then health insurance coverage could not be required to cover the costs except for medical counseling. The only conditions under which a woman's medical costs would be covered by health insurance due to a 'unlawful' abortion were (1) if the abortion fails, and to then protect the health of the unborn, (2) to protect the health of the woman, particularly in regards to complications from the abortion and (3) protect the health of any future children, which refers to protecting the woman's ability to become pregnant. Lastly the law stated that women who are financially unable to pay for Section 218a 'unlawful' abortions were able to receive support under the "Women's Aid Act Concerning Abortions in Special Cases" Act. This was a social welfare provision separate from health insurance applying only to women with a limited income and without other means of financial support. The Länder were obligated to provide such funds under these conditions. To remove any social stigma a woman might have when applying for this welfare payment, women were allowed to apply through their mandatory health insurers for payment, who would then be reimbursed by the Land (Ibid.).

Summary and analysis of the federal abortion policy response

As in the Canadian case, abortion is part of the criminal law in Germany, which is under federal jurisdiction. With one criminal abortion statue determined by the federal government for the country, there was no way for federal legislature to 'avoid' addressing the issue, as compared to the United States where the responsibility for the criminal law is largely been left to the states. When the German parliament passed the Section 218 revision after reunification, support for the bill crossed all party lines (though only those that crossed the CSU line were women). In addition, it was understood that there could be a likely constitutional challenge to the new legislation, given the presence of the 'abstract review' procedure, therefore most proposals explicitly tried to consider, but not in all cases accept, the requirements laid out by the Constitutional Court in its previous *Abortion I* decision. Even with the cross-party support in Parliament for the new legislation, the institutional feature of abstract review empowered minority forces to appeal to the Constitutional Court to get around the majority proposal.

In addition, the Bundesrat became a non-factor because of the abstentions--those Länder with coalition governments (CSU/SPD or CSU/FDP) who could not come to a unanimous agreement in how to cast their votes and therefore could not vote (another institutional requirement). It was not surprising that these Länder could not come to agreement, since the CDU's partners in these Länder, the SPD or FDP, had overwhelmingly supported the legislation in the Bundestag. The question then is this: why did the Berlin/Saxony/Saxony-Anhalt governments support the legislation when they were also led by the CDU? One likely explanation is because in the east, CDU members are mostly Protestant while in the west they are Catholics (Prützel-Thomas 475). In addition, these eastern Länder were from the former GDR, which had liberal abortion policies for decades.

The role of abstract review, enabling direct appeal to the Constitutional Court, was omnipresent in the reform of Section 218. This institutional feature was used three times, once in the 1970's and twice in the early 1990's, by both a Land government and a minority of Parliament members. Even with Parliament's attempts to integrate the Court's precepts from its *Abortion I* decision and cross-party support of the 'group proposal', it was still not enough to prevent an abstract review appeal to the Constitutional Court. The Court, again as it did in the 1970's, responded with its own lengthy decision detailing precise guidelines regarding the conditions for a legal abortion, abortion counseling requirements and other support policies. In neither the *Abortion I* decision in 1975 nor almost 20 years later in *Abortion II*

(1993), did the Court made any statements indicating it would refrain from policy-making and defer to parliamentary majority. This lack of deference to the legislature contrasts with both the Canadian and US Supreme Courts, both of whom provided justifications in their decisions as to why they were 'deferring' (Canada) or 'not' deferring (United States) to the legislative branch on the abortion issue. Relative to the German Constitutional Court, Canada and the United States Supreme Court have fewer institutional features supporting the exercise of a strong judicial authority and perhaps this explains why these two Courts would 'justify' their exercise of judicial review, whereas the German Constitutional Court makes no concessions in its exercise of authority.

In both major abortion decisions, the German Constitutional Court consistently asserted its own interpretation of Basic Law guarantees as the primary basis for its policy determinations. One might argue that perhaps the policy preferences (attitudes) of the Constitutional Court judges explains the Court's relatively consistent position on abortion across time. However, Constitutional Court justices are appointed through a process providing relatively 'equal' partisan representation on the Court, ensuring that no one political point of view may dominate the Court. Second, with the presence of an institutional rule restricting justices to only one non-renewable twelve-year term on the Court, this feature also limits the possibility of having the same like-minded judges dominate the Court for a long period of time.

In summary, the abstract review procedure enabled the Court to intervene in the policy process quickly and repeatedly. Given its explicit authority to interpret the Basic Law and to exercise judicial review, these factors helped insure that the Court's views of abortion policy (in light of its interpretations of the Basic Law) were complied with by the federal government, even when there was a significant parliamentary majority (and public) supporting a less restrictive position on abortion.

BAVARIA

Land political orientation and brief summary of land activity on abortion

Bavaria is a Land that considers itself distinct from the rest of Germany (and the rest of Germany feels the same way about Bavaria). Bavaria has a distinct culture, from its unique dialect to the large concentration of Roman Catholics who populate the state. Bavaria's political orientation has been largely socially conservative, with notable pockets of liberalism, like its largest city Munich, which has long had a SPD mayor. The Christian Social Union (CSU) has governed the state since its inception after WWII, and is the only party in Germany that does not seek election in any other German state. The party maintains very close relations with the national CDU party and essentially represents the CDU's interests in Bavaria.

These features of Bavaria politics dominated its approach to abortion policy. Bavaria consistently sought stricter policies limiting abortion at both the federal and land levels. When their preferred policies were not be enacted by their CDU partners at the federal level, they initiated abstract review appeals seeking Court intervention. This approach was largely successful, until Bavaria found its own onerous abortion regulations reviewed and rejected by the Constitutional Court. Bavaria found itself constrained by the Court due to three significant conditions; 1) the expansive and detailed nature of the Basic Law protecting professional freedom, 2) the constitutional complaint procedure, which provides the opportunity for individuals to seek redress directly from the Constitutional Court, and 3) the Court's authority to mediate the appropriate division between federal and land authorities. The Court sanctioned Bavaria for passing legislation which violated Basic Law guarantees and overstepping its jurisdictional authority by attempting to enact policies that had been explicitly rejected by the federal parliament.

Bavaria enacts abortion regulations and prosecutes abortion doctors-1970-1980.

After the parliament's implementation of the new Section 218 and its supporting legislation in response to the *Abortion I*, one year later in 1977, the state of Bavaria quickly passed its own supporting legislation detailing the counseling and certification procedures for obtaining an abortion in the state. As discussed in chapter four, Germany's federal logic allows Länder to establish implementation regulations whose purpose is to support legislation passed on the federal level. Therefore, Bavaria passed the "Schwangerenberatungsgesetz" (SchwBerG) "The Law on social counseling of pregnant women" (1977). The law stated that a woman had the right to obtain free, personal and confidential counseling and that the appropriate resources necessary for the counseling were to be provided by the state, its counties and municipalities.

The law specifically described the topics to be covered during the counseling session and the types of support to be offered to the woman. The regulations stated that the counselors must certify that the pregnant woman was informed about available monetary and social support that would be available to her should she choose not to abort. The certificate had to include personal biographical information and the records of the counseling session had to be kept on file for 5 years and destroyed thereafter (Ibid).

In regards to where and what organizations would be able to provide counseling, such organizations had to be certified by the state government. Certification would be granted based upon the fulfillment of specific criteria, which included staffing requirements, collaboration with outside professionals (including doctors, psychologists, etc.), facility requirements, required hours and proven previous counseling experience. These requirements were quite extensive and detailed, which critics said limited the number of counseling centers available in the state (Klein-Schonnenfeld119).

Since the constitutional division of competencies between the federal government and the Länder enabled each state to create its own implementation laws regarding abortion counseling, the extent of these counseling requirements varied among Länder. As noted in the previous section, more liberal Länder, like North-Rhine Westphalia, largely accepted the federal directives and imposed minimal regulations and requirements on counseling centers, enabling women to gain easy access to abortion. The result of this variation among Länder was that "there was considerable [increase of] traffic of women seeking abortions in states where the restrictions were not strictly enforced" (Van Zyl Smit 307). As compared to the US and Canada, Germany is fairly small in size and traveling from the southern part of the country to the north where the regulations were less strict was a feasible option for women. Therefore, during the late 1970's and 1980's 'abortion tourism' began to increase both within the country and to neighboring countries like the Netherlands.

In addition to the existence of less strict abortion policies elsewhere, there were a number of state-supported counseling centers run by religious organizations due to Bavaria's conservative orientation and the influence of the Roman Catholic Church, which also turned women away from obtaining abortions within the Land. By the early 1990's only 3 of the 40 counseling centers in the entire Land were secular-run organizations (Klein-Schonnenfeld119). The dominance of the Catholic Church in the region was also a contributing factor to the prosecution of Dr. Theissen in the Memmigen trials of the late 1980's.

Given Bavaria's conservative orientation, its increasing opposition to 'abortion tourism' and its authority to dictate abortion-counseling requirements, in June 1988, the Ministers of the Interior and Labor and Social Affairs issued a joint MinisteriallBlatt (Ministerial Paper, akin to an 'executive order'), outlining a labyrinth of rules as to how execute the Bavarian counseling law (SchwBerG 1977). In order for a counseling center to be recognized or licensed, the following conditions had to be met: 1) only licensed social workers or those who had not yet graduated a social work program but received state recognition were able to work as abortion counselors, psychologists or nurses would not be eligible; 2) each center was required to have a waiting room and an indoor, sound-proof room; 3) counseling centers also had to maintain regular contact with other counseling services like marriage, family and social counseling services, and centers were required to provide regular evidence of this relationship to the state welfare office (Vollzug des Schwangerenberatungsgesetz- Execution of the Law on the Counseling of Pregnant Women, 1988). In order for doctors to participate in the abortion process, they had to prove that they were "sufficiently knowledgeable of the public and private help available to pregnant women, families, mother and children" The doctor had to be able to fulfill these obligations, and this would be verified by the government through a personal discussion (Ibid).

The MinisterallBlatt was highly detailed and specific. Regarding how the counseling session should proceed, first, the counselor had to determine how many weeks the woman was pregnant. Second, the law stated that the "Counseling must not be limited to the handing over of brochures and leaflets. A counseling session by telephone does not suffice either" (Ibid). Counseling centers had to inform doctors of their hours and maintain a close relationship with them. According to the federal 218 law, counseling was to occur at least 3 days prior to the abortion. The counseling session had to take at least an hour, and was to include a thorough conversation in which the woman's living situation and the difficulties of the pregnancy were discussed. Available public and private aid had to be discussed, and it would not be sufficient to simply refer the woman to such organizations; rather it was required that the counselors insured that the woman would receive the necessary help. Therefore the counseling center had to contact all social welfare, youth welfare, and housing benefit offices, as well as health and family insurance companies and church and charitable organizations, in order to insure the woman would receive help (Ibid).

In addition, counselors had to provide instruction on family planning in regards to being a responsible parent. The order stated, "It is the foremost task of the state to prevent the killing of unborn lives by providing instruction on preventative contraception", a citation to the Constitutional Court's directive in its 1976 *Abortion I* decision that the state's duty and obligation is to protect life (Ibid). The second to last section of the MinisterialBlatt stated that the woman's identity must be confirmed in order to receive the counseling certificate and that the social counseling requirement was separate from the doctor's determination that the proscribed legal requirements (proper indications were present or that the woman was not more than 12 weeks pregnant) were met in order to obtain an abortion (Ibid). Lastly, extensive statistics had to be compiled regarding the number of women counseled and those who chose not to terminate their pregnancy.

Bavaria pressures federal government to reform the federal abortion law, defeated in parliament, it's views find favor with the Constitutional Court--1980-1995

As noted in the previous section focusing on the federal level, during the late 1980's the CDU gained control of the federal government with its governing partner, the FDP. Now that the Bavarian ruling government (CSU) had its governing partner at the federal level in power, the Bavarian government begun to put pressure to reform Section 218 at the federal level. In addition, as also noted earlier, the Bavarian government in early 1990 chose to submit an abstract review appeal to the Constitutional Court which asserted that the 1976 law was essentially abortion on demand and that if abortion was considered 'illegal' but not punishable, as stated by the Court, then it should not be paid for by any state health insurance (Prützel-Thomas 473). Bavarian Prime Minister Max Streibel announced the action as a confirmation of a promise he made to CSU members at a state party convention a year earlier (Streibel 1990). In a newspaper editorial outlining the justification for the appeal, Steibel explicitly referred to the Constitutional Court's *Abortion I* decision, declaring the 1976 federal reforms that allow abortion within the first 12 weeks of pregnancy (Fristenloesung) as incompatible with the Basic Law (Ibid). Yet, outside forces intervened during this time to alter the course of abortion policy reform, as the fall of Berlin Wall and reunification consumed the country.

As the reunification treaty required the federal government to pass a new federal abortion law, the Bavarian government continued to assert that the new law should not allow health insurance to cover abortion procedures in any Land, including the former GDR states where liberal abortion policies included insurance coverage of abortion procedures (Der Tagesspeigel 1990). CSU party elites made numerous public statements attempting to influence the direction of the federal negotiations over section 218, asserting that the Basic Law (and the Constitutional Court's interpretations of the Basic Law) demanded more restrictions on abortion. For example, Bavarian State Social Minister Stamm said that Bavaria's stance in protecting unborn life was demanded by the Constitutional Court's interpretations of the Basic Law, and should be imitated by SPD-led states like Saarland or North Rhine-Westphalia (Lechtleitner 1990). In addition to the abstract review lawsuit over the Fristenlosung (time-period) indication, the Bavarian government officials threatened they would immediately make an abstract review appeal to the Constitutional Court in two years, if the new federal law did not meet Bavarian expectations regarding the protection of unborn life (Deutsche Tagespost 1990). That threat was carried out immediately after Parliament passed the revised federal abortion law in 1992. Frustrated with the direction the negotiations in federal parliament had taken, and the Constitutional Court's delay in responding to Bavaria's normkontrolle appeal in late 1991, Bavarian Prime Minister Steibel publicly prodded the Constitutional Court by stating it needed to provide a clarifying statement on the necessary protections for unborn life, which in his view was overdue (Frankfurter Allegemeine 1991).

As the CDU/CSU proposals had failed to garner a sufficient number of votes in the Bundestag, the 'Group Proposal' was passed in June 1992. The legislation was then sent to the Bundesrat, where most

Länder supported the new legislation and the three Länder with CSU-coalition led governments abstained. Bavaria was the only Land that voted against it. The Bavarian government immediately took its case to the Constitutional Court. While the Federal law was suspended from taking effect due to the Constitutional Court's injunction and review of the new law, within Bavaria there were public complaints that the state was not providing opportunities for out-patient abortions (Frankfurter Rundschau 1992). Since the previous federal abortion law stated that only abortions could be performed in Land licensed institutions, some Länder had never passed licensing rules, allowing institutions to provide out-patient abortions (Klein-Schonnenfeld 119). If licensing regulations did not exist, then only hospitals were able to provide abortions. In many places in Bavaria only religious institutions operate hospitals (even though they are state funded). This meant that through their employment contracts, these hospitals could prohibit their staff from performing abortions and therefore, in many places, particularly rural areas where there were only religious-run hospitals, access to abortion was non-existent (Ibid).

In response to these criticisms, the Bavarian Interior Minister issued a statement saying, "Right now, we don't see the necessity and we don't see opportunities to create options for out-patient abortions" (Frankfurter Rundschau 1992). Given that the new federal law requiring available out-patient abortion options was enjoined, and the Constitutional Court had not yet begun to hold hearings on the law, the Bavarian government made no attempt to address these concerns. In addition, Bavaria believed that since they included their opposition to out-patient clinics in their appeal to the Constitutional Court in 1990, they did not have to implement this part of the original 1976 Section 218 federal law on abortion (Emundts1993). Bavaria's resistance to implementing the federal directive was similar to the Alberta and Nova Scotia provincial governments' opposition to license out-patient abortion clinics as a means to limit abortion. The jurisdictional authority of the Canadian provinces and German Länder to regulate medical licensing and hospitals provided these sub-national actors a means to control abortion policy.

In May of 1993, the Constitutional Court issued its ruling in *Abortion II*, agreeing with Bavaria that state health insurance should not pay for socially indicated abortions. Its decision also echoed many of the counseling directives Bavaria had set out in the MinisterialBlatt of 1988. The Constitutional Court's *Abortion II* decision of 1993 was a victory for Bavaria, affirming its approach to strictly regulating abortion counseling and access to abortion. While the Parliament quickly responded to the Court's decision by revising Section 218 according to the Court's directives, there was no immediate policy response to the Court's decision in Bavaria.

Bavaria passes controversial implementing legislation on abortion counseling and faces review by the Constitutional Court – 1996

However, soon after Parliament passed the new Section 218 regulations on abortion in July 1995, Bavaria prepared its new implementing regulation on abortion counseling, replacing the 1977 state law (Law on the Counseling of Pregnant Women). The new law specifically stated that its purpose was to protect the unborn and to care for the pregnant woman through counseling and support (BaySchwBerG 1996). The law explicitly outlined the topics to be covered during counseling and that the goal of pregnancy counseling was to protect the life of the unborn (there was no mention of the rights/interest of the woman as part of the counseling 'goal'). The law also required that only after the woman disclosed her reasons for wanting to terminate her pregnancy could the counselor issue the counseling certificate.

Other political actors in Germany strongly opposed Bavaria's requirement for the woman to disclose her reasons for having an abortion. A number of national parliament members believed that this requirement jeopardized the quality of the counseling interview and contradicted the spirit of Section 218 (Holzhaider1996). The recently passed federal law stipulated that the pregnant woman would have to communicate the reasons why she was considering an abortion, but that the character of the counseling interview would be such that a pregnant woman would not be coerced into a "willingness to converse and cooperate" (Ibid). Bavarian Social Affairs Minister Stamm said that this wording in the federal law did not sufficiently regulate a woman's obligation to cooperate and that if the woman did not disclose her reasons directly then no 'conflict' counseling took place and a certificate should not be issued (Ibid). Ms. Stamm referred to the Constitutional Court's 1993 decision in her comments by noting that the Court had said in its ruling that a disclosure of reasons by the woman was 'indispensable' (Ibid). However, the Minister failed to mention the

Court *also* ruled that the woman could not be coerced into a willingness to cooperate. The Bavarian Minister was picking and choosing which parts of the Court's decision to use as support for Bavaria's new policy. The Minister did acknowledge, however, that only communications of those reasons are sufficient and that those reasons did not have to be verified in order for the woman to receive the counseling certificate.

In addition, Ms. Stamm announced additional regulations that Bavaria planned to enact limiting the number of providers able to perform abortions. Bavaria wanted to ensure that no doctors or clinics would come to Bavaria solely to perform abortions. Therefore, any out-patient institutions or private doctors not included in the state hospital budget plan were to receive no more than *one-quarter* of their annual income through performing abortions. They would be required to inform their local government of the number abortions they performed in the previous year, and the revenue received for those services (Ibid).

As these proposed implementation laws received more outside attention and criticism, Bavarian officials continued to assert that these laws were constitutional and that Bavaria was the only government in Germany correctly implementing the will of the Constitutional Court. In an editorial in the Bayern-Kurier, Bavarian Social Minister Stamm justified these regulations by stating that "Bavaria is only clarifying where federal regulation remains incomplete" (Stamm 1996). In addition, she asserted that since the federal law did not determine the legal consequences if a pregnant woman was unwilling to disclose her reasons for having an abortion, the Land governments had the authority to 'fill this gap' in the law (Ibid). Stamm also stated that contrary to public criticism, counseling in Bavaria was not patronizing and nobody was being pressured. To support her assertions, Minister Stamm again cited the 1993 Constitutional Court *Abortion II* decision; "conflict counseling is only possible if a pregnant woman discloses the principal reason for considering an abortion"(Ibid). Therefore, Bavaria claimed it was only following what the Court required conflict counseling to look like as opposed to what the federal legislation outlined (Ibid).

Echoing public complaints from local SPD and Green party leaders, Federal government officials also began complaining about these proposed laws. Federal Justice Minister Jortzig (FDP) believed that the new Bavarian counseling regulations were unconstitutional and violated the Basic law, and he sent a letter to the Bavarian Justice

Minister stating his concerns (Frankfurter Rundshau 1996). Not surprisingly, since the CDU controlled the federal government in coalition with the FDP, the federal government chose not to intervene and file an 'abstract review' appeal in order to stop Bavaria from passing these additional abortion regulations (Schlötzer-Scotland 1996). However, with federal government's failure to intervene, and increasing nation-wide public attention over the Bavarian regulations, the leader of the FDP faction in Parliament threatened to start proceedings against Bavaria given Parliament's and Bavaria's conflicting interpretations of the Constitutional Court's directives regarding abortion counseling (Fietz 1996). Responding to the FDP's threat of abstract review, Bavarian State Interior Minister Leeb warned that those willing to challenge the Bavarian law might 'end up getting a slap in the face' if the Court did not agree with their petition (Bayern-Kurier 6/1/96).

By August 1996, Bavaria defied its critics and adopted the Law on Counseling of Pregnant Women (BaySchweBerG 1996) and supplemental counseling regulations, the Bavarian Pregnant Woman Assistance Auxiliary Law (BaySchwHEG 1996). In addition to requiring women to reveal their reasons for wanting an abortion, the new law made abortion counseling free and open to the woman's partner. These supplemental regulations created onerous regulations on abortion providers. In order to receive state authorization to perform abortions, a written application would have to be submitted proving that only gynecologists and anesthesiologists will be performing the abortion procedures (Ibid). This meant that no other doctors could be authorized to perform abortion procedures, yet another means by which to limit abortion-related services.

As was outlined by Minister Stamm, the law required abortion providers, such as private doctors or medical institutions, including hospitals to fill out and submit state forms certifying that revenue from abortions could not exceed 25% of all revenues collected during one calendar year (Ibid). The government could also demand the doctor's financial statements at will. Also, all gynecologists performing abortion procedures would have to provide evidence that they participated in training sessions by the Chamber of Doctors (State Medical Board) related to the performance of abortions (Ibid). State health authorities had to receive certificates indicating that the doctors have received such training (Ibid). State health authorities were authorized to inspect rooms and equipment of those providing abortions at any time during normal business hours. In addition, state officials could also take evidence and make copies of information found if necessary to 'prevent urgent dangers to the life and health of third parties' (Ibid). The law also included a stipulation that those working in these institutions may be called as witnesses if such institutions were found to be performing abortions without state authorization (Ibid). Lastly, the law instituted a criminal penalty for those who violated the above provisions with up to a year prison sentence or a fine (Ibid).

The immediate response to these laws was that given such onerous requirements, no doctor in Bavaria would be willing or be in a position to perform out-patient abortions. As one doctor who had been performing abortions in the Land noted: "The government has designed the law consciously in a manner that no doctor performing abortions in his/her office will be able to do so anymore" (Thelen 1996).

Bavarian doctors bring a constitutional complaint to the Constitutional Court over the new Bavarian regulations- 1996-1998

While federal politicians were debating as to whether they would file an abstract review appeal regarding these new regulations, in October 1996, five Bavarian doctors filed a constitutional complaint with the Constitutional Court. Their complaint stated that these laws, particularly the Bavarian Pregnant Woman Assistance Auxiliary Law, violated their professional freedom and that the Bavarian regulation violated the federal law-making capacity (Neumann 1996). As detailed in chapter three, Article 93(1, 4a) of the Basic Law allows constitutional complaints (in which a "public authority" has violated a person's rights) against not only governmental actions, but judicial decisions, administrative acts, and legislative acts (Kommers 1997: 15).

Eight months later, in June 1997, the Constitutional Court issued a temporary injunction against the Bavarian law stating that Bavaria could not prohibit those doctors who were *not* gynecologists and had performed out-patient abortions from continuing to perform such procedures until a decision on the merits could be issued (Federal Constitutional Court Press Release 1997). In addition, the requirement that no more than a quarter of a doctor's income come from abortions could not be implemented. The Court did not extend the temporary stay to the other parts of the regulation dealing with the notification and submission requirements; these parts of the law would not immediately harm the interests of the doctors.

While most of the law was temporarily suspended, the Constitutional Court heard the full case on its merits during the following year. During the hearing on June 23 1998, the lawyer representing the doctors asserted that Bavaria could not impinge upon the Basic Law guarantee of professional freedom. The Bavarian regulation limited the doctors' ability to contract (through limiting their income from abortion) with patients and violated their professional freedom (Frankfurter Allegemeine 1998). In Germany, individuals have the right to make a direct constitutional complaint to the Constitutional Court and have it reviewed by the Court if the case is constitutionally significant and/or the government action/law imposes a grave hardship on the complainant. Even though complaint asked the court to the review Bavaria's actions impinging upon the doctor's freedoms, constitutional complaints allow the Court to review the entire legislation that gave rise to the action (Ipsen 128).

The hearing also addressed the issue of whether Bavaria had overstepped its Land law-making authority by promulgating the regulations in the first instance. Echoing her earlier public statements, Bavarian State Minister Stamm asserted that Bavaria had only fulfilled the guidelines set out by the Constitutional Court's 1993 ruling. Bavaria argued that the federal Section 218 abortion regulation set out only the minimum guarantee, leaving room for the Bavarian legislature to pass complementary regulations (Frankfurter Allegemeine 1998). In response to that argument, the doctors' lawyer asserted that Bavaria was attempting to circumvent the federal law by making the federal law harsher than was intended, thereby violating the unification contract which required a uniform abortion law across East and West Germany (Ibid). Constitutional Court Judge Grassof noted that the unification contract did not give the federal parliament any additional competencies and that the Länder had the authority to regulate the medical law and that they too are 'obligated to protect life'. However, Constitutional Court Judge Kuehling noted that the federal law created a complete counseling system in which any additional changes would change the entire federal counseling model (Ibid).

The Constitutional Court upheld the doctor's Basic Law claims and struck down other significant parts of the Bavarian regulations-1998.

Issuing its decision on October 27, 1998, the Constitutional Court upheld the doctors' claim that the Basic Law's (Article 12) guarantee of freedom of profession prohibited Bavaria from putting limits on how much of their income could come from performing abortion procedures (Knapp 1998). In addition, the Court ruled that the doctors may not be prohibited from performing an abortion if the woman does not disclose her reasons for requesting the procedure (Ibid). In regards to the requirement that only gynecologists may perform abortions, the Court upheld this restriction but stated that Bavaria must implement transitional regulations for the other doctors who had been previously performing abortions in Bavaria without incident (Ibid).

The main thrust of the Court's decision relied on not only the Basic Law guarantee of freedom of profession but also on the appropriate division of federal-provincial competencies. The Court ruled that since the federal government had the jurisdictional authority over criminal law, Bavaria had no authority to create criminal sanctions, such as a prison sentence or fines for doctors failing to meet the notification requirements on the number of abortions performed (Handelsblatt 1998; Leclerque1998). This aspect of the ruling is similar to the Canadian Supreme Court ruling in *Morgentaler III,* in which the Court asserted that the Nova Scotia regulations were in 'ultra vires' and violated the federalism principle because they imposed criminal sanctions on doctors performing out-patient abortions.

Further, the Constitutional Court ruled that Bavaria could not adopt many of its other regulations because the Federal government had already made 'conclusive' regulations of abortion in its 1995 legislation (Knapp1998). For example, the Court noted that the Federal Parliament had debated whether to include income limits on women seeking abortions but that this amendment had been explicitly rejected and not included in the final version of the law, thereby prohibiting Länder from establishing similar legislation on this issue (Graupner 1998).

In regards to the abortion counseling issue, the Court also noted that the federal 1995 law stated that women *could not be forced* to divulge their reasons for pursuing an abortion, which clearly contradicted and superseded the Bavaria legislation (Ibid). The Court asserted that since the federal law had provided specific rules allowing the pregnant woman to express her reasons for requesting an abortion but not creating conditions *where she would be forced to do so*, doctors could not turn down the woman's request to perform an abortion if the woman did not provide explicit reasons for requesting the procedure. Therefore, since the federal government had previously ruled on this issue, there was no room for a complementary Land law (Neues Deutschland 1998). This part of the ruling clearly rebuked Bavarian Minister Stamm's arguments that the Land had only created the Bavarian legislation in order to 'fill the gap' left by the federal law.

The Constitutional Court also upheld the Bavarian requirement that Bavarian doctors obtain a Land permit to perform abortions since the federal legislation did not provide such regulation. The Court's position was that the sub-national government had the authority to create supporting legislation in so far as the federal government had not conclusively determined to regulate or not to regulate in a particular area. In determining what would be the proper division of authority between the federal and Land governments, the Court was asserting that if the federal government had actively or conclusively chosen *to provide* or *not to provide* regulation regarding a particular policy area (over which it had jurisdiction), then the Land could not impose its own regulations. This interpretation of German federalism, which meant that intended action and 'inaction' by the Federal government pre-empted subsequent Land regulation, clearly tipping the 'balance of power' in favor of the federal government over the Länder.

In contrast to the majority opinion, which focused on determining the appropriate division of authority between the federal and land government, the minority opinion argued that the federal government had not correctly implemented the Constitutional Court's 1993 decision when it revised the federal abortion law. Therefore, if Parliament had not sufficiently implemented the 1993 decision then there could be no 'barring' effect for Bavaria to impose such a regulation (Handelsblatt 1998). The majority opinion 'responded' to that point by stating that Länder are bound and limited by the federal law as long as they have not made a 'normkontrolle' appeal to the Court regarding the constitutionality of the federal law, and until the Court subsequently determines the federal law unconstitutional (Ibid). A Land could not simply unilaterally make corrections retroactively to a federal law through its own regulatory authority (Graupner 1998). By making its assertion in this fashion, the Constitutional Court was not only reinforcing an adherence to a hierarchal logic of policy-making (Parliament → then Land) but also re-asserting its own significance in the political process by scolding Bavaria, since it had failed to 'defer' to the Court and use existing legal procedures to challenge a federal statute rather than independently challenge the federal government's interpretation of the 1993 decision through passage of its own legislation. This rebuke is reminiscent of the Canadian Supreme Court reprimanding the government's lawyer in the *Borowski* case for wanting the Court to quash the appeal without properly asking the Court to do so. These instances indicate that courts are willing to assert their authority over political elites when they can rely on legal rules/institutional features justifying their position.

The Bavarian government's response to the Constitutional Court's decision striking down much of the Bavaria law was not surprising. Bavarian Social Minister Stamm immediately responded to the decision by stating that Bavaria would consider filing a petition, but noted that it would first have legal experts review the Court's decision in detail (Die Welt 1998). In an analysis determining the likelihood of whether such a petition would be successful, Focus magazine stated that the recent change in party control of the federal government (SPD-Green) coalition had made it politically less viable to push for the changes that Bavaria wanted through the federal legislature (Baumslisberger, Hilbig and Kistenfeger 1998). In addition, the Court's decision put into question whether other types of Land regulation could now be struck down as exceeding a Land's competencies, which was something that did not bode well for Bavaria. In the end, the Bavarian government backed down, and did not end up taking formal steps to file an abstract review petition and the federal law stood without challenge from Bavaria.

Summary and analysis of Bavaria Case

The Bavaria case shows how the institutional arrangements in Germany supported the Court's authoritative role in the policy process and enabled the Court to shape the direction of abortion policy. First, Bavaria and the CSU members in parliament were able to file an abstract review/'normkontrolle' complaint in order to defeat a policy supported by a broad based coalition in Parliament. Second, due to the constitutional complaint procedure and the expansive and detailed nature of the Basic Law with its guarantee to professional freedom, doctors in Bavaria were immediately able to bring their case to the Constitutional Court. Due to this direct link to the Constitutional Court, it took only two years (with an injunction imposed within a year) for the Constitutional Court to issue a ruling regarding Bavaria's restrictive regulations. In contrast, it took six years for the case against Utah's restrictive legislation to reach the Supreme Court in the United States and it took 5 ½ years for the Canadian Supreme Court to strike down Nova Scotia's abortion regulations in *Morgentaler III*.

Both *the nature and timing of* these procedures enabled the German Court to remain an integral player in shaping the direction of abortion policy. By getting involved quickly, the Court could be part of an ongoing policy dialogue rather than only commenting after the fact. For Bavaria, it is somewhat ironic that the institutional features enabling the Court to determine the constitutionality of abortion (the Basic Law's numerous and detailed rights guarantees, the direct appeal procedures), which initially affirmed Bavaria's approach to abortion policy, are also the same features that allowed the Court to step in and restrain Bavaria from overstepping its legislative authority.

Lastly, the Constitutional Court interpretation of Germany's federal logic also limited Bavaria competencies, in that the Court ruled that the federal government's power pre-empts Land authority in situations where the federal government has legislated in a particular area and even where it has explicitly *chosen not to* legislate. Similar to the case of Nova Scotia in Canada, the proper division of power between the federal government and the Länder as determined by the Constitutional Court also limited Bavaria's ability to enact restrictive abortion policies. In conclusion, direct access to court adjudication through abstract review and constitutional complaint procedures, the expansive Basic Law guarantees, and the 'interlocking' federal logic were the conditions shaping Bavaria's abortion policy and the Court's adjudication of that policy.

NORTH RHINENE-WESTPHALIA

Land political orientation and brief summary of Land activity on abortion

From 1966-2005, North Rhine-Westphalia had a SPD (Social Democratic Party) Prime Minister and the SPD has dominated Land politics. For most of its history, the coal and steel industries have dominated the state economy. The SPD's strong relations with unions in these industries (and others) formed much of the party's support, particularly during the early decades of the party's rule in the state. In the north-west region of Germany, North Rhine-Westphalia politics have been fairly liberal and minimally influenced by religion as compared to southern states like Bavaria. It is also the most populous Land in Germany. Given this political orientation, the Land government's activities on abortion policy were relatively minimal and much less intrusive than Bavaria's.

Overall, the Land adopted the basic implementing legislation necessary in order to effectuate the federal laws in regards to counseling pregnant women and the administrative oversight of counseling and abortion providers. The Land made no attempt to enact legislation hindering access to abortion or to create onerous regulatory requirements of abortion providers. North Rhine-Westphalia did take some active steps to ensure access to abortion and abortion counseling by providing subsidies to facilities that would be willing to provide abortion counseling and meet Land and federal requirements, therefore making it easier for women to obtain abortions if necessary and to follow the time limit regulations in the criminal law. In addition, the Land's guidelines on counseling services published in June 1998, after the 1996 federal revisions went into effect, echoed the requirements laid down by the Constitutional Court and the Federal Parliament regarding the nature of the counseling process ('hilfe nicht strafe') and that a woman would not be forced into revealing why she is seeking an abortion.

While the overall the tone of the Land's regulations tended to emphasize the needs and rights of the woman over rights of the fetus, in contrast to Bavaria's regulations, the Land was careful to craft its regulations as to be consistent with the legal guidelines as laid out by the federal government and the Constitutional Court directives. As one

Land legislator noted in a discussion of the Constitutional Court's decision that had struck down the onerous Bavarian abortion regulations, "We in North Rhinene-Westphalia have done our homework. The approval guidelines in force are almost letter by letter the federal law in force" (Plenarprotokoll 1998).

North Rhinene-Westphalia implements the revised federal regulations on Abortion- 1974-1983

Three days after the federal law went into effect, on June 24th 1976, North Rhine-Westphalia enacted preliminary guidelines regarding the approval and recognition of counseling centers, counseling doctors and institutions performing abortions. The regulation outlined the acceptable indications for abortions, and stated that all private and public options "must be exhausted to allow the continuation of the pregnancy and alleviate the situation of the mother and child." (Vorläufige Richlinien-Preliminary Guidelines for the recognition of counseling centers, counseling doctors and approval of institutions that perform abortions according to paragraph 218 of the penal code 1976).

In regards to defining the counseling process the regulations stated the counseling was more than mere instruction and was to encourage the pregnant woman to continue the pregnancy and to offer help, with the goal of saving developing life. The state provided blanket recognition of all existing institutions that "perform tasks related to pregnancy counseling" and general social counseling centers such as community health departments, youth welfare offices, church bodies, family planning centers, marriage and life counseling centers and the state association of Pro Familia (Planned Parenthood in Germany) (Ibid). In order to receive continued recognition from the state, the law required that such centers must publicize their services, open at least one work day, and that counseling must be made free of charge and counselor should be willing to issue a certificate that such counseling took place (Ibid). The regulation did not detail what the certificate should look like or require. This law contrasts with the Bavarian regulations stipulating that a certificate must be issued including biographical information and such certificates must be kept on file for five years. In addition, the Land authorized individual doctors to perform social counseling as long as they were associated with a recognized counseling center or recognized as a counselor by a local governing body (district president) (Ibid). Such unaffiliated doctors could get recognized by participating in a one day seminar for counseling doctors or work in a publically sponsored counseling center for six months (Ibid).

Regarding which institutions would be authorized to perform abortions; all hospitals were recognized, even in the case of out-patient services. Established individual doctor's offices also could be recognized as long as the doctor performing the abortion was experienced in gynecology and had an assistant (nurse) working with him or her (Ibid). Any institutions providing abortions had to have the necessary medical instruments and medications necessary to revive patients and to treat breathing complications and provide an aftercare room (Ibid). Individual doctors had to work with a local hospital should a complication warrant in-patient admission to the hospital. Lastly, the Land simply stated the medical license of the doctor or the institution would be revoked if these requirements were not met or if an institution did not meet its obligation [of providing such services] (Ibid).

This preliminary regulation remained in effect until 1979, when the Minister of Work, Health and Social Services issued permanent regulations, which essentially reaffirmed the preliminary guidelines. The only significant difference was in the elaboration of the counseling process. The permanent regulations removed the statement that counseling 'should encourage the pregnant woman to continue the pregnancy, with the goal of saving developing life'. This statement was replaced with an emphasis on understanding the woman and her conditions:

> The counseling shall serve to illuminate psycho-social conflicts and to procure any public and private aid that would help her cope. The counselor must comprehensively deal with the woman's concrete situation and must consider her whole living situation in personal, economic and social respects. The goal is for the pregnant woman to make a responsible decision in the context of the legally available options (Richtlinien für die Anerkennung vonBeratunsstellen, beratenden Ärzten und Aulassung von Einrichtungen zur Durchführung eines Schwangerschaftsabbruchs nach 218 a des Strafgesetzbuches-Guidelines for the recognition of counseling centers,

counseling doctors and approval of institutions that perform abortions according to paragraph 218 of the penal code 1979).

Consistent with the federal law (Section 218), North Rhrine-Westphalia also issued guidelines naming which legal authorities would be responsible for recognizing pregnancy counseling centers and abortion providers. District presidents were responsible for recognizing counseling centers and churches were responsible for recognizing church run centers. District presidents were responsible for authorization and accrediting institutions performing abortions, as well as responsible for prosecuting and penalizing misdemeanors according to the federal criminal law (Section 218). The medical association of North Rhine-Westphalia was responsible for determining which doctors may determine indications as preconditions for abortion (Verordnung über Zuständigkeiten bei Schwangerschaftsberatung und –abbruch-Regulations regarding the responsibilities in the case of pregnancy counseling and abortion. 1978). This law was later repealed and replaced with a virtually identical law on December 6, 1994, in response to the second federal revision of Section 218.

During the 1970's-1980s, there were no significant legal controversies or debates over abortion services within the Land. There was only one significant regulatory activity that the state engaged in beyond counseling regulations and administrative oversight procedures. The Land passed regulations providing financial incentives in the form of subsidies for existing counseling centers or for the establishment of new counseling centers to provide both social and medical counseling as required by the federal criminal law on abortion. North Rhine-Westphalia first enacted these administrative regulations in November 1977, and reaffirmed them in 1983 with new monetary amounts.

The 1977 regulations stipulated the institutional requirements needed in order for counseling centers to receive the subsidies. Counseling centers must have a doctor, social worker/therapist and psychologist on staff (Verwaltungsvorschriften über die Bweilligung von Landeszuschüssen und die Träger von Beratungsstellen für Schwangerschaftsprobleme und Familienplannung-Administrative Regulations regarding the approval of state subsidies directed at the responsible bodies of centers offering counseling on pregnancy problems and family planning 1977). These funds were to support centers with their personnel and material expenses as well as expenditures for the potential expansion of services (Ibid). Centers could apply for these additional subsidies with their local district president and providing evidence of use of funds in the form of a report every 6 months (application and evidence forms provided) (Ibid). As noted above, the law was updated in 1983, listing new monetary amounts for the subsidies.

The 'preamble' of the regulations restated the requirements of the federal criminal law on abortion. The law was enacted in order to address the time intensive nature of the counseling process and to avoid delays that could threaten a women's health. The regulation defined the counseling process as such;

> [C]ounseling must consider the medical and social uniqueness of each case and must consider the full living circumstances of the advice seeking person. If abortion is desired, counseling shall in principle motivate to maintain the unborn life and in this way accommodate the plurality of viewpoints among all advice seeking persons. The goal of counseling cannot be to support each wish for abortion or the categorical recognition of a serious emergency situation as an indication for abortion. Conflict situations during pregnancy require, if at all possible, fast help including an examination of the motives behind the desire to abort. Psychological long term consequences resulting from inconsiderate decision-making can effectively be countered by means of thorough discussion and counseling, which permit the pregnant woman to reach a thoughtful conclusion (Ibid).

The regulations also stated that the 'social counseling' should also discuss the help that can be made available to the pregnant woman and the persons influencing her to maintain unborn life (Ibid).

Land implements new and updated regulations after the second revision of the federal abortion law in response to the Constitutional Court Abortion II decision -1983-1998.

During this time period, the Minister of Work, Health and Social Services of North Rhine-Westphalia intermittently reported to the Land President about the status of abortion counseling in the Land, publishing lists of all available counseling centers in the Land both state sponsored and religious organizations (Sicherstellung und Finanzierung von Beratungsstellen für Schwangershaftsprobleme und Familienplanung in Nordrhein-Westphalen- Securing and financing of Advising Centers for Pregnancy Problems and Family Planning in North Rhine-Westphalia 1996).

There was also little substantial legislative debate or discussion in the Land legislature about the constitutionality of abortion policies. Occasionally CDU members posed questions regarding the number of counseling centers in the Land or asking whether students at universities were getting adequate access to family planning counseling (Kleine Anfrage 238 1996). On the other side of the ideological spectrum, Green party members inquired whether funding for family planning and abortion counseling was sufficient and whether more funds should be provided (Kleine Anfrage 587 1997). None of these inquiries led to any changes or alteration in Land policy.

After the revision of the federal abortion laws went into effect in 1996, the Minister of Work, Health and Social Services of North Rhine-Westphalia proposed new guidelines for advice centers, counselors and doctors regarding implementation of the federal law. These regulations were formally published May 7, 1998. Overall, these Land regulations closely reflected the Courts directions in *Abortion II* and implemented the federal "Pregnancy Conflict Act" almost word for word regarding the nature of the abortion counseling process (Richtlinien zur staatlichen Anerkennung der Beratungsstellen und der Ärztinnen und Ärzte als Beraterinnen oder Berater nach den §§ 8 und 9 Schwangerschaftskonfliktgesetz (SchKG) Guidelines for the state recognition of advising centers and the consulting doctors or advisors to Paragraphs 8 and 9 of the Pregnancy Conflict Law 1998).

As noted above, the Land regulations largely echoed the 1996 federal criminal law revision and the Constitutional Court's decision in *Abortion II*. The regulations stated that, "it is necessary that advising is to be result-open [ergebinsoffen]" and for the woman to make the final decision. "Counseling should be understood as encouraging and inspiring, not patronizing or teaching. Abortion counseling serves to protect unborn life" (Ibid).

In addition, the regulation included verbatim parts of the federal law that stated the counseling session should provide "the necessary medical, social and legal information regarding possible assistance available for 'mother and child' in particular information that would make it easier for the woman to continue her pregnancy and that would address the woman's concerns regarding the obtaining and financing of an abortion" (Section 2.2.1 of the Guidelines). The regulation also reaffirmed the requirements of the federal social legislation passed in conjunction with the revision of the federal criminal law, noting that counseling services must also offer to help the woman with housing, child care or employment (Section 2.2.3 of the Guidelines).

North Rhine-Westphalia's implementation guidelines clearly stated that the counseling session could not be characterized as "forcing the conversation and the cooperation of the pregnant woman. It is expected that the pregnant woman announce the reasons she is seeking consultation to the person advising her. The counseling certificate may not be withheld from a woman who chooses not to name her reasons" (Section 3.2 of the Guidelines) As the Constitutional Court noted in *Abortion II*, the woman may request to have the counseling session conducted anonymously. The Land regulation included this option and in order to insure her anonymity, an authorized employee other than the attending counselor could confirm that the counseling had taken place and issue the counseling certificate to the woman (Section 3.2.2). In addition, the Guidelines stipulated that records of the counseling sessions should be kept secure and that the records could not include information that would reveal the identity of women who were counseled (Section 4.2 of the Guidelines).

Consistent with the federal law and the Court's decision, the Land regulation stated, with the approval of the pregnant woman, the counselor may also counsel persons who were assisting the woman with her situation. Afterwards, the advisor or doctor would record that the advising has taken place by filling out the form provided in the regulation. In addition, the regulation emphasized that "[t]he certificate shall not be denied nor the continuation of the consultation be delayed so that compliance with the period of twelve weeks after conception is impossible" (Section 3.7 of the Guidelines). This language was clearly references the 12 week window that woman had in obtaining an 'unlawful' yet 'unpunishable' abortion. The remainder of the law outlined the administration procedures regarding the recognition of counseling centers and consulting doctors; this section was largely a restatement of previous regulations regarding recognition of advising centers, counselors and doctors.

The only part of the regulations that went beyond either Court's decision or the federal revisions of the abortion laws was a section discussing the laws of discretion and the right to refuse to testify by counselors and doctors. The regulation stated that within state approved advising centers such workers were bound to secrecy within the meaning of these directives. The institution of the advisory body has the obligation to secrecy as guaranteed in the Federal Criminal Law (referencing Sect 203 sub 4a of Federal Criminal Law) and "is hereby notified of the criminal consequences of the violation of professional secrecy" (Section 5 of the Guidelines).There was no legislative record or other supporting documents to explain why this section was included, but it is plausible to deduce that this section was included as a response to the well-publicized and controversial Memmigen trials that occurred in Bavaria in the late 1980's. Given the language, it seemed that the Land wanted to make a statement clarifying that it would protect the rights of doctors and counselors as well as possibly deter any doctors or counselors opposed to abortion to provide information about women seeking abortions that could be used in a criminal trial.

Summary and analysis of North Rhinene-Westphalia case with comparison to Bavaria

In comparison to the Bavaria, whose implementing legislation was challenged and eventually struck down by the Constitutional Court, North Rhinene-Westphalia implemented a counseling law conforming to the major provisions of the federal laws and was consistent with the Court's decision in *Abortion II*. One could argue that the language used in the regulations was not as emphatic as Bavaria's in emphasizing the rights of the unborn. In addition, by detailing the specifics of how the counseling process may be conducted anonymously and threatening doctors and counselors of the consequences for violating laws of professional secrecy, North Rhine-Westphalia's regulations emphasized the rights and concerns of the pregnant woman whereas such language was absent in Bavaria's implementing regulations. This emphasis is not particularly surprising since North Rhine-Westphalia was consistently governed by the SPD, who consistently supported policies protecting women's rights.

Similar to the Conservatives in Alberta, Canada, albeit from a different ideological perspective, the SPD led North Rhinene-Westphalia government constructed its regulations so they adhered to the 'letter of the law'. There was little attempt to implement regulations that could be construed as exceeding the Land's competencies or that were substantially inconsistent with the federal law or the Constitutional Court's *Abortion II* decision. If anything, the Land was careful to use identical language from the federal abortion law or to clearly cite federal laws in its regulations. Similar to Alberta, this likely explains why there was no substantive controversy over North Rhine-Westphalia's implementing regulations, thereby providing no avenue for legal challenges and judicial oversight. In one of the few substantive legislative discussions in the Land regarding abortion policy, a CDU member of the North Rhine-Westphalia legislature criticized the Land for providing just as much money for pregnancy counseling as it did to support poor women who could not afford an abortion, and asserted that Bavaria provided a greater range of services for expectant mothers than North Rhine-Westphalia (Dinther, Plenarprotokoll 1998). While other CDU members made similar assertions that North Rhine-Westphalia didn't 'do enough' to protect pregnant women and to provide services for them, none of these statements included accusations that the Land was violating the federal law or the decisions of the Constitutional Court. If anything, SPD and Green members cited the Constitutional Court decision striking down Bavaria's regulations as affirmation of the constitutionality of North Rhine-Westphalia's regulations. As one legislator noted,

> I am very happy that our state guidelines for recognizing pregnancy counseling centers are very close to the federal law and that only where it makes sense; we have made things more concrete, without changing the quality of the content. The Federal Constitutional Court decision following Bavarian's special route can also be read as an explicit confirmation of our route in North Rhine-Westphalia" (Huerten Plenarprotokoll 1998).

Lastly, another Land or the federal government could have brought an abstract review appeal asserting that the North Rhinene-Westphalia did not correctly implement the federal legislation consistent with Court's *Abortion II* decision. However, without any clear deviation from the federal law, there was little constitutional basis upon which to argue that Land was exceeding its competencies. The Land did chose to subsidize counseling centers in order to insure that women could access counselors and receive counseling certificates thereby providing access to abortions in a timely manner. North Rhine-Westphalia's regulations and financial supports encouraged the expansion of counseling centers and services, while Bavaria's regulations were an attempt to limit access and services.

In conclusion, the following chapter will compare and contrast in more detail how the different 'intrinsic' and 'extrinsic' features present in the three cases shaped the role and influence of high courts in Canada, US and Germany and discuss the implications of these differences for understanding the influence of courts in federal systems.

CHAPTER 8

Comparing the Power of Courts in Federal Systems

INTRODUCTION

This project generally asserts that high court power is shaped and conditioned by a number of institutional and political features, both intrinsic and extrinsic to high courts. Drawing upon the empirical data presented in the previous chapters, I posit three conditions under which such courts are likely to be powerful political actors: (1) A high degree of court policy comprehensiveness and specificity, (2) a high likelihood of court oversight/intervention in the policy process, and (3) a limited diffusion or overlap of legislative competencies between federal and sub-national governments. I find that particular institutional features, including the comprehensiveness and nature of constitutional rights guarantees, the structure of judicial review and the constitutional division of powers between the federal and sub-national governments enable these conditions. In addition, the following outlines the implications this analysis has for examining court power in other contexts and provides directions for future research. Lastly, I suggest how these concepts may apply to a more general approach to understanding institutional power.

HOW DO INTRINSIC INSTITUTIONAL FEATURES AFFECT THE QUALITY AND CONTENT OF COURT DECISIONS?

One argument this project has asserted is that the greater number of clear, uncontested institutional supports a court has, such as an extensively detailed guarantee of rights (both positive and negative) or unqualified judicial review, the more likely a court will provide policy directives (through its decisions) that are comprehensive, detailed and prescriptive. Conversely, if those features are absent or weak, a court is more likely to refrain from making comprehensive, detailed and prescriptive decisions. In addition, this study also finds that the courts with limited or constrained institutional supports are more likely to depend on court/legal rules and/or to 'defer' authority to legislative institutions in order to justify their interventions or non-interventions in the policy process. On these measures, the Canadian Supreme Court abortion decisions were the least comprehensive, detailed and proscriptive, while the German Constitutional Court's decisions were the most comprehensive, detailed and proscriptive.

The Canadian Supreme Court, with fewer independent institutional supports for the exercise of its authority as compared to the other two courts in this study, was the court that most often utilized legal rules such as mootness and standing in its decision-making. The Canadian Court was authoritative in its decision-making when reviewing lower court interpretations of the law, but restrained when exercising judicial review, particularly when the federal government was sending contradictory signals about whether the Court should 'interpose its friendly hand'. For example, as we saw in chapter five, the Court employed the 'mootness' standard to evade a charge of policy-making in *Borowski*, but chose to assert its judicial authority in *Daigle*. In *Daigle* the Court was resolving lower court conflicts regarding interpretations of civil and common law, whereas in *Borowski,* had the Court issued a ruling on the merits of the case, it would have had to review the acts of another branch of government.

In terms of comprehensiveness, the Canadian Supreme Court rulings were narrowly focused, often avoiding substantive questions such as where life begins and whether women have right to abortion. In regards to how or where abortions are to be performed, the Court decreed only that provinces may not use criminal sanctions to regulate abortions. Regarding rights issues, the Court did not address whether or not provincial health care services must provide and/or pay for abortion services. It also consistently asserted that it was the federal government's responsibility to establish a new criminal law on abortion and refused to provide direction as to what reforms would pass constitutional muster. Overall, the Canadian Supreme Court's decisions were relatively restrained, narrow and not proscriptive.

Comparatively, the United States Supreme Court did not provide as much evidence of 'deference' to federal government actors in its decisions, but that is likely due to the fact that criminal law is largely a state matter within the US system. In addition, the United States federal government took little substantive action on abortion policies (during the time period examined in this study); therefore most of the legislative action on abortion occurred at the sub-national level. The US Supreme Court, while addressing more aspects of abortion policy than the Canadian Supreme Court, still left significant questions unresolved. The US Court only obliquely addressed the fetal life question. It provided a constitutional right for women to obtain abortions, yet weakened that right over time by replacing a specific test (trimester framework) with a broader and less specific one (undue burden). With a less stringent rule in place, states were encouraged to establish stricter abortion regulations.

Lastly, the German Constitutional Court specifically addressed the initial questions raised by abortion policy, evaluated abortion policy in detail and provided prescriptive, substantive directives for rewriting abortion regulations. If anything, over time, the Court's rulings on abortion became more proscriptive and comprehensive, rather than more diffuse, as what occurred in the United States. For example, as one commentator on the German Constitutional Court's *Abortion II* decision noted,

> Although the Court formally left the regulation of counseling to the legislature, its directives with respect to the "normative" contents of counseling do not leave much leeway. The Court itself has extensively "regulated" the content, procedure and organization of counseling held due for decriminalized, yet non-indicated early abortion by virtue of the *Grundgesetz* (Walther 397).

This assessment was consistent with other court scholars estimating the impact of the of the Court's ruling on any future legislative revision of abortion policies. Court scholar Sabine Klein-Schonnenfeldpredicted, "the future [legislative debates] will be characterized by more or less detailed legal discourse on how to organize and control advice centers and the medical profession" (Klein-Schonnenfeld132). Her prediction was accurate, as chapter seven illustrated how Bavaria passed complicated regulations limiting counseling centers and ability of doctors to provide abortions by mandating only a percentage of their income derived from performing abortions.

In comparison to the other two high courts, the German Constitutional Court established the limits of abortion policy and provided firm and detailed answers to the policy questions within those bounds. The US Supreme Court also determined both the parameters of abortion policy and some of the policy interior but not to the extent that the German Court did. The US Supreme Court left some policy areas untouched and provided only limited 'substance' in others. The Canadian Court provided the least amount of guidance on abortion policy, barely outlining abortion policy boundaries and leaves most of the interior policy terrain to be decided by other political actors.

Comparing across the cases presented, Germany's Basic Law was the most detailed and proscriptive regarding rights guarantees, providing both negative rights and positive guarantees that the state is obliged to uphold. Given the comprehensiveness and positive rights inherent in the Basic Law, as compared to the other two courts in the study, the German Constitutional Court had a stronger basis on which to base its decisions and to oblige state actors to conform to its interpretation of the Basic Law. In contrast, both the US and Canadian Supreme Courts started with constitutional documents that were less detailed and provided few (if any) positive rights guarantees requiring government intervention on the issue of abortion.

In regards to the nature of judicial review and its impact on court influence, this study confirms that abstract review significantly enlarges a court's influence and ability to intervene in the policy process. What is key, however, is not just the presence of such a procedure but that (1) multiple actors have access to this process and that (2) court decisions resulting from said review are to be binding on those actors. While both the Canadian and German systems provide for some type of 'abstract' review, in Canada that review may only be exercised by the ruling party in either the federal or provincial government. The opposition or minority faction in the Canadian parliament does not have access to the reference procedure as in Germany. In addition, in Canada, the 'reference' is only an advisory opinion that is not legally binding. In practice, the presence of the reference procedure actually inhibited the Canadian Supreme Court from making more substantive policy decisions in its concrete cases. Whereas, Germany's abstract procedure is definitive and legally binding; having such influence emboldens the German Constitutional Court to interject itself forcefully into the legislative process.

The Canadian government had the opportunity to make a 'reference' to the Canadian Supreme Court during the revision of the federal abortion law, but it chose not to do so. It sent contradictory messages to the Court on whether or not it wanted the Court to address the abortion issue. In its attempt to reform the criminal abortion law, the Mulroney government seemingly set itself up to fail, by allowing a free vote and too many amendments to its bill. In addition, government lawyers tried to make a 'mootness' claim in the *Borowski* case, when it should have asked for the case to be dismissed in the first instance. Lastly, the Prime Minister publically stated that the government would not take any further legislative action on abortion until after the *Borowski* ruling, which could have been interpreted as a 'deferral' to the Supreme Court However, the Canadian Court did not see it that way.

It was never publically stated why the Canadian government chose not to make a reference to the Court, but as noted, the reference procedure is only an advisory opinion while an abstract review appeal (Germany) is binding on all governmental organs. Without the presence of a binding constraint, the reference procedure might not have provided enough political cover for the Mulroney government to decide to use the reference procedure. As Graber's asserts, judicial review can benefit elites when they can point "to their obligation to obey the law, while insisting that they disagree with the Court's holding" (Graber 1993: 43). Yet, without the binding constraint, the Mulroney government could not say 'we're amending the law in this way because the Supreme Court said so and we have to abide by its decision'. In other words, the Canadian government could not use the reference procedure to effectively 'defer' to the Canadian Supreme Court, insuring that the Court could be held responsible instead of the Mulroney government.

Conversely, since the government *did not* make a reference, the Court could have surmised that if it *had* made a substantive policy decision in *Borowski*, its legitimacy would be threatened if its decision was met with public opposition (which was likely to some extent given the controversy over the issue). The Mulroney government could have 'safely' criticized the Court for both an inappropriate exercise of judicial review and on the nature of the ruling itself. One could argue that the lack of the binding constraint of the reference procedure led *both institutions* to defer making a substantive policy decision.

Another background condition present in the Canadian case was that at the time the Canadian Supreme Court was not firmly established as a political actor equal to Parliament, as was the Constitutional Court in Germany. Early Canadian constitutional documents established limited independent authority of the Canadian Supreme Court. The Court had long operated under these conditions until the Charter of Rights and Freedoms, which had been in effect less for less than decade when the abortion debate took place in the Canadian Parliament. Therefore expectations of judicial review and constitutional supremacy were not as established at the time as it was in Germany. However, one could argue that these expectations have developed further over recent years, and perhaps if the Canadian Court was presented with such issues today, the Court would be less deferential in its decision-making.

Besides the binding nature of abstract review, the fact that more political actors may access the procedure in Germany has enabled its use, and by extension facilitated the Constitutional Court's intervention in the policy process. Alec Stone has argued that abstract review allows courts to act as 'third legislative chambers'. This was apparent in Germany, where the opposition had the opportunity to employ the abstract procedure, creating conditions under which legislative policies negotiated and passed by a majority could be overturned via a court's abstract review decision. However, in light of the Canadian case, if abstract review is an option but underutilized and/or is not sufficiently binding upon political actors, the presence of such review may inhibit a Court from issuing substantive policy decisions in *concrete* cases thereby diminishing the court's overall influence. Abstract review which results in only advisory opinions may also diminish the likelihood of its use and subsequently, the authority and influence of a high court. Therefore, both the level of access to and the binding nature of abstract review are significant determinants as to whether courts are empowered as 'third legislative chambers'. Future research comparing across high courts with varying 'types' of abstract review, in terms of the number of actors able to initiate such review and the 'finality' of said review, could confirm or refine this finding.

HOW DO THE EXTRINSIC FEATURES OF FEDERALISM SHAPE LEGISLATIVE RESPONSES TO COURT DECISIONS?

This project asserts that the distribution of both policy and legislative competencies between federal and sub-national governments significantly shapes whether and how governments advance their interests regarding abortion policy. Most notably, the determination of whether abortion is primarily a health or a criminal policy was a necessary but not sufficient condition in determining responsibility for abortion policy and how said government would legislate. In addition, whether or not sub-national governments were largely responsible for implementing federal abortion policies or establishing their own substantive regulations conditioned sub-national legislative responses to high court decisions. The *presence* and *nature* these features provided particular avenues in which legislative actors could act and shaped the conditions that facilitated or inhibited court oversight of such actions. Notably, sub-national governments who successfully avoided court challenges to their policies were those that strategically sought to enact their preferences by working within the policy and institutional competencies available to them. However, when sub-national actors exceeded either their policy or legislative (or both) competencies they were likely to face judicial review. Regardless of ideological or party affiliation, sub-national governments who avoided judicial oversight employed particular competencies, such as utilizing their fiscal authority or promoting their actions as falling clearly under sub-national policy authorities (such as health policy) thereby insulating their actions from legal challenge.

HOW DID THE FEDERAL LOGIC SHAPE THE INTERACTIONS BETWEEN THE FEDERAL AND SUB-NATIONAL GOVERNMENTS?

In Canada, the division of jurisdictional authority between the federal government and the provinces contributed to the competitive dynamic between the two levels of government. Since the Conservative Mulroney government did not reform the federal criminal law on abortion, the provinces, under the auspices of their authority to regulate health care policy, attempted to either enable or inhibit access to abortion. Alberta and Nova Scotia attempted to regulate out-patient clinics and billing procedures, which impacted abortion access. Under the leftist NDP government, Ontario provided travel grants and approved out-patient abortion clinics. When the Liberals gained control of the federal government, it attempted to coerce provinces to provide access to abortion through the Federal Health Act and withholding federal transfer payments to the provinces, however it did not seek to reform the federal criminal law on abortion (S.251). Had the Canadian federal government successfully revised S.251 of the criminal law, there still may still have been conflicts between the federal government and provinces, due to constitutional authority of provinces over health policy. If the federal policy was in conflict with the policy interests of particular provinces, such provinces may have imposed convoluted and complicated health regulations, 'deinsured' abortion to prohibit access, or determined that abortion was not a 'medically necessary' health procedure.

Conversely, in the United States, the most significant legislative act (during the time period examined) by the federal government was to *withhold* the distribution of federal funds to the states by prohibiting the use of Medicare monies to fund abortions, effectively limiting access to abortion for poor women. In addition, since criminal law is primarily under the jurisdictional authority of the states, the majority of legislative activity on abortion occurred within the states. Given this distribution of jurisdictional authority, there was little evidence of a competitive dynamic between the federal government and the states. In this case, the federal government seemed to 'wave the flag' of federalism in order defer the issue of abortion onto the states and the Supreme Court (through its review of state abortion legislation). As noted in Chapter two, this is consistent with both Mark Graber's and

Keith Whittington's observations regarding federalism as a condition which supports judicial review and influence.

However, if the US federal government passes legislation outright banning all abortions or prohibiting the regulation of abortions, this could lead to conflicts between the federal government and the states. It is not clear on what constitutional basis the federal government could take such action. Recently, the US federal government passed the Partial Birth Abortion Act (2003), prohibiting the use of a late term abortion procedure. Five years later in *Gonzales vs Carhart (2007)* the United States Supreme Court upheld the federal law. This legislation mirrored statutes that had been in effect in about half of the states in the US. The constitutional justification for the exercise of Congressional authority in order to pass the law was based nominally on the commerce clause (said justification was not addressed by the court). One could raise the argument, based on Supreme Court's own federalism jurisprudence (see *Lopez, Morrison),* that there is not a significant enough connection between late term abortions and interstate commerce in order to justify the law. Conversely (and somewhat ironically), since access to late term abortions has declined within states due to increased state regulations (enabled by Supreme Court decisions), this condition has de facto made abortion an 'interstate commerce' issue since women are more likely to travel across state lines in order to obtain an abortion.

In Germany, since the Constitutional Court was interjected relatively early into the policy debate over abortion through abstract review and subsequently issued detailed, proscriptive and comprehensive decisions, which were largely complied with by Parliament. Since the criminal law is the province of the federal government in Germany and the Länder do not have significant jurisdictional authorities which conflict with the federal government, there was not much of the policy area left for the Länder to exercise control over. As noted previously, Klein-Schönfeld's prediction that what would be 'left' after Constitutional Court's *Abortion II* decision were details about counseling centers and the medical profession was accurate. Both Bavaria and North Rhine Westphalia created legislation that addressed the former, while Bavaria also addressed the latter. By attempting to limit the amount of income doctors could garner from performing abortions, Bavaria attempted to restrict the number of abortion performed in the Land.

In summary, while these cases revealed that the division of jurisdictional policy authority between the federal government and sub-national government conditioned legislative responses regarding abortion policy, this division was not always sufficient in determining which level of government would play a more significant role in establishing abortion policy. In Canada, the federal government had clear responsibility over criminal law, but chose not to exercise that authority, effectively leaving abortion regulation to the provinces through their authority over health policy. In the United States, the federal government could have easily deferred the responsibility of abortion regulation to the states, since criminal law is largely under state jurisdiction. In Germany, there is limited diffusion of legislative competencies between the federal government and the Länder. The federal government is largely responsible for criminal law and most other substantive policy areas, whereas the Länder are responsible for administering or implementing said federal laws, leaving few areas where the Länder have sole jurisdiction to establish substantive policies. Future research could examine additional federal cases, such as Brazil, Australia and even the European Union to further understand how different divisions of legislative authority in federal systems impacts the responses of legislative actors to high court decisions and subsequently court influence.

COMPARING COMPLIANCE ACROSS SUB-NATIONAL CASES

All three 'liberal' sub-cases (Ontario, Oregon and North Rhine-Westphalia), generally complied with the Court decisions on abortion and at various points utilized their own finances to ensure or promote access to abortion services. All three also took actions that were within their legislative and jurisdictional competencies, and generally did not pass legislation or take other actions that were highly controversial or could lead to a substantive legal challenge. When Ontario was ruled by the NDP (New Democratic Party) government it provided provincial funds supporting counseling and outpatient abortion services. In Oregon, the state government (through the Governor) chose to use its own funds to support counseling centers when federal funds were to be withheld. North Rhine-Westphalia provided subsidies to counseling centers that provided both social and medical counseling, ensuring such counseling centers would remain available to women. North Rhine-Westphalia was also careful to mimic both the language in the federal criminal abortion regulations and the Constitutional Court's abortion decisions in its regulations.

These activities contrast with the legislative actions taken in three of the 'conservative' sub-national cases of Nova Scotia, Utah, and Bavaria, where abortion regulations were eventually struck down by high courts. Nova Scotia attempted to prohibit the establishment of out-patient abortion clinics by attaching a criminal sanction to the regulation. Canadian courts struck down this criminal sanction as infringing upon the federal authority over the criminal law. Utah attempted to regulate abortions beyond the constitutional standards set out by previous US Supreme Court decisions. Bavaria attempted to limit the amount of income doctors could receive from performing abortions and to impose convoluted regulations of abortion counseling procedures. The US and Canadian Supreme Courts, in their review of the legislative policies of Utah and Nova Scotia respectively, avoided addressing substantive issues regarding abortion regulation, whereas the German Court did address these to some extent in its decision reviewing Bavaria's abortion regulations. However, the major justifications for the German Court's decision were based on some issues not directly related to the nature of abortion policy; the constitutional 'right to free employment' and the division of legislative competencies between the federal and state governments.

Why did the conservative states/provinces/Länder test the boundaries of their authority by passing controversial legislation? In Utah and Bavaria it appeared that these states passed their respective regulations in part they believed that the high courts would support them based upon the previous decisions by these courts. The Utah legislature passed a law that was unconstitutional as a response to Supreme Court decisions that essentially invited states to enact stricter abortion regulations. Similarly, the Bavarian government believed that its regulations were more consistent with the dictates of the Constitutional Court's *Abortion II* decision than the federal parliament's revision of the criminal abortion law. Both sub-national governments were vociferous that their actions were in compliance or at least consistent with previous court decisions. However in both cases courts eventually struck down these legislative actions.

In Canada, Nova Scotia was comparatively less confident in the constitutionality of its legislation as it attempted to 'shore up' the constitutional justifications for its regulations by passing supplemental legislation that fell under its authority to regulate hospital policy. Alberta chose a different route in evading compliance with the Canadian Supreme Court decisions on abortion. Alberta was consistent in casting its attempts to restrict abortion within its provincial authority to regulate health policy. Alberta also refrained from taking actions that appeared to impose criminal sanction. However, because of the jurisdictional overlap between the federal government and the provinces, the Canadian federal government was able to provide some oversight by withholding federal transfer payments to Alberta, eventually forcing the province to back down on its attempts to deinsure abortion.

These sub-national cases suggest that regardless of political orientations, sub-national governments who seek to exceed their competencies, are likely to have their actions reviewed by courts and those that take actions clearly within their competencies may insulate themselves from court oversight. This finding is both consistent with and extends arguments made by 'strategic scholars' by providing empirical evidence of the role "institutional arrangements play in structuring choices made by strategic actors." (Epstein et al 2004: 171). In this case, jurisdictional authority helps determine what actions sub-national actors might take and also help us understand under which conditions they are likely to be successful or unsuccessful in evading court oversight. As Epstein et al note,

> Policy formation…. emanates not from the separate actions of the branches of government but the interaction among them. Thus it follows that for any set of actors to make authoritative policy—be they justices, legislators, or executives—they must take account of this institutional constraint by formulating expectations about the preferences of other relevant actors and what they expect them to do when making their decisions (Ibid: 174).

What this research adds to that observation is that formulating expectations about what courts might do is necessary but not sufficient (as seen in the cases of Utah, Nova Scotia and Bavaria). Such actors must also be aware of other institutional structures which enable institutional interaction and subsequently may impact their ability to enact their preferred policy.

GENERAL THEORIZING, INSTITUTIONAL INTERACTION AND 'COMPLEX INTERDEPENDENCE'

As this project has demonstrated, one must consider the multi-dimensional structuring and 'complex interdependence' of institutional relationships in order to understand high court power and the responses of sub-national actors to court decisions. Based upon the cases presented this study posits that there are three conditions that significantly contribute to the influence of high courts in federal systems (1) a high degree of court policy comprehensiveness and specificity, (2) a high likelihood of court oversight/intervention in the policy process and (3) a limited diffusion or overlap of legislative competencies between federal and sub national governments. Future research may find that these conditions apply to predicting the influence of non-judicial institutions. Given these factors, we then may be able to compare across institutions to determine when and how institutions may exert influence. For example, the nature and degree of institutional integration or interaction may be a more reliable indicator of influence or power than whether compliance is dictated by a particular type of institution (i.e., a court or by a legislature). It may not be the functional differences (e.g., the lack of enforcement powers of courts) as much as the 'institutional matrix' in which these various institutions operate which provides incentives and disincentives for particular responses. Therefore we must continue to examine the complex interdependence among institutions and between levels of government, noting not just the preferences of other actors but the institutional structures which will hinder or enable their ability to make authoritative policy.

References

Almond, G. (1958). "Research Note: A Comparative Study of Interest Groups." *American Political Science Review* 52 (1): 270-282.

Almond, G., Verba, S. (1965). *The Civic Culture.* Boston, MA: Little, Brown and Company.

Bacharach, P. and M. Baratz (1963). "Decisions and Nondecisions: An Analytical Framework." *The American Political Science Review* 57(3): 632-642.

Bagley, G. (1992). "Bombing of Toronto abortion clinic raises stakes in bitter debate." *Canadian Medical Association Journal, 147*(10):1528-1531.

Baier, G. (2002). "Judicial Review and Canadian Federalism," in *Canadian Federalism: Performance, Effectiveness and Legitimacy*, H. Bakvis & G. Skogstad (eds.). Oxford: Oxford University Press.

Bakvis, H., and G. Skogstag (2002). "Canadian Federalism: Performance, Effectiveness, and Legitimacy," in *Canadian Federalism: Performance, Effectiveness, and Legitimacy*, H. Bakvis and G. Skogstag (eds). Oxford: Oxford University Press.

Barnes, J.. (2007). "Bringing the Courts Back In: Interbranch Perspectives on the Role of Courts in American Politics and Policy Making." *Annual Review of Political Science* 10:25-43.

Baum, L. (1998). *American Courts: Process and Policy.* Boston: Houghton Mifflin.

Baum, L. (2003). "The Supreme Court in American Politics". *Annual Review of Political Science* 6: 161-180.

Baumgartner, F. and B. Leech (1998). *Basic Interests: The Importance of Groups in Politics and in Political Science.* Princeton: Princeton University Press.

Bennett, A. and A. George (2001). "Comparative Methods: Controlled Comparison and Within-Case Analysis." *American Political Science Association Annual Meeting,* San Franscico, CA.

Berube, B. (1988). "Now private clinics to be funded in Ontario. *" Medical Post,* June 14, 1988: 2,46.

Bickerton, J. (2001). "Nova Scotia: The Political Economy of Regime Change." in *The Provincial State in Canada: Politics in the Provinces and the Territories,* K. Brownsey & M. Howlett (eds.) Peterborough, Ontario: Broadview Press. 49-74.

Birkenfeld-Pheiffer, D. (1991-1992) "Abortion and the Necessity for Compromise" *German Politics and Society (24&25):* Winter 1991-1992

Biskupic, J., and Witt, E. (1997). *The Supreme Court at Work.* Washington DC: Congressional Quarterly Press.

Blair, P. and P. Cullen (1999). "Federalism, Legalism, and Political Reality: The Record of the German Constitutional Court," in *Recasting German Federalism,* eds. C. Jeffery. London, Pinter: 119-154.

Blankenburg, E. (1996) "Changes in Political Regimes and Continuity in the Rule of Law in Germany" in *Courts, Law and Politics in Comparative Perspective,* H.Jacob, E. Blankenburg, H. Kritzer, D.M. Provine, and J. Sanders (eds.). New Haven, CT: Yale University Press.

Brace, P. and M. Gann Hall. (1997). "The Interplay of Preferences, Case Facts, Context, and Rules in the Politics of Judicial Choice." *Journal of Politics* 59(4): 1206-31

Brace, P. and M.Gann Hall. (1990). "Neo-Institutionalism and Dissent in State Supreme Courts." *The Journal of Politics* (52): 54-70.

Brodie, J., Gavigan, S. A. M., & Jenson, J. (1992). *The Politics of Abortion.* Toronto: Oxford University Press.

Bullock, C. and H. Rodgers., (1976). "Coercion To Compliance: Southern School Officials and School Desegregation Guidelines," Journal of Politics: 987-1011.

Campbell, D.and Pal, L. (1991). *The Real Worlds of Canadian Politics.* Peterborough: Broadview Press.

Canon, B. (1991). "Courts and Policy: Compliance, Implementation and Impact," in *The American Courts: A Critical Assessment,* eds. J. B. Gates and C. A. Johnson Washington DC: CQ Press.

Carr, R. K. (1942). *The Supreme Court and Judicial Review.* New York: Farrar and Rinehart.

Clayton, C.W. (1992). *The Politics of Justice: The Attorney General and the Making of Legal Policy.* New York: M.E. Sharpe.

Cole, R. T. (1984). "Federalism: Bund and Länder.", in *Politics and Government in the Federal Republic of Germany: Basic Documents,* C.-C. Schweitzer, D. Karsten, R. Spencer, R. T. Cole, D. Kommers and A. Nichols. (eds.)Leamington Spa: Berg Publishers Limited.

Collier R. and D. Collier (1991). Shaping the Political Arena: Critical Junctures, the Labor Movement, and Regime Dynamics in Latin America. Princeton: Princeton University Press.

Collins, L. (1982). "The Politics of Abortion." *Atlantis,* 7(2), 2-20.

Committee on the Operation of the Abortion Law. (1977). "Report of the Committee on the Operation of the Abortion Law." Ottawa.

Cross, F., Tiller, E. (1998). "Judicial Partisanship and Obedience to Legal Doctrine: Whistleblowing on the Federal Court of Appeals" *Yale Law Journal* 107: 2155-76.

Dahl, R. (1959). "*Decisonmaking in a Democracy*: The Supreme Court as a National Policy-Maker," *Journal of Public Law* 6: 279-295.

Dahl, R. (1961). *Who Governs? Democracy and Power in an American City.* New Haven: Yale University Press.

Des Rosiers, N. (1997). "Federalism and Judicial Review", in *Challenges to Canadian Federalism,* M. Westmacott and H. Mellon (eds.). Scarborough: Prentice Hall Canada. 63-75.

DiMaggio, P, Powell, W. (1991). *The New Institutionalism in Organizational Analysis.* Chicago: University of Chicago Press.

Dunsmuir, M. (1998). "Abortion: Constitutional and Legal Developments." Ottawa: Library of Parliament, Research Branch, Law and Government Division.

Epp, C. (1998). *The Rights Revolution: Lawyers, Activists, and Supreme Courts in a Comparative Perspective* Chicago: University of Chicago Press.

Epstein, L., and J. Knight. (1998). *The Choices Justice Make.* Washington, DC: CQ Press.

Epstein, L., J. Knight, and A. Martin. (2004). "Constitutional Interpretation from a Strategic Perspective" in *Making Policy, Making Law: An Interbranch Perspective,* ed. M. Miller and J. Barnes. Georgetown University Press.

Epstein, L and J.A. Segal. (2005). *Advice and Consent: The Politics of Judicial Appointments.* New York: Oxford University Press.

Eskridge, W., P.Frickey and E. Garrett. (1999). *Legislation and Statutory Interpretation.* West Publishing Company.

Esser, A. "Reform of German Abortion Law: First Experiences", *American Journal of Comparative Law* (34): 369-383.

Faird, C. (1997). "Access to Abortion in Ontario: From *Morgentaler 1988* to the Savings and Restructuring Act." *Health Law Journal* 5:119-45.

Foster, N. G. (1996). *German Legal System and Laws*: Blackstone Press Limited.

Frymer, P. (2003). "Acting When Elected Officials Won't: Federal Courts and Civil Rights Enforcement in U.S. Labor Unions, 1935-85." *American Political Science Review* 97(3): 483-499.

Funston, B. W, E Meehan. (1995). *Canada's Constitutional Law in Nutshell.* Toronto: Carswell.

Gely, R. and Spiller, P. (1990). "A Rational Choice Theory of Supreme Court Statutory Decisions with Applications to the State Farm and Grove City Cases," *Journal of Law, Economics and Organization.* 6(2): 263-300

George, A. (2000). "Case Studies and Theory Development: The Method of Structured, Focused Comparison." In *Diplomacy: New Approaches in History, Theory, and Policy*, ed. P. G. Lauren. New York: The Free Press.

Gillman, H. (1993). *The Constitution Besieged: The Rise and Demise of Lochner Era Police Powers Jurisprudence.* Durham: Duke University Press.

Gillman, H., Clayton, C. W. (1999). *Supreme Court Decision-Making: New Institutionalist Approaches.* Chicago: University of Chicago Press.

Gillman, H., Clayton, C. W. (1999). *The Supreme Court in American Politics: New Institutionalist Interpretations.* Lawrence, KS: University Press of Kansas.

Ginsburg, T. (2003). *Judicial Review in New Democracies: Constitutional Courts in Asian Cases.* Cambridge: Cambridge University Press.

Goldstein, L. (2004). "From Democracy to Juristocracy." *Law & Society Review* 38 (3):611-29.

Graber, M. A. (1993). "The Nonmajoritarian Difficulty: Legislative Deference to the Judiciary." *Studies in American Political Development* 7:35-73.

Graber, M. A. (2005). "Constructing Judicial Review." *Annual Review of Political Science* 8:425-51.

Guarnieri, Carlo, and Patrizia Pederzoli. (2002). *The Power of Judges: A Comparative Study of Courts and Democracy.* Oxford: Oxford University Press.

Gunlicks, A. B. (1999). "Fifty Years of German Federalism: An Overview and Some Developments." In The Federal Republic of Germany at Fifty, ed. P. H. Merkl. New York: Palgrave.

Hall, P. (1986). *Governing the Economy: The Politics of State Intervention in Britain and France.* New York: Oxford University Press.

Hall, P. and Taylor, R. (1996). "Political science and the three new institutionalisms." *Political Studies.* 44: 936-957.

Hilbink, Lisa. (2007). *Judges beyond Politics in Democracy and Dictatorship: Lessons from Chile.* New York: Cambridge University Press.

Hirschl, R. (2004). *Towards Juristocracy: The Origins and Consequences of the New Constitutionalism.* Constitutional Courts in Asian Cases. Cambridge: Harvard University Press.

Hogg, P. W. (2007) Constitutional Law of Canada. Scarborough, Ontario: Carswell.

Immergut, E. (1992). *Health Politics: Interests and Institutions in Western Europe.* Cambridge: Cambridge University Press.

Ipsen, J. (1983). "Constitutional Review of Laws." In *Main Principles of the German Basic Law*, ed. C. Starck. Baden-Baden: Nomos Verlagsgesellschaft.

Jackman, M. (1995). The Status of the Foetus Under Canadian Law. *Health Law in Canada 15*(3): 1-11.

Jaeger, Renate (2000). Interview. Karlsruhe, Germany , 2/21/00.

Kellough, G. (1996). *Aborting Law: An Exploration of the Politics of Motherhood and Medicine.* Toronto: University of Toronto Press.

Klein-Schonnenfeld, S. (1994). "Germany" in *Abortion in the New Europe: A Comparative Handbook* , ed. B. Rolston and A.Eggert. Westport, CT: Greenwood Press 119-138.

Kokott, J. (1996). "German Constitutional Jurisprudence and European Integration". *European Public Law 2*: 237.

Kokott, J. "Report on Germany", in *The European Court and the National Courts—Doctrine and Jurisprudence: Legal Change in Its Social Context.*, A-M Slaughter, A. Stone Sweet and J.H.H Weiler. (eds.) Oxford: Hart Publishing, 1998.

Kommers, D.P. (1977) ""Abortion and the Constitution: The Cases of West Germany and the United States" in *Abortion: New Directions for Policy Studies,* E. Manier, W. Liu, and D. Solomon, South Bend: University of Notre Dame Press, 1977: 83-116.

Kommers, D. P. (1997). *The Constitutional Jurisprudence of the Federal Republic of Germany.* (Second edition). Durham: Duke University Press.

Krasner, S. (1991). "Global Communications and National Power: Life on the Pareto Frontier." *World Politics* 43:336-66.

Landfried, C. (1988). "Constitutional Review and Legislation in the Federal Republic of Germany." In *Constitutional Review and Legislation*, ed. C. Landfried. Baden-Baden: Nomos Verlagsgesellschaft.

Leonardy,U. (1991). *"The Working relationships between the Bund and the Länder in the Federal Republic of Germany"* in *German Federalism Today.* C. Jeffery and P. Savigear (eds.). London: Leicester University Press.

Lijphart, A. (1968). *The Politics of Accommodation. Pluralism and Democracy in the Netherlands*. Berkeley: University of California Press.

Lijphart, A. (1971). "Comparative politics and the comparative method." *American Political Science Review* 65(3): 682-693.

Lovell, G. (2003). *Legislative Deferrals; Statutory Ambiguity, Judicial Power and American Democracy.* Cambridge: Cambridge University Press.

Macdermid, R. and Albo, G. (2001). "Ontario: Divided Province, Growing Protests: Ontario moves Right" in *The Provincial State in Canada: Politics in the Provinces and the Territories,* K. Brownsey & M. Howlett (eds.). Peterborough: Broadview Press: 163-202.

Magiera, S. (1983). "Application of the Basic Law." in *Main Principles of the German Basic Law*, C. Starck (ed). Baden-Baden: Nomos Verlagsgesellschaft.

Malcolmson, P. and R. Myers. (1996). *The Canadian Regime.* Ontario: Broadview Press.

Maltzman, F., and P. Wahlbeck. (1996). "Strategic Policy Considerations and Voting Fluidity on the Burger Court." *American Political Science Review* 90: 581-592.

Maltzman, F., J.F. Spriggs III, and P. Wahlbeck. (2000). *Crafting Law on the Supreme Court: The Collegial Game.* Cambridge, UK: Cambridge University Press.

Manfredi, C. (2001) *Judicial Power and the Charter: Canada and the Paradox of Liberal Constitutionalism.* Ontario: Oxford University Press.

March, J. and J. Olsen. (1989). *Rediscovering Institutions: The Organizational Basis of Politics.* New York: Free Press.

Mattli, W., and A-M Slaughter. (1998). "Revisiting the European Court of Justice." *International Organization* 52 (1):177-209.

McCann, M. (1994). *Rights at Work.* University of Chicago Press.

McCann, M. (1996). "Causal versus Constitutive Explanations (or, On the Difficulty of Being so Positive…)" *Law and Social Inquiry.* 21 (2): 457-482.

McConnell, M. L. (1994). "Abortion-Provincial Legislation-Control over Health Care- *R. v Morgentaler.*" *The Canadian Bar Review, 73*: 417-430.

McMahon, K. (2003). *Reconsidering Roosevelt on Race: How the Presidency Paved the Road to Brown.* Chicago: University of Chicago Press.

McMahon, K., and M. Paris. (1998). "The Politics of Rights revisited: Rosenberg, McCann and the New Institutionalism," in *Leveraging the Law: Using the Courts to Achieve Social Change*, D. Schultz (ed). New York: Peter Lang.

Meisel, J. (1995). Multinationalism and the Federal Idea: A Synopsis" in *Rethinking Federalism: Citizens, Markets and Governments in a Changing World*, K. Knop, S. Ostry, R. Simeon & K. Swinton. (Eds.). Vancouver: UBC Press.

Morton, F. L. (1992). *Morgentaler v Borowski: Abortion, the Charter and the Courts.* Toronto: McClellan and Stewart, Inc.

Murphy, W. (1962). *Congress and the Supreme Court.* Chicago: University of Chicago Press.

Murphy, W. (1964). *Elements of Judicial Strategy*, University of Chicago Press.

Murphy, W..; Pritchett, C. H. (1961). *Courts, Judges, and Politics: An Introduction to the Judicial Process.* New York: Random House.

Neuman, G. (1995) "Casey in the Mirror: Abortion, Abuse and the Right to Protection in the United States and Germany" *The American Journal of Comparative Law,* 43(2): . 273-314

Nicholls, A. J. (1997). *The Bonn Republic: West Germany Democracy, 1945-1990.* London: Longman.

North, D. (1990). *Institutions, Institutional Change and Economic Performance.* Cambridge: Cambridge University Press.

Olson, D., & Franks, C. (1993). "Representation in the Policy Process" in Representation and Policy Formation in Federal Systems. Berkeley: Institute of Governmental Studies, University of California.

Orren, K. and S. Skowronek (1994). "Beyond the Iconography of Order: Notes for a New Institutionalism" in *The Dynamics of American Politics,* eds. L. Dodd and C. Jillson. New York: Westview Press.

Pacelle, R. (2002). *The Role of the Supreme Court in American Politics: The Least Dangerous Branch?* Boulder, CO: Westview Press.

Peretti, T. (1999). *In Defense of a Political Court.* Princeton, NJ: Princeton University Press.

Perry, H.W. (1994). *Deciding to Decide: Agenda Setting in the United States.* Cambridge: Harvard University Press.

Pickerill, J. M. (2004). *Constitutional Deliberation in Congress: The Impact of Judicial Review in a Separated System.* Durham, N.C.: Duke University Press.

Pierson, P. (1994). *Dismantling the Welfare State? Reagan, Thatcher and the Politics of Retrenchment.* Cambridge: Cambridge University Press.

Pierson, P. (2000). "Path Dependence, Increasing Returns, and the Study of Politics." American Political Science Review 94(2): 251-267.

Powe, Lucas. 2000. The Warren Court and American politics. Cambridge, Mass.: Bellknap Press. Pritchett, C. Herman.

Pritchett, C.H. (1961). *Congress versus the Supreme Court, 1957-1960.* Minneapolis: University of Minnesota Press.

Provine, D. (1999). "Revolutionizing Rights : Epp's Comparative Perspective" *Law & social inquiry: Journal of the American Bar Foundation.* 24: (4)

Prützel-Thomas, M. (1993) "Abortion Issue and the Federal Constitutional Court" *German Politics* (2)3: 467-484.

Quass, M. (1984). *"Federal Republic of Germany" Abortion Law and Public Policy*. Dordrecht: Martin Nijhoff Publishers, 41-60.

Ress, G. (1994). "The Constitution and the Maastricht Treaty: Beyond Cooperation and Conflict." *German Politics,* 3 (3): 47-73.

Richards, M. and H. Kritzer,, (2002)"Jurisprudential Regimes in Supreme Court Decision Making" *American Political Science Review* (96): 305-320

Riker, W. (1964). "Some Ambiguities in the Notion of Power." American Political Science Review 58(2): 341-349.

Riker, W. H. (1964). *Federalism: Origin, Operation, Significance.* Boston: Little, Brown and Company.

Roberts, G. K. (2000). *German Politics Today*. Manchester, UK: Manchester University Press.

Roche, M. (2001). Interview. Portland, OR, 10/5/01.

Rodgers, H. and Bullock, C. (1976). "School Desegregation: A Multivariate Test Of The Role Of Law In Effectuating Social Change," *American Politics Quarterly*: 153-176.

Rohde, D., and H. *Spaeth. (1976)*. *Supreme Court Decision Making*. San Francisco: W.H. Freeman and Co.

Rosenberg, G. (1991). *The Hollow Hope: Can Courts Bring About Social Change?* Chicago: University of Chicago Press.

Russell, P. (1987). *The Judiciary in Canada: the third branch of government.* Toronto: McGraw-Hill Ryerson.

Russell, P. H., Knopff. R.and Morton F.L.. (1989). *Federalism and the Charter: Leading Constitutional Decisions.* Ottawa: Carleton University Press.

Scharpf, F. W. (1988). "The Joint Decision Trap: Lessons From German Federalism and European Integration." *Public Administration* 66:239-78.

Schlegel, C. "Landmark in German Abortion Law: The German 1995 Compromise compared with English Law" *International Journal of Law, Policy and the Family* (11) 1: 36-61

Schmidt, M. G. (2003). *Political Institutions in the Federal Republic of Germany*. Oxford: Oxford University Press.

Schubert, G. (1958). "The Study of Judicial Decision Making as an Aspect of Political Behavior." *American Political Science Review* 52: 1007-25.

Segal, J. and H. Spaeth. (1993). *The Supreme Court and the Attitudinal Model.* New York: Cambridge University Press.

Shapiro, M. and A. Stone Sweet. (2002). *On Law, Politics and Judicialization.* Oxford: Oxford University Press.

Shepsle, K. (1986). "Institutional equilibrium and equilibrium institutions," In *The Science of Politics,* Herbert Weisberg (ed.). New York: Agathon.

Silverstein, H. (1996) *Unleashing Rights: Law, Meaning, and the Animal Rights Movement.* Ann Arbor, Michigan: University of Michigan Press.

Skcopol, T. (1992). *Protecting Soldiers and Mothers: The Political Origins of Social Policy in the United States.* Cambridge: Belknap Press of Harvard University Press.

Slaughter, A-M. and W. Mattli (1997)."The Role of National Courts in the Process of European Integration: Accounting for Judicial Preferences and Constraints" in *The European Courts and National Courts: Doctrine and Jurisprudence.* Slaughter, A-M, A. Sweet, and J.H.H. Weiler, (eds.) Oxford: Hart Publishing.

Smiley, D.V. (1980). *Canada in Question: Federalism in the Eighties.* Toronto: University of Toronto Press.

Smiley, D.V. and R.L. Watts. (1985). *Intrastate Federalism in Canada.* Toronto: University of Toronto Press.

Smith, P. (2001). "Alberta: Experiments in Governance-From Social Credit to the Klein Revolution, in *The Provincial State in Canada: Politics in the Provinces and the Territories,* K. Brownsey & M. Howlett (eds.). Peterborough: Broadview Press: 277-308.

Smith, R. (1988) "Political Jurisprudence, the 'New Institutionalism,' and the Future of Public Law," *American Political Science Review* 82: 89-108.

Snyder, R. (2001). "Scaling Down: The Subnational Comparative Method." *Studies in Comparative International Development* 36(1): 93-110.

Songer, D. Segal.J. & Cameron. C.(1994). "The Hierarchy of Justice: Testing a Principal-Agent Model of Supreme Court-Circuit Court Interactions" *American Journal of Political Science* 38:673-696

Spiller, P. and Gely, R. (1992). "Congressional Control or Judicial Independence: The Determinants of U.S. Supreme Court Labor-Relations Decisions, 1949-1988," *RAND Journal of Economics.* 23(4): 463-492,

Spriggs, J. (1997). "Explaining Federal Bureaucratic Compliance with Supreme Court Opinions." *Political Research Quarterly* 50: 567-593.

Spriggs, J. (1996). "The Supreme Court and Federal Administrative Agencies: A Resource-Based Theory and Analysis of Judicial Impact." *American Journal of Political Science* 40: 1122-1151.

Stern R., E. Gressman, S. Shapiro, and K. S. Geller (2007) Supreme Court Practice Arlington, VA: BNA Books

Stone Sweet, A. (1999). "Judicialization and the Construction of Governance." *Comparative Political Studies,* 32: 147-84.

Stone Sweet, A. (2000) *Governing with Judges: Constitutional Politics in Europe* Oxford: Oxford University Press.

Tarrow, S. (1994). *Power in Movement: Collective Action, Social Movements and Politics.* Cambridge University Press.

Tate. C. N. (1992). "Comparative Judicial Review and Public Policy: Concepts and Overview" in *Comparative Judicial Review and Public Policy,* Jackson, D. W. and C. N. Tate (eds.). Westport: Greenwood Press.

Thelen, K, with S. Steinmo and F. Longstreth, eds. (1992). *Structuring Politics: Historical Institutionalism in Comparative Analysis.* Cambridge: Cambridge University Press.

Thorlakson, Lori (2003). "Comparing Federal Institutions: Power and Representation in Six Federations." *West European Politics* 26 (2):1-22.

Tribe, L. H. (1992). *Abortion: The Clash of Absolutes.* New York: W.W.Norton.

Truman, D. (1951). *The Governmental Process.* New York: Knopf.

Tuohy, C. J. (1992). *Policy and Politics in Canada: Institutionalized Ambivalence.* Philadelphia: Temple University Press.

Van Dam, Paul. (1991). *Letter.* Salt Lake City, UT, January 24, 1991.

Van Zyl Smit, D. (1994) "Reconciling the irreconcilable? Recent Developments in the German law on abortion", *Medical Law Review,* 2(3), 320-320.

Wahlbeck, P. J.; J. F. Spriggs; and F. Maltzman. (1998). "Marshalling the Court: Bargaining and Accommodation on the United States Supreme Court." *American Journal of Political Science* 42:294-315.

Walther, S. (1993) "Thou Shall Not (But Thou Mayest): Abortion after the German Constitutional Court's 1993 Landmark Decision", *German Year Book of International Law*. (36) 391.

Ward, N. (1987). Dawson's The Government of Canada (6 ed.). Toronto: University of Toronto Press.

Wasby, S. (1970). *The Impact of the United States Supreme Court: Some Perspectives*. Homewood Ill: Dorsey Press.

Watts, R. (1987). "The American Constitution in Comparative Perspective: A comparison of Federalism in the United States and Canada", *Journal of American History*. 74(3), 769-792.

Weisman, N. (1996). "Provincial Political Cultures." in *Provinces: Canadian Provincial Politics*, in C. Dunn (ed.). Peterborough, Ontario: Broadview Press: 21-62.

Whittington, K. E. (2003). "Legislative sanctions and the strategic environment of judicial review." *I Con: The International Journal of Comparative Law* 1 (3):446-74.

Whittington, K. E. (2005). ""Interpose Your Friendly Hand": Political Supports for the Exercise of Judicial Review by the United States Supreme Court." *Ameican Political Science Review* 99 (4):583-96

Wright, C. and Miller, A, et al. (2001). *Federal Practice and Procedure*. West Publishing

Wuertenberger, T. (1994). "The principle of Subsidiarity as Constitutional Principle." in *Jarhbuch zur Staats-und Verwaltunswissenschaft*, G. F. Schuppert (ed.). Baden-Baden: Nomos Verlagsgesellschaft.

Media Sources

Another Abortion Law Fight? ACLU, Doctors to Decide Today. (1993a, B1). *Salt Lake Tribune*, B1.

Ballot Initiative prompts showdown over state abortion funding. (1986). *The Oregonian*, p.B6.

Bayern mahnt Spruch des Bundesverfassungsgericht. (1991, December 9) *Frankfurter Allegemeine*.

Bayern prüft Abtreibungs-Urteil. (1998, October 29). *Die Welt*.

Die Sorgen der Elke H. (1992, November 28). *Frankfurter Rundschau*.

Doctors are warned not to ask pay in advance of treatment. (1980, August 2). *The Globe and Mail*.

Kontroverse um Beratung von Schwangeren in den neuen Ländern. (1990, March 10). *Der Tagesspiegel.*

Legislators Should Steer Away From Costly Abortion Crusade. (1991, January 23). *Salt Lake Tribune* p. A6.

Marleau ready to go after renegade provinces. (1994, May 21) *The Medical Post,* p. 34.

May set up an Abortion Clinic in Halifax, Morgentaler says. (1985, March 3). *The Globe and Mail,* p. 5.

Medical Bill Challenged. (1989, June 14th). *The Daily News.*

Morgentaler to Take Government to Court. (1994, January 25). *The Medical Post,:* p. 13.

Nation Watches Oregon's test of abortion issue. (1990, July 22) *Statesmen Journal,* p. G1.

Notes. (2001) *Canadian Medical Journal* 164 (6):847.

Schmidt-Jortzig rügt bayerischen Sonderweg. (1996, May 20). *Frankfurter Rundschau,.*

Schwangersschaftsabbruch als "qualifizierte Dienstleistung"? (1998, June 24). *Frankfurter Allgemeine.*

Sonderregelung Bayerns verfasungswirdrig. (1998, October 28) *Neues Deutschland.*

Streibl bekräftigt: Fristenlösung und Grundgesetz sind unvereinbar.. (1990, September 8). *Deutsche Tagespost.* Utah Lawmaker Drafts Another Abortion Law. (1993b, May 18.) *Salt Lake Tribune,* May 18: D12.

Verfassungsgericht stoppt Sonderweg. (1998, October 28) *Handlesblatt.*

Allen, G. (1990, October 25). Rae hinting at court challenge of abortion law. *The Globe and Mail.*

Ames, S. B. (1989, July 16). Abortion likely to dominate Oregon politics for years. *The Oregonian,* p. A20.

Associated Press. (1992, November 27). 'Give Up 'Foolish' Abortion Fight, Bangerter Tells Law's Supporters. *Salt Lake Tribune,*p. D2.

Athon, A. (1995, May 23). Teen Abortion Bill Fails House. *Statesman Journal,*p. A1.

Bangerter, N. (1991). Statement by Governor Norman Bangerter. Salt Lake City, Utah.

Bauman, J. (1996, June 17). Court Overturns Rejection of Abortion Law." *Deseret News,* p.1.

Baumlisberger, B, Hilbig M. and H. Kistenfeger.(1998, November 2). Der Kater kommt noch. *Focus,* November 2.

Blackwell, T. (1994, August 31). Keep away from Clinics, judge orders pro-life protestors. *Ottawa Citizen,* p. A5.

Borsellino, M., Gagnon, L., Pole, K., Walker, R., & Driver, D. (1995). Penalties for Alberta Could reach $5 million with smaller amounts for other provinces. *Medical Post,* p. 1;51.

Bray, D., & Fisher, M. (1994, November 19). "Klein turns tables on Marleau." *Calgary Sun,* p, 21.

Brent, B. (1992, May 19). Opposing sides in abortion issue decry violence. *Toronto Star.*

Bundesverfassungericht. (1997, June 24)."Presstelle." No. 58/97.

Canadian Press (1988, February 2). OHIP to cover private abortions. *Edmonton Journal.*

Canadian Press (1980, April 3). Fee double for abortion review told. *Toronto Star.*

Canadian Press (1985, April 27). Alberta, P.E.I latest provinces to reject Morgentaler clinic. *Ottawa Citizen.*

Canadian Press (1987, December 18). Abortions out at women's clinic awarded to Catholic hospital. *Toronto Star,* p. 16.

Canadian Press (1989a, November 7). Clinic in Halifax hit with injunctions. *Toronto Star.*

Canadian Press (1989b, May 25). N.S. rejects Morgentaler clinic offer. *The Globe and Mail,* A10.

Canadian Press (1995a, October 7) Alberta Doctors refuse request to help rewrite abortion laws. *Ottawa Citizen.*

Canadian Press (1995b, November 7) Alberta plan rejected to end health clinic row. *The Globe and Mail..*

Canadian Press (1995c, October 11). Alberta retreats in attempt to change abortion policy. *The Globe and Mail.*

Cernetig, M. (1995, April 12). Ottawa accused of ruining medicare." *The Globe and Mail.*

Collins, L. (1996, February 21). House oks 2 Anti-Abortion Bills Despite Possibility of Lawsuits. *Deseret News,* p. 1.

Costanzo, J. (1996, December 24). "Appeals Court Strikes Down Abortion Law." *Deseret News,* p.1.

Cox, K. (1989, March 17). Nova Scotia bans abortion clinics. *The Globe and Mail,* p. 1.

Crosby, C. (1990, November 22). Governor Undecided on Pending Bill: Threats Won't Dictate Abortion Policy. *Salt Lake Tribune*, p. 2B.

Cunningham, J., & Kondro, J. (1986). Doctors warned against refusing abortions. *Calgary Herald*, October 8.

Dedyna, K., & Creswell, D. (1985, January 4). Morgentaler faces battle in Alberta. *Edmonton Journal*, p. 1.

Delacourt, S. (1986, July 2). Curtailing of abortions shows need for clinics, pro-choice groups say. *The Globe and Mail*.

Emundts, C. (1999, March 22). Bayern: Hürden für legale Abtreibung. *Die Tageszeitung*.

Fahys, J. (1993). Lawmakers Tack 24 Hour Waiting Period Onto Utah's Abortion Law. *Salt Lake Tribune*, A1.

Fendick, R. (1989, March 17). Abortion clinics banned in NS. *The Daily News,*p.1.

Fendick, R., & Lightstone, M. (1989, June 7). Medical Bill scorned as cover to fight abortion clinic suit. *The Daily News,*p. 1.

Ferguson, D. (1995, January 7). Fee-charging clinics face ban. *The Toronto Star,*p.A6.

Ferguson, D., & Brent, B. (1992, May 21). Ontario beefs up abortion clinics' security. *Toronto Star*, p.A1, 7.

Feschuk, S. (1995a, July 20). Alberta may stop funding abortions. *The Globe and Mail*, p. A1,A2.

Feschuk, S. (1995b, July 20). PM rejects Klein's medicare ideas. *The Globe and Mail*, p. A1,A9.

Fietz, M. (1996, March 24). Ich werde nicht weichen. *Die Welt*.

Flavelle, D. (1986, June 30). Abortion too hard to get in some areas. *Toronto Star*, p. A11.

Gilbert, T. (1989, February 12). League battle abortion cut. *Calgary Herald*.

Graupner, H. (1998, October 28). Der Sonderweg wird zur Sackgasse. *Süddeutsche Zeitung*.

Greenspon, E. (1995, October 16). "Ottawa tallies clinic' fees. *The Globe and Mail*, p. A5.

Ha, T. (1995, March 18). Marleau, PM vow to protect medicare. *The Globe and Mail*, p. A1; A9.

Harrie, D. (1992, December 22). Levitt, Bangerter Meet. *Salt Lake Tribune*, p. B2.

Harrie, D. and Cilwick, T. (1995). Levitt revives abortion law fight. *Salt Lake Tribune*, p. A1.

Harrington, D. (1986, March 13). Alberta will continue seeking extra-billing ban, official says. *Toronto Star*.

Heinrich, J. (1988, February 19). Abortion clinics get $1m to grow. *The Citizen*, p. C1.

Henton, D. (1986, October 15). Abortion dilemma not my fault, it's a federal issue, Scott says. *Toronto Star*.

Henton, D. (1995, October 12). Alberta asks for delay in clinic fight. *Toronto Star*, p. A3.

Holzhaider, H. (1996, April 18). CSU begrüsst Mitwirkungspflict. *Süddeutsche Zeitung*.

Hortsch, D. (1986a, November 5). Abortion measure failing. *The Oregonian*, p. D2.

Hortsch, D. (1986b, September 27). Fiscal Statement ordered removed from Measure 6. *The Oregonian*, p. C1.

Hortsch, D. (1986c, October 13). Tight contest seen on measure to ban abortion funding. *The Oregonian*, p. C2.

Hortsch, D. (May 30 1991). Governor to redirect family planning funds. *The Oregonian*, p. B4.

Hossie, L. (1985, November 2). Doctors demanding advance payment for abortion services, women charge. *The Globe and Mail*, p. A19.

Hossie, L. (1990, November 1). Ontario to inure abortion bill be dropped. *The Globe and Mail*.

House, D. (1991, September 11). Defend Abortion Law Now, Rules Judge. *Salt Lake Tribune*, p. A1.

Hunt, S. (1997, June 17). Utah Abortion Law Legal Battle is Over. *Salt Lake Tribune*, p. A1.

Kaufmann, B. (1995, September 24). MDs Uneasy with guidelines task. *Calgary Sun*, p.5.

Kennedy, M. (1987, March 14). Ontario rejects special clinics for abortions. *The Ottawa Citizen*, p. A1,2.

Kennedy, M. (1997, September 30). "Provinces continue to flout Medicare." *The Ottawa Citizen*, p.A6.

Kennedy, R. (1986, October 22). Medical Legal Fee for Therapeutic Abortion. *Calgary Sun*, np.

Knapp, U. (1998, October 28). Bayerns Abtreibungsgesetz ist verfassungswirdig. *Frankfurter Rundschau*, np.

Knapp, U. (1998, October 28). Karlsruhe und die Farbe Lila. *Frankfurter Rundschau*, np.

Laatz,J. (1986). Oregon has relative calm in litigation's choppy seas. *The Oregonian*, p. B5.

Laghi, B. (1995, August 13). Abortion battle heating up. *Calgary Herald*, p. A12.

Lechtleitner, U. (1990, September 22). Im Dienst für die Menschen. *Der Tagesspeigel*, np.

Leclerque, J. (1998, October 28). Bundesverfassungsrichter waren erstmals Fernsehstars. *Badische Neueste Nachrichten*, np.

Leeb, H. (1996, June 1). Gemäss dem Grundgesetz. *Bayern-Kurier*, np.

Leeson, F. (1990, March 14). State high court hears arguments on initiative to curb minors' abortions. *The Oregonian*, np.

Legge, L. (1995, September 24). Doctors are wary of abortion debate. *Calgary Herald*, p.A10.

Legge, L. (1989a, March, 22). Abortion Battle Lines Set. *The Chronicle-Herald*, p.1.

Legge, L. (1989b, March 17). Abortion Clinics Outlawed. *The Chronicle-Herald*, p.1,20.

Legge, L. (1989c, September 5). N.S. Abortion Law challenged. *The Chronicle-Herald*, p.1.

Legge, L. (1989d, June 7th). New N.S. bill prohibits non-hospital abortions. *The Chronicle-Herald*, np.

Legge, L. (1989e, January 18). No Need for Clinic-Leaders. *The Chronicle-Herald*, p.1,16.

Legge, L. (1989f, January 27). Province Pursues plan to block abortion clinic. *The Chronicle-Herald*,p.1,12.

Legge, L., & Proctor, S. (1989, May 25th). Morgentaler delays opening abortion clinic. *The Chronicle-Herald*, p. 1.

Lightstone, M. (1995, January 12). N.S. still won't fund abortions. *The Daily News*, p.3.

Locherty, L. (1986, November 17). Abortion travel aid offered. *Calgary Herald*, np.

Locherty, L., & Pratt, S. (1986, November 13). "No action by minister on abortion." *Calgary Herald*, np.

MacDonald, D. (1982). "Tougher Laws on Abortion Favoured." *Chronicle Herald*, June 16.

Massey, B. (1995, May 20). Judges Grill Utah Abortion Law Defender. *Salt Lake Tribune*, p. B2.

Matheson, S. (1981). Salt Lake City, April 3, 1981.

Maychack, M. (1987, March 7). Ontario urged to license clinics and abolish abortion committees. *Toronto Star*, np

Maychack, M., & Millar, C. (1991, February 2). Surge in abortion protests forecast as federal bill dies. *Toronto Star*, np.

McGarry, J. (1980, May 10). Alberta urged to probe abortion committees. *The Catholic Register*, p. 8.

McLaren, C. (1988, June 4). Provincial bill aims to limit spread of abortion clinics.*" Globe and Mail*, p. A5.

McMonagle, D., Hossie, L., & Silversides, A. (1986, February 25). MD's criticized for quitting abortion committee. *Globe and Mail*, np.

Mickleburgh, R. (1993, April 20). Ontario seeks court order. *Globe and Mail*, p. A5.

Miller, M. (1984, June 24). Board vetoes local abortions. *Fort McMurray Today*, p.1.

Mitchell, A. (1995, September 25). "Alberta to restrict abortion access.*" Globe and Mail*, p. A1, 2.

Morningstar, L. (1986, October 17). Doctors want fee for reports to abortion committees. *Edmonton Journal,*p. B2.

Moulton-Barrett, D. (1990, April 17). Abortion Group gets a split decision from N.S. court. *The Medical Post*, p. 51.

Moulton-Barrett, D. (1991a, August 6). Round three imminent in N.S.fight with Morgentaler. *The Medical Post*, p. 43.

Moulton-Barrett, D. (1991b, December 3). Supreme Court to allow N.S. to appeal Morgentaler case. *The Medical Post*, p. 50.

Moysa, M. (1988, September 29). Group fears cuts in access to abortion. *Edmonton Journal*, np.

Network, S. S. (1995, September 24). Defining 'medically necessary' abortions will be a challenge, Alberta doctors say. *Ottawa Citizen*, p. A6.

Neumann, C.(1996, October 10). Klage gegen Sonderweg bei Paragraph 218. *Süddeutsche Zeitung,* np.

Payne, E. (1994, February 8). Ontario government moves abortion battle into court. *Ottawa Citizen*, p. A4.

Pole, K. (1995). Feds won't lead quest to define medical necessity *Ottawa Citizen*, p. A33.

Rich, P. (1988, June 28). Ontario College sets medical standards for abortions. *Medical Post*, np.

Roberts, R. (1989, August 9th). Clinic Ban challenge delayed. *The Daily News*, p. 1.

Schifrin, L. (1986, November 17). Alberta situation fuels pro-choice advocates. *Toronto Star*, p. A17.

Schlötzer-Scotland, C. (1996, May 13). Der Bund lässt Bayern frieie Hand. *Süddeutsche Zeitung*, np.

Semerad, T. (1994, October 11). Leavitt didn't know of Abortion Filing. *Salt Lake Tribune*, p. C1.

Silversides, A. (1986, June 25). Health Act behind move on billing. *Globe and Mail*, np.

Sisco, C. (1991, January 26). Bangerter Signs Nation's Toughest Abortion Bill. *Salt Lake Tribune*, p. A1.

Slotnick, L. (1983, June 6). OHIP pays doctor for illegal abortions. *Globe and Mail*, p. 9.

Speirs, R. (1987, November 21). Caplan ducks real question about clinics. *Toronto Star*, p. D1.

Speirs, R. (1988, June 4). Liberals have brainwave on abortion. *Toronto Star*, p. D5.

Stamm, B. (1996, April 27). Bayerns klare Position. *Bayern-Kurier*, np.

Streibel, M. (1990, March 10). Warum Bayern in Karlsruhe klagt. Bayern-Kurier, np.

Terry, M. (1983, March 12). Morgentaler loses bid on lease in Calgary. *The Catholic Register*, p. 19.

Thalman, J. (1989, April 10). Oregon awaiting decision. *The Register-Guard*, p. A1.

Thelen, S. (1996, August 2). Das Abtreibungsrecht landet wieder in Karlsrue. *Stuttgarter Zeitung*, np.

Tibbetts, J. (1989, October 18). Abortion Law appeal dismissed. *The Chronicle-Herald*, np.

Todd, P. (1990, November 29). Ontario plans full funding for abortions. *Toronto Star*, np.

Ubelacher, S. (1986). *Canadian Press*, June 6.

Valorizi. (1986). *Canadian Press*, June 25.

Walker, R. (1986, October 24). Abortion Crisis hitting Alberta. *Calgary Herald*, p. A1-2.

Walker, R. (1988). Patients now need second opinion for Alberta Abortion. *Medical Post*, np.

Walker, R. (1991, September 23). 20 Weeks new limit on abortion. *Calgary Herald*, p. A1.

Walker, R. (1996, June 11, 1996). Alberta settles dispute over private clinic. *Medical Post.*

Walker, W. (1986, September 27). Toronto hospital could be abortion centre, Scott says. *Toronto Star,* np.

Walker, W., & Moloney, P. (1993, March 24). NDP pursuing ban on abortion protests. *Toronto Star,* p. A13.

Ward, B. (1995, October 20). N.S. Willing to pay the price on abortion policy-Stewart. *The Mail-Star,* p. 1.

White, S. (1986). *Canadian Press,* February 24.

Wright, Jeff. (1990, November 7). Oregonians shoot down both abortion measures. *The Register-Guard,* p. A1, 4.

Canada

Law

British North America Acts, 1867 to 1964.

Criminal Code, RSC 1970, c C-34, s.251

Criminal Code (R.S.C., 1985, c. C-46)

Supreme Court Act, R.S. 1985, c. S-26, 53 (1, 2)

Supreme Court Act, R.S. 1985

Federal and Provincial Documents

Committee on the Operation of the Abortion Law. (1977). *Report of the Committee on the Operation of the Abortion Law.* Ottawa.

Dunsmuir, M. (1998). *Abortion: Constitutional and Legal Developments* (No. 89-10E). Ottawa: Library of Parliament, Research Branch, Law and Government Division.

Government of Ontario (1991). *Brief of the Government of Ontario to the Senate on Bill C-43 An Act Respecting Abortion.* Toronto: Government of Ontario.

MacLean, L. (1995). *Province wants better solution for private clinics.* Halifax: Department of Health.

Ministry of Health (1993). *New Abortion Services for Ottawa.* Toronto: Ministry of Health.

Ministry of Health (1994). *Morgentaler proposal accepted for Ottawa abortion clinic.* Toronto: Ministry of Health.

Supreme Court of Canada, *Transcript of Appeal Proceedings* 10/3/1988 *Borowski* case

Provincial Legislative Debates

House of Assembly, (1982). *Debates and Proceedings*, Nova Scotia. 53rd, 1st session 82-76 Session. 3936-3942

House of Assembly (1991). *Assembly Debates*, 55th, 2nd Session. *Nova Scotia.* 7865-7867

Legislative Assembly, (1987a). *Legislative Debates*, Alberta 21st, 2nd Sess. 234

Legislative Assembly (1987b). *Legislative Debates*, Alberta 21st, 2nd Sess. 1351-1352

Legislative Assembly of Alberta (1988) *Legislative Debates*, 21st Legislature, 3rd Session, Alberta.

Legislative Assembly of Ontario (1990). *Legislative Debates*, 35th Legislature, 1st Session. Ontario. 2198-2199

Supreme Court of Canada Court Cases

A-G Ontario v A.G Canada (*Reference Appeal case)* (1912)
Anti-Inflation Act Reference (1976) 2 S.C.R. 373
Borowski v. Canada (Attorney general), (1989) 1 S.C.R. 342
Canada Assistance Plan Reference (1991) 2 S.C.R. 525
Constitutional Patriation Reference (1981), 1 S.C.R. 753
Manitoba Language Rights Reference (1985) 1 S.C.R. 721
Morgentaler v the Queen (1975) (Morgentaler I) 20 CCC 2nd 449, 491
Ng Extradition Reference (1991) 2 S.C.R. 858
Nova Scotia Board of Censors v McNeil (1976) 2 SCR 271
Operation Dismantle v the Queen (1985) 1 SCR 441
Provincial Court Judges Reference (1997) 3 S.C.R. 3
Quebec Sales Tax Reference (1994) 2 S.C.R. 715
Quebec Veto Reference (1982) 2 S.C.R. 793
R. v Morgentaler (1988) *(Morgentaler II)* 1 SCR 30, 183
R. v Morgentaler (1993) (*Morgentaler III*) 3 *S.C.R.* 463
R. v Oakes (1986) 1 S.C.R. 103
R. v. Crown Zellerbach (1988) 1 S.C.R. 401
Secession of Quebec Reference (1998). 2 S.C.R. 217
Smith v AG Ontario (1924) 1 SCR 331
Thorson v the Queen (1974) 1 SCR 138
Tremblay v Daigle (1989) 2 SCR 571

United States

Federal Legislation and Law
Detainee Treatment Act of 2005 (H.R. 2863, Title X)
Judiciary Act of 1925 (43 Stat. 936)
Military Commissions Act of 2006 HR-6166
US Constitution

State Legislative Acts, Court Cases and other state documents
Evans, R. M. (1989). "Request for Legislation." Salt Lake City, UT.
Graves, Clark C. (1985). Salt Lake City, March 11, 1985.
Hancock, Janetha. 1989. "Notes on Abortion amendments."
———. 1991. "Abortion Legislation." Salt Lake City, UT: Office of Legislative Research and General Counsel.
———. 1993. "Abortion Law Modification." Salt Lake City: Office of Legislative Research and General Counsel.
Planned Parenthood et al vs Department of Human Resources of the State of Oregon; Leo Hegstrom., Director of the Department of Human Resources for the State of Oregon. (1984). 297 Oregon Supreme Court 562.
Tinker, P. Assistant Attorney General. (1977). "Opinion." Salt Lake City: Office of the Attorney General of the State of Utah.
Tinker, P., Assistant Attorney General. (1981). "Opinion." Salt Lake City: Attorney General of State of Utah.
Utah State Legislature. (1981). Abortion Restrictions. HB 83.
Utah State Legislature. (1991). Abortion Litigation Trust Account and Clarification Amendments. HB No.257.

United States Supreme Court Cases
Adair v US (1908) 208 U.S. 161
Adkins v Children's Hospital (1923) 261 U.S. 525
Alden v Maine (1999) 527 U.S. 706
Allen v Wright (1984) 468 U.S. 737
Baker v Carr (1962) 369 U.S. 186
Barron v Baltimore (1833) 32 U.S. 243
Boumediene v Bush (2008) 553 U.S. ___
Bush v Gore (2000) 531 U.S. 98
City of Boerne v Flores (1997) 521 U.S. 507
Clinton v City of New York (1998) 524 U.S. 417

Cohens v Virginia 19 U.S. 264 (1821)
Coppage v Kansas (1915) 236 U.S. 1 (1915)
Doe v Bolton, 410 U.S. 179 (1973)
Epperson v Arkansas (1968) 393 U.S. 97
Ex Parte McCardle (1868) 74 U.S. 506
Flast v Cohen (1968) 392 U.S. 83
Garcia v San Antonio (1985) 469 U.S. 528
Gibbons v Ogden (1824) *22 U.S. 1*
Gideon v Wainright (1963). 372 U.S. 335
Grizwold v Connecticut (1965) 381 U.S. 479
Hamdan v Rumsfeld (2006) 548 U.S. 557
Hein v Freedom From Religion Foundation (2007) 551 U.S. ____
Kimmel v Board of Regents (2000) 528 U.S. 62
Lochner v New York (1905) 198 U.S. 45
Lujan v Defenders of Wildlife (1992). 504 U.S. 555
Marbury v Madison (1803) 5 U.S. 137
Massachusetts v Environmental Protection Agency (2007) 549 U.S. 497
McCulloch v Maryland (1819) 17 U.S. 316
Mills v Green (1895) 159 US 651
Morrison v US (2000) 529 U.S. 598
Muller v Oregon (1908) 208 U.S. 412
Muskrat v US (1911)219 US 346
National League of Cities v Ursery (1976) 426 U.S. 833
New York v US (1992) 505 U.S. 144
NLRB v Jones (1937). 301 U.S. 1
Planned Parenthood v Casey (1992) 505 U.S. 833
Printz v US (1997) 521 U.S. 898
Roe v Wade (1973) 410 U.S. 113
Seminole Tribe v Florida (1996) 517 U.S. 44
Sierra Club v Morton (1972) 405 U.S. 727
US Term Limits v Thorson (1995) 514 U.S. 779
US v Lopez (1995) 514 U.S. 549
US v Richardson (1974)418 US 166
US v SCRAP (1973) 412 U.S. 669
Washington v Glucksberg (1997) 521 U.S. 702
Webster v. Reproductive Health Services (1989) 492 U.S. 490
West Coast Hotel v Parrish (1937) 300 U.S. 379

Germany

German federal and Constitutional law
Grundgesetz (Basic Law) (GG)
"The Law on the Federal Constitutional Court", *Bundesgesetzblatt
(Federal Law Gazette - BGBl),1951.*
Law on the Federal Constitutional Court *(Federal Law Gazette 1951
and German Bundestag 2001)*
Strafgesetzbuch, (StGB) (Criminal Code)

Laender Laws, Regulations and Legislative Debates
587 Schwangerschaftsabbrüche an allen Uniliniken möglich? Kleine
Anfrage, *Drucksache* 12/1669 Lantag Nordrhein-Westfalen,
February 1, 1997.
Bayerisches Schwangerenhilfeergänzungsgesetz (BaySchwHEG)
(Bavarian Pregnant Woman Assistance Auxiliary Law). (1996).
Bayerisches Gesetz und Verordnungsblatt (GVBl) No. 16 August
9: 328
Bundesverfassungsgericht bestätigt auch das nordrhein-westfälische
Konzept für Lebensschutz - Hilfe und Beratung statt Strafe -
Klares "Nein" aus Karlsruhe für Sonderwege! (Federal
Constitutional Court confirms North Rhine-Westphalia's idea of
the protection of unborn life—help and counseling instead of
punishment—A clear "no" from Karlsruhe in response to "special
routes"), Aktuelle Stunde SPD, *Plenarprotokoll,* Lantag
Nordrhein-Westfalen, *12/100 ,* Nordrhein-Westfalen, June 11,
1998: 8249-8265
Erste Richtlinien für die Anerkennung von Beratungsstellen,
beratenden Ärzten und Aulassung von Einrichtungen zur
Durchführung eines Schwangerschaftsabbruchs nach 218 a des
Strafgesetzbuches. (Preliminary Guidelines for the recognition of
counseling centers, counseling doctors and approval of institutions
that perform abortions according to paragraph 218 of the penal
code. *MinisterialBlatt für das Land Nordrhein-Westfalen,* February
9, 1978.
Gesetz über die soziale Beratung schwangerer Frauen
(Schwangerenberatungsgesetz –SchwBerG) (Law regarding the
social advising of pregnant women), 1977. *Bayerisches Gesezt und
Verordnungsblatt (GVBl),* No. 19 August 12: 401.

Gesetz über die Schwangerenberatung (BaySchweBerG1996) (Law on Counseling of Pregnant Women), 1996. *Bayerisches Gesetz und Verordnungsblatt, (GVBl)* No. 16 August 9: 320

Richtlinien für die Anerkennung vonBeratunsstellen, beratenden Ärzten und Aulassung von Einrichtungen zur Durchführung eines Schwangerschaftsabbruchs nach 218 a des Strafgesetzbuches. (Guidelines for the recognition of counseling centers, counseling doctors and approval of institutions that perform abortions according to paragraph 218 of the penal code). *MinisterialBlatt für das Land Nordrhein-Westfalen.* March 5, 1979

Richtlinien zur staatlichen Anerkennung der Beratungsstellen und der Ärztinnen und Ärzte als Beraterinnen oder Berater nach den §§ 8 und 9 Schwangerschaftskonfliktgesetz(SchKG) (Guidelines for state recognition of the advisory bodies and the doctors as consultants or advisers in regards to Paragraphs 8 and 9 of the pregnancy conflict law) *MinisterialBlatt*, Düsseldorf, North Rhine-Westfalen No.29, May 7, 1998: 468-478

Sicherstellung und Finanzierung von Beratungsstellen für Schwangershaftsprobleme und Familienplanung in Nordrhein-Westphalen. (Securing and financing of Advising Centers for Pregnancy Problems and Family Planning.) *Minsterium für Arbeit, Gesundheit und Soziales des Landes Nordrhein-Westfalen*, October 6, 1996.

Van Dinther, CDU Sind in Nordrhein-Westfalen als Beraterinnen und Berater für Schwangerschaftskonflikte anerkannte Ärztinnen und Ärzte nach der Neuregelung des § 218 weiterhin in der Beratung tätig? Kleine Anfrage 238, *Drucksache 12/605* Lantag Nordrhein-Westfalen January 17, 1996

_____,Anzahl der von den anerkannten Ärztinnen und Ärzten seit der vom Bundestag am 29.06.1995 verabschiedeten Neuregelung des § 218 in NW abgerechneten Beratungen in Schwangerschaftskonfliktfällen; Richtlinien für die Beratungstätigkeit von Ärztinnen und Ärzten" Antwort, *Drucksache 12/778* Lantag Nordrhein-Westfalen, August 6, 1996.

Verordnungen über die Zuständigkeiten im Falle einer Schwangerschaft Beratung und Abtreibung (Regulations regarding the Responsibilities in the Case of Pregnancy counseling and abortion.). *Gesetz und Verordnungsblatt für das Land Nordrhein Westfalen.* December 12, 1978. No 75.

Verwaltungsvorschriften über die Bweilligung von Landeszuschüssen
and die Träger von Beratungsstellen für
Schwangerschaftsprobleme und Familienplannung-Administrative
Regulations regarding the approval of state subsidies directed at
the responsible bodies of centers offering counseling on pregnancy
problems and family planning *MinisterialBlatt für das Land
Nordrhein-Westfalen.* November 1977.

Vollzug des Schwangerenberatungsgesetz (Execution of the Law on the
Counseling of Pregnant Women),1988 *Allgemeinen
Ministerialblatt (AllMBl)* , No. 12 Vol. 1, June 15: 521.

Voräufige Richlinien für die Anerkenneung von Beratunsstellen,
beratenden Ärzten und Zulassung von Einrichtungen zur
Durchführung eines Schwangersschaftsabbruch nach dem
Fünfzehnten Strafrechtssänderungsgestetz. (Preliminary Guidelines
for the recognition of counseling centers, counseling doctors and
approval of institutions that perform abortions according to the 15th
penal code." *Ministerialblatt für das Nordrhein-Westphalen.* No. 2
August 6, 1976:1536.

Constitutional Court Cases

Abortion I Case (1975) 39 BVerfGE 1
Abortion II Case (1993) 88 BVergGE 203
Bank Standing Case (1968) 23 BVerfGE 153
Maastricht (1993) decision 89 BVerGE 155
*Mental Deficiency Case (1951),*1 BVerfGE 87
State Radio Cases (1971) 31 BVerfGE 314
Television Case (1961) 12 BVerfGE 205

Index